Praise for Ken Dornstein's THE BOY WHO FELL OUT OF THE SKY

"It's only as time passes and the pain softens that what was complicated about the relationship between survivor and deceased emerges. And it's in teasing out those complications that we learn something about what it is to be human, something beyond the fact that the pain of losing someone you love seems unbearable. In seeking to understand, as well as tell, the past, Dornstein employs the full power and grace of the genre of memoir. The effect is extraordinary."   —*The Atlanta Journal-Constitution*

"Dornstein makes his brother into a character whom we feel we've already, always known. . . . Whether or not David was a great artist, he was a devastating confessor of love, a love so presciently conveyed that one is left, even secondhand and decades later, dumbfounded. . . . Even had David lived, there couldn't have been a more knowing biography."   —*The Village Voice*

"A mesmerizing tale of family crisis, mental illness and unfulfilled promise."
                   —*The New York Times*

"Dornstein's memoir is always compelling and frequently stunning, as in his hauntingly described visit to Lockerbie. . . . *The Boy Who Fell Out of the Sky* is a quiet but powerful affirmation of life."   —*The San Diego Union-Tribune*

"Dornstein's investigation of his brother David's life and death is a considerable, multifaceted achievement. . . . It's rare for a memoir to demand such intense emotional involvement from the reader, and rarer still for it to be so amply rewarded."   —*Time Out* (London) "Book of the Week"

"Gripping. . . . Having spent his brief life dreaming of literary fame, David finally achieved it, posthumously, as the subject, not the writer, of a book. He would surely have been pleased by the book—exciting, astonishing, moving, profound; he'd have loved being in it."
                   —*Daily Mail* (London) "Critic's Choice"

"A remarkable book on many levels, not least for Ken Dornstein's dogged honesty and winsome personality. . . . By its conclusion, however, he has created something unusual and unforgettable: a heartfelt but unsentimental honouring of his brother that takes this brutal waste of life and reworks it into a sensitive and uplifting meditation on living."   —*The Herald* (Glasgow)

"What an expressive range Dornstein has! Humour, absurdity, bathos, drama, tragedy, excitement—he combines them all in this shocking, complex and profoundly thoughtful study of loss and survival. Anyone wanting an insight into ambivalence and emotional repair and how to write a good memoir should read this book."

—Alexander Masters, author of *Stuart: A Life Backwards*

"This book stands on its own. . . . Dornstein imitates his dead brother, parallels [Joan] Didion and [Mikal] Gilmore, but somehow, in the process, Dornstein has proven he has his own style, his own memoir, his own writer's life, and, much to our surprise and his, his own life." —*Chicago Tribune*

"[Dornstein's] memoir is an elegy, a love letter, but also a necessarily mechanistic performance of what Freud called 'the work of grief'—the only way of perpetuating that love which we do not want to relinquish."

—*The Boston Phoenix*

"Riveting." —*Entertainment Weekly*

"Vivid, brilliant. . . . This book isn't easy reading, and it's not for those looking for neat resolutions, but Dornstein has written an unflinching, graceful portrait of grief and the hope that comes after it." —*The Hartford Courant*

"The story of Ken's quest begins with a near-pitch-perfect chapter devoted to a trip he made to Lockerbie eight years after the bombing. . . . Powerful. . . . Revelatory." —*Newsday*

"[Dornstein's] clear-eyed and unsentimental account of how he stopped his fall just short of impact is a remarkable story. It leaves the reader astonished and grateful that Pan Am Flight 103 didn't take one more soul down with it."

—*The Plain Dealer*

"Dornstein succeeds precisely because he eschews melodrama and oversimplification in favor of a fairly straight, modest, and often conflicted recounting. He does his brother justice and learns, finally, to let him go. In the process, he discovers himself." —*Star Tribune* (Minneapolis)

KEN DORNSTEIN
The Boy Who Fell Out of the Sky

Ken Dornstein has been published in *The New Yorker*
and has received two Yaddo artist residencies. He is the
series editor at PBS's *Frontline* and lives near Boston
with his wife and two children.

THE BOY

WHO FELL

OUT OF THE SKY

THE BOY
WHO FELL
OUT OF THE SKY

—— *A True Story* ——

KEN DORNSTEIN

VINTAGE BOOKS

A Division of Random House, Inc.

New York

FIRST VINTAGE BOOKS EDITION, JUNE 2007

Copyright © 2006 by Ken Dornstein

The Library of Congress has cataloged the Random House edition as follows:
Dornstein, Ken.
The boy who fell out of the sky : a true story / Ken Dornstein
p. cm.
1. Pan Am Flight 103 Bombing Incident, 1988.   2. Bombing investigation—
Scotland—Lockerbie—Case studies.   3. Victims of terrorism—
United States—Case studies.   4. Dornstein, David, 1963–1988.
5. Brothers—Death—Psychological aspects.   I. Title.
HV6431.D665 2006
973.91'092'2—dc22   2005042683
[B]

Vintage ISBN: 978-0-375-70769-8

Author photograph © Jessica Boyatt

www.vintagebooks.com

Printed in the United States of America
10   9   8   7   6   5   4   3   2   1

There was a time in our lives when we were so close that nothing seemed to obstruct our friendship and brotherhood, and only a small footbridge separated us.

Just as you were about to step on it, I asked you: "Do you want to cross the footbridge to me?"—immediately, you did not want to any more; and when I asked you again, you remained silent.

Since then mountains and torrential rivers and whatever separates and alienates have been cast between us, and even if we wanted to get together, we couldn't. But when you now think of that little footbridge, words fail you and you sob and marvel.

—Friedrich Nietzsche, "Over the Footbridge"

CONTENTS

LAST THINGS

———

There was a hill not above a mile from
me, which rose up very steep and high. . . .
I traveled for discovery up to the top of
that hill. After I had with great labor and
difficulty got to the top, I saw my fate to
my great affliction. . . . The island was barren.

Daniel Defoe, *Robinson Crusoe*

I

THE NIGHT MY BROTHER DIED, I slept fine, back in my old bed in my old room in the old house where I grew up. I came downstairs late the next morning. My father and stepmother had left for work, but I was on my first day of Christmas break from college. I had nothing to do, and the entire day to do it. I found the newspaper laid out on the kitchen table. The headline ran in giant letters across the front page—PLANE WITH 259 ABOARD CRASHES, DESTROYS 40 HOMES IN SCOTLAND. I started to read:

> LOCKERBIE, Scotland—A Pan Am jumbo jet bound for New York with 259 people, many of them Christmas travelers, crashed last night into this Scottish village, exploding into a huge fireball and setting ablaze dozens of homes and cars. No survivors from the Boeing 747 were found. The cause of the crash was not immediately clear, although speculation centered on either structural failure or sabotage.

There were other stories on the bombing as well: "Fire Fell from the Sky 'Like Liquid.'" "All On Jet, 11 in Town Are Killed." There were also pictures—a Scottish police officer peering into the plane's crushed cockpit lying in a field; houses and cars on fire; a woman collapsed on the floor of JFK airport (she'd just been told that her daughter was on the plane). I skimmed the stories. I also checked the sports page and the police blotter in the suburban "Neighbors" section. A pizza delivery man had been robbed of $120 at knifepoint not too far from where I lived. News is just news to those not immediately affected, and my brother, David, was not supposed to fly until later in the week.

I finished breakfast and puttered around. At around noon, I turned on the television. Again, the bombing. Now there was news footage from Scotland. I remember the blue lights of the ambulances streaking into town and the hospital doctors looking useless waiting for injured passengers who would never arrive. There would be no injured, the anchorman said, "only dead." I remember the houses on fire and that cockpit in the field still looking sort of like a cockpit. It was Thursday, December 22, 1988. David had been dead on the ground since early Wednesday night, but I didn't know it.

I have come to think of the impact of my brother's death in dramatic terms: a curtain dropping on my youth, a terrible storm that left me shipwrecked, the start of a new life. But this language came much later. Events unfolded in a much more everyday way: The phone rang and my father, home early from work, answered it. A sales agent from the airline said she might have some unfortunate news about a David Dornstein. *Is this the family of David Dornstein?* The agent said she needed to check the final passenger list. She said she needed to cross-reference one thing with another. She said she needed to speak with her supervisor. She said she needed to get people in London or Scotland or New York or somewhere to "sign off." She said things were still a little confused. *So could you please bear with us? Could you please hold?*

My father waited on hold by himself initially, and then he called upstairs to me. I found him at his desk. "Pan Am is on the phone," he said. David boarded the plane at Heathrow, the woman from the airline had told him, but for some reason she wasn't ready to say that David had been on the plane when it exploded. My father held the phone away from his ear and let his head slump. I could hear the airline's hold music through an amplifier my father had put on the phone because of a bad ear: Dionne Warwick's "Do You Know the Way to San Jose" . . . a Muzak version of "When I'm Sixty-Four" . . . that trumpet song by Chuck Mangione—*Do do dooooo, do do-do do-dooooo, da da da da-daaaaaaaaa*. The phone call from Pan Am was strange, and the news likely tragic, but the experience of being on hold was familiar. It was as if we had called the airline to book a flight, a winter getaway. Except we hadn't. The airline had called us, and this, we knew, could not be good.

When the woman from Pan Am came back on the phone, my father mainly listened. If he said anything it was on the order of "Hmm hmmm" or "Yes, I understand." Maybe he said nothing. Then he set down the receiver. The message had been delivered.

Neither of us spoke. If we said nothing, if we shut off the lights, if we stood perfectly still, would the news go away? No. My father and I both had heard the final ax blow land, even if the tree had not yet tipped and fallen. We took a last quick look at the world as we had known it, and as the world still seemed to be—but for the fact of that phone call—and then it all came crashing down.

What happened next for my father is not for me to tell. He may not even recall the details; we've never spoken about it. But I remember my own reaction, and it still troubles me. I didn't cry or put my head in my hands or collapse like the lady from the picture at JFK. I was still. I understood the loss as my father's, for the most part, and I thought about how to console him. I looked down from above as the scene in the bedroom played out: those two pitiable souls, my father and I, rats in a maze of grief they had just begun to feel their way around. I felt sorry for them, but sorry like I might feel for the survivors of an earthquake somewhere (there was one in Armenia that same month); sorry like I'd initially felt for the victims of Flight 103 when I read about them in the paper that morning—which is to say, not that sorry at all. It was intolerable for me to have a personal connection to this story, so I simply decided not to.

My father began making calls—one to a friend to cancel dinner plans, another to my sister, who said she'd be right over. My stepmother walked in from work a few minutes later and collapsed in the doorway after hearing the news. My father helped her to a chair. I didn't know what to do. I walked back upstairs. The book I'd been reading was still propped open at the place where I'd left off. A glazed chocolate doughnut sat on a white napkin, half eaten. I am embarrassed to say that I finished it. I was hungry. *Now what?*

David's old room was next door. I peeked inside. The room was just as he had left it, but now, I knew, it had become a room in a museum. I lay down on David's bed, thinking maybe I could channel his spirit through his sheets and blankets. The house was quiet for a while.

Time had been suspended, a giant parenthesis had opened up in my life, and I could have stayed there a long time. But then the doorbell rang and the parenthesis closed. Men and women in their hats and coats were arriving at a house of mourning. Well-wishers. They walked through the front door on the verge of tears. They talked in small groups, with hushed voices. Someone asked me where we kept our drinking glasses, almost apologetic for wanting something to drink *at a time like this.* I pointed someone else to the bathroom. A dozen or so people were in the house within an hour.

Soon the Eyewitness News team would be in the living room. David's picture, yearbook-pose false, would be beamed throughout the tri-state area, the local angle to the international news story. Mothers mixing noodle casseroles would glimpse my brother's face and think, How handsome (my father would later mistake a picture of JFK, Jr., for David). And then: How awful.

I was overwhelmed by a sense of the wrongness of what was happening, or if not by the wrongness, then by the sheer pace of events. I felt that David would have been disappointed at how quickly we had accepted the news of his death, and how readily we had set in motion the machinery of memorialization. One minute he was alive in our minds, headed home from a long time away; the next minute the phone rang and we were burying him.

I refused to be enlisted into this gathering army of the

bereaved. I slipped out the door and into the backyard. I dropped to my knees on the frozen ground, thinking I should pray, but I didn't know any prayers. Then I lay down, looking up. It was cold, but I couldn't be bothered with so small a matter as my own warmth. I had ventured out into the winter night to make some kind of celestial connection with my dead brother and I assumed I would be insulated from such worldly concerns by the sheer drama of the situation.

I don't know how long I was outside. At one point a jet flew overhead, and I watched the blinking lights on the wings and tail move across the sky. I thought of the snug world inside the cabin, the ice clinking in the first-class glasses, the reading lights being dimmed, the endless rearrangements of blankets and pillows at the start of a night flight. And then I wondered what it would look like if the plane suddenly split in two and all of the people inside spilled out. Which is to say: I tried that night, but it would be years before I could even begin to imagine David's fall.

II

I HAVE STARTED THIS STORY a hundred times in the years since David died, but never finished. Let me begin again.

Once upon a time, I had a brother. He was older, bigger, wiser, more daring, more passionate, better spoken, and much better looking. He traveled farther away from home than I ever imagined I would. I admired him. I was nineteen when he died, a sophomore in college. Now I am in my midthirties. I have some memories of my brother, but not as many as I'd like to think. And each time I check, I seem to have one fewer. If at first I found it hard to believe that David was dead, now I find it hard to believe that he ever lived. David's life has come to seem like a story I made up, a fairy tale, no more real than words on a page. I sometimes find it dispiriting to think that this is what a life comes to, that this is how it ends. But I can imagine David smiling about it. Words were his life. And now the words he left behind would be more vital than ever.

David was a writer. In the years before he died, he was working on something big and, at least to me, mysterious. He wrote night and day, filling dozens of spiral notebooks with his fevered thoughts and phantasmagorical dreams. For a time, he told people he was trying to write down every thought that had ever occurred to him. When he slept it was on the floor, surrounded by books and papers. He renounced beds. Later, he swore off banks, keeping his money thoroughly liquid—a wad of cash tucked inside the pages of a book called *The Irrational Man*. This was David: He played out every idea to the end.

One day David left home. He left the country. He said he had to go, but beyond his initial destination he didn't know where, and he didn't know when he would be back. He was twenty-five. He pledged not to return until he had written something substantial or until he had otherwise settled the question of his future as a writer. Before he left, David copied into his notebook a passage from the novelist Thomas Wolfe about the extraordinary troubles Wolfe had with an early novel:

> I had been sustained by that delightful illusion of success which we all have when we dream about the books we are going to write instead of actually doing them. Now I was face to face with it, and suddenly I realized that I had committed my life and my integrity so irrevocably to this struggle that I must conquer now or be destroyed.

We know this story: A boy heads off into the wild to kill a bear, and he returns to the village a man. But in this case, the boy did not come back. A newspaper feature called this "A Tragic Twist on a Young Writer's Life." According to the article, David carried a manuscript with him onto Pan Am Flight 103, the draft of a brilliant first novel finally on its way to expectant American publishers. But the novel was presumed lost in the wreckage, loose pages of it spread across Scotland along with seat cushions and insulation and other bits of the disintegrating 747. Coming-of-age stories usually end with some obstacles being overcome and the way ahead finally clear. But this one seemed to have ended, at least in part—at least for David—at the bottom of the North Sea with the rest of the lightest debris from Flight 103.

Was the "Tragic Twist" story true? I didn't know. I remember meeting David's best friend, Billy, a month or so after the bombing and talking to him about what we should do with David's writings. Even if there were no novel to publish, I argued that we could put together an edited collection of some kind. David had filled a giant cardboard box with his notebooks and manuscripts. He labeled it in thick Magic Marker: THE DAVE ARCHIVES. I told Billy that there must be material in there for several books. I remember thinking we needed to strike fast, while the world still cared about the people on Flight 103, but Billy and I never formed anything like a plan.

David's papers sat unread for a long time. At one point, I decided to catalog them. I ordered the notebooks chronologically and straightened them on a shelf. I sorted loose typescripts into color-coded files. I was careful to read only enough of each thing to fix a label to it: FICTION, POETRY, PLAYS, LETTERS, etc. I told myself it was too sad to read these pages, too difficult, too soon, too much, but my reasons were much simpler. I feared what David himself had feared: that what was inside those notebooks, what was typewritten on all of those loose sheets, was not good enough to justify all of the big noises he'd made about it. I feared that the grand plan had never been realized and that David had hidden this fact from himself in a mass of paper. I feared page after page of throat-clearing about a book that David would forever be on the verge of writing. Wasn't the "Tragic Twist" story a much better way to leave things?

If I wasn't reading David's writing, I also couldn't leave it be. On visits home, I spent long stretches among his papers. I'd look at the urgent loops of his writing and remember David sitting in the corner of a room scrawling it down, every word so crucial, every sentence potentially the sentence that would bring a new clarity, finally launching him on his way. The pages cried out to be read. One manuscript seemed to address me directly: "You cannot put me on the shelf with all of your other documents. I WILL NOT TOLERATE BEING CATALOGUED. When you file me I die. I DIE. And I am not reborn until you read me again." I would read and sometimes cry and puzzle over what to do, and then I'd decide, effectively, to do nothing. This went on for years.

A story: One day I was in David's room reading when my

father walked in. I was in the far corner, my back up against a dresser, and David's notebooks were laid out on the bed. I felt caught in the act of something, as if I had violated the ground rules that we had set down in those first moments after the phone call from the airline. I didn't know if my father came into David's room when I was not at home, but I suspected that he did. We each had our rituals where David was concerned, but they were private. (Question: How do things become unspeakable?)

My father picked up one of David's notebooks and began thumbing through it. It felt good to see that he, too, could be curious about what was inside, but I'm not sure if he was really reading. He turned the pages with a fixed expression, as if he'd long ago appraised their value. Neither of us spoke. After a minute or two he closed the cover and neatly returned the notebook to the spot on the bed where he'd found it. He got up to leave. I remember him brushing off his pants like a man who had just fallen from a horse. He said, "What a waste." And then he walked out.

I wasn't sure what my father meant by this, but it felt like a powerful idea. The words seemed to settle over David's room. *What a waste.* I looked around at the posters still taped to the wall since high school, the bad posters of bad classic rock bands that came free with all of those bad albums that David collected when he was a teenager. Inside a dresser drawer, I found old socks and underwear, the ones deemed not good enough to make the trip abroad, the worst of David's whole sad, soiled fleet. There were also shirts that David had ripped the necks from in a fit of 1980s *Flashdance* fashion consciousness. The white walls of David's room seemed dirtier, and the shag rug shaggier. The furniture, a bedroom set done in faux wood and brass, seemed cheaper and more out of date. The turntable, the eight-track player, the pot-smoking supplies in the desk drawer, the Cape Canaveral commemorative plaque from the first moon landing. At the time that he died, these relics held only marginal sentimental value for David. Now, to me, they looked like really old exhibits in the Dave Museum. I thought, maybe for the first time, that some of this stuff should be put away somewhere. Or tossed.

But then there was the question of those notebooks and the

manuscripts. Had these been a waste, too? In the box of papers that David left behind, I found a strange and often impenetrable web of fictions. An example: *The Memoirs of an Unknown Author* was written by "D. Avid Dornstein," who refers to himself as "the author of the bestselling novel *Aunt Peggy's Nursery School*," a work that not only was not a bestseller, but was also never actually written. A different series of stories takes place in "South Coprophilia," a kind of dystopian Winesburg, Ohio. (I had to look up *coprophilia*—a "marked interest in excrement; especially: the use of feces or filth for sexual excitement." *What was this about?*) There were three or four different drafts of "A Chronological Incest," each version penned under a different variation of David's own name: "D. Avid Dornstein," "David Dorrance-Dean," "Dr. David Dornheimer." For a time, it seemed, David wrote exclusively under the name "Kristian Santini."

My idea was this: I would help David finish whatever it was that he had started to write. But the more I read, the less clear I grew about what that really was. There were notes about how a number of his different stories might be fitted together into a larger work, but there was no evidence that he'd ever attempted it. And this map he left, once I tried to follow it, led only to imaginary places.

III

A curious thing: I was not alone with the problem of what to do with David's notebooks and papers now that he was dead. David himself was there to answer a lot of my questions. He had prepared his "literary estate" for posterity, believing that a tragic early death would ensure his literary greatness. He wrote notes in the margins of his notebooks "for the biographers"; he instructed his correspondents to "save this letter or you'll be sorry." He imagined scholars trying to figure out the riddle of his life in light of his untimely death. He suggested topics for graduate student theses: "The Nature of Chance Violence in Dornsteinian Thought"; "Dornstein and the Notebook Form of the Novel." He pictured his friends poring over his pages to see what he had been working on all of those years, to look for their own names if nothing else. I felt stuck with the knowledge that no one ever came.

David seemed prepared for this as well. If need be, he would burnish his own legend. He cut out words from magazines and pieced together, ransom-note style, his own jacket copy for the first posthumous collection of his writings:

AN ARTIST WHOSE SHORT CAREER WAS TROU-
BLED BY BOTH PSYCHOLOGICAL AND PHYSICAL

TRAUMA LEFT JOURNALS AND OTHER WRITTEN
RECORDS OF TRAGIC LIFE AND INTENSE COM-
MITMENT TO WORK.

Inside, I found a page with this sentence written over and over:

> Humorously, tragically, I really am starting to believe that the
> only way any of these notebooks will mean anything is if I die
> an early death.

David gave a lot of thought to the manner in which he would die,
and he concluded, at least for a time, that only a sudden, violent
death would do. The title page of his *Memoirs* features a headline
from *The New York Times*—DIES IN AIR CRASH—along with
this caution to his imagined biographers: "There is NOTHING
accidental or random in any of Dornstein's work, especially in this
early work."

It was oddly consoling to think that David knew his fate,
accepted it, and made provisions, even if the rest of us had been
caught off guard. But there was also some adolescent romance in
his idea of an early death, and maybe some very rational calcula-
tion: If only a fiery death would ensure posthumous interest in his
writings, then why not die in the most dramatic way our modern
age affords? He would die in an air disaster, or at least this would
be the story. He explained the idea more fully in the preface to his
"posthumous" work:

> Initially, this work began with a fervent belief that I would die
> very young and would be mythologized as such. "Sad young
> comet, shined brightly, blazed, burst. . . ." But then I realized
> that I was afraid of dying, and I did not want to sacrifice
> myself for the potency of my scrawl. So I conceived of an
> autobiographical fiction wherein the story of my struggle and
> my death and my ultimate recognition could be told without
> actual personal decease occurring. . . . Work on this project
> has only just begun. I shall spend no less than eight years on
> this, at the completion of which I shall either die in reality, or

I shall spend an additional seventeen years creating a book that will keep the critics and biographers and scholars busy for their natural lifetimes. In order to ensure endurance I have decided to create something so powerful and so universal that it will not be allowed to perish.

David's plan was straightforward. He would take himself apart, piece by piece, and reassemble himself on the pages of his notebooks. He would remake himself in words, and those words would live forever. If he succeeded, "David Dornstein" would be David Dornstein's most fully realized creation. It began as an elaborate high-literary joke—a young man's search for himself; a young writer's first shot at immortality—but then David died, and the joke was on him. And on me. David had put his life into his pages. Now those pages were his life, and I had moved them to the floor of my closet. What was I supposed to do with them? *With him?*

A painful recollection: The night David died, I dumped a drawerful of his old letters to me onto the floor of my bedroom and began to reread them. It was an astounding output of pages, dozens of thick envelopes filled with tens of thousands of words for "Dear Ken." I picked up pages at random, not sure what I was looking for. And then I settled on those last letters from Israel. "Dear Ken, I have an address and an Israeli phone number. I crave hearing from you. . . ." "Dear Ken, Absurd to know how much time has elapsed without contact. . . ." "Dear Ken, I wish with every petal on my flower that you would write to me. Are we still pals? It pains me to be so groping, but there is INSTABILITY here. . . . Please write soon."

Why had I let so many of David's appeals go unanswered? I found one of his old spiral notebooks and began writing on the unused pages. I sat at his old desk and wrote while the well-wishers came and went from the house. It's what David would have done, I thought. *It's what I should do.* This was the new logic that would govern my life.

I tried to be a journalist, reporting the story of the aftermath of David's death. I was writing for a very small audience—just David, really. I thought he'd want to know all of the details. I thought he'd be pleased to know that I'd picked up his pen, that his notebook was once again filling up with words. It felt good to respond to him in the way that he'd wanted me to for so long. I wrote for David, and after a few paragraphs, I began to write in his style as well. It was code, all very private between the two of us—the notebook as direct line between us. When it came time to hold a memorial service for David, I thought I'd write a proper eulogy, but I didn't. All I had were those notebook pages I'd been writing in the few days since he'd died. So that's what I read.

This was a mistake. For one thing, the sheets were difficult to decipher. I had used the backs and fronts of pages, covered every inch with ink, stuck Post-it notes all over to squeeze in one more thing. Some sections were obscured by big patches of blood that had dried, brown and crusty. (One night, while writing at David's desk, I had started to cry. To stop the tears, I pressed my face hard into the desk; something snapped out of place and my nose started to bleed over the words.)

My Awful Eulogy was painfully obscure, filled with references to things David had written to me in letters, lyrics to his favorite songs, passages from books I knew he'd read—nonsense speech at times, free association, and lots of wordplay in David's style. It was not an appreciation of David so much as an impersonation of him. And it was long, tremendously long, a river of words. It felt as if David were alive as long as I spoke, so I kept going with long quotes from books I'd been reading (Nietzsche and Beckett, especially) and liberal doses of the Old Testament. (I cast David as the prophet Jeremiah and myself as his assistant Baruch, writing down his words for posterity.) I had been so silent with David those last few months of his life, but now I was telling all, hoping it would make a difference.

After forty-five minutes or so, my father got up from his seat, walked past the soured faces of the rabbis—stood in front of hundreds of gathered mourners—and tried in the gentlest way possible to ease me away from the microphone. He whispered in my ear, "We're proud of you, son." But I don't think he would have come up like that had he simply been feeling proud.

Back in my seat a few moments later, I thought: I have probably made some people uncomfortable and annoyed others and quite possibly been profane. The shame took a few days to develop, like a bruise, as I reread those bloodied notebook pages and thought about the faces of the people listening. After that first week, I stopped writing in David's notebook. I stopped talking about him as well. Where David was concerned, I went largely silent. And this silence would last for years.

David's body was cremated. His ashes were put in a box, flown to JFK Airport, and driven out to a cemetery on Long Island, where my father's father had established a Dornstein burial plot.

I remember seeing this box of David—a standard overnight shipping carton—before it went into the ground. It was sitting in the back of a flatbed truck beside a handful of Hispanic men with shovels. The truck made its way through the cemetery to the grave site. I watched as the men tore through the cardboard, removed the vessel with the ashes, and placed it near the open grave. We paid a rabbi $250 to recite a few psalms and get us through some kind of ceremony in a brief and reasonably dignified way. I remember the rabbi rushing around beforehand asking how old David was and *what did he do for a living?* and *was he married?* Then the vessel with the ashes was lowered into the ground, and the rabbi shoveled some dirt onto it. We each laid a shovelful on top ourselves, and then it was done.

I went back to college—the same college David had attended—and tried to complete my coursework. When I graduated, I moved far away and found work that bore no resemblance to anything David had done. I tried to go my own way, but David was hard to shake. He returned in dreams. He cried out from his notebooks not to be ignored. *When you file me, I die.* Many years after his death, the top story in my life still felt largely the same: PLANE WITH 259 ABOARD CRASHES, DESTROYS 40 HOMES IN SCOT-LAND. I was stuck. This is when I decided to take a trip to Lockerbie. It had been eight years since the bombing, but I told myself I could still save David's life if I went right away.

IV

To get to Lockerbie, I walked to the edge of the city of Dumfries, located some twelve miles west, and I waited for the 81 bus. I stood alongside kids in school uniforms, and women with packages, and pensioners who'd maybe come to the city to see a doctor. A light rain forced us close together under a bus shelter, shoulder to shoulder, the kids' books pressed up tight against their chests, the old ladies jostling to keep their packages out of the weather. It was oddly intimate.

The aging diesel coach rounded to a stop in front of us, with LOCKERBIE spelled out in block letters above the driver. The doors opened. I could hear people ahead of me naming Lockerbie as their stop and paying their fare. Then it was my turn. For years Lockerbie had felt like the name of my own private grief, nothing I had discussed much with anyone. Now, standing before the driver, I felt as if I were being pressed for an admission I wasn't ready to make. Lockerbie. I couldn't remember the last time I had said the word aloud. I found a seat near the back.

During the twenty-five-minute ride, I did not take pictures and I did not take notes. I spoke to no one. I looked out the Plexiglas window, which was almost opaque from dirt and age, and tried to remember everything I was seeing. My ears were tuned for talk of the bombing, but I heard nothing. It was November of 1996, almost eight years since Flight 103 went down, so I would have heard such talk only by extraordinary chance. But I was not thinking this way at the time. For me, the bombing had just happened and I was streaking into town to search for survivors.

We passed by lochs and glens, by woods and wide-open fields. Signs advertised castles and golf courses. At one point we approached some housing developments, a traffic signal, a pub, a church, a town square. *Was this Lockerbie?* No.

Through some dense woods, we crossed a major road. It was the six-lane A74 highway to Edinburgh; a road sign said the Lockerbie exit was just ahead. On the night of the bombing, parts of the plane had come down here. Some cars and trucks were abandoned, some were burnt down to their frames. The wings of Flight 103 had fallen on the far side of the road, setting aflame a line of homes at Sherwood Crescent and blasting a crater into the ground that ran some 250 feet. It looked peaceful there now. A new housing complex had been built on the site, and the landscaping betrayed not a hint of what it had replaced.

After dropping some passengers at the new Kwik-Mart supermarket on the edge of town, the 81 bus headed up the high street toward the center of Lockerbie. We passed an impressive church and cemetery. The grounds were packed tight with grave markers the height of grown men. The imposing sandstone slabs lurched forward as if to tell you secrets about the once-feuding clans of Maxwells, Johnstones, and Jardines buried beneath. Further on, some windowless pubs. Years of sentimental news features about Lockerbie had consistently portrayed a quaint, bustling little burgh, all crackling fires, stout glasses of beer, and good cheer. But the initial view from the bus revealed a cheerless-looking town with many empty storefronts and few people walking around.

The bus came to a stop in a flat, empty part of town, near a livestock auction yard. When the driver announced that this was the end of the line, I was the only one left on board to hear him. I stepped down, not sure where I was. I thought I saw areas significant to the bombing, but I was mistaken. It didn't matter. I looked up at the hills above the town where I knew bodies had fallen on the night of the bombing. Every town has its secrets, but I felt as if I knew Lockerbie's, and the knowledge warmed me. I walked to the town square and looked around. *So this is Lockerbie.* For the next ten days I would punctuate most of my observations with this same dull recognition: *So this is Lockerbie.* I had arrived.

There are so many ways to lose someone you love. Even limiting the field to those losses we think of as particularly tragic does not narrow the list much. A fire burns the home of a sleeping family. A train derails. And in the aftermath, memory can become bound up with place; sites of loss can be sanctified, obliterated, or simply marked, like the cross by the side of the mountain road where the station wagon, kids asleep in the back, skidded off. For me, the whole knot of feelings I had for my brother became fixed around the town where he fell to earth. I did not know what to do with these feelings, not for a long time, but I could make a trip to Scotland, so that is what I did.

A lot of the American relatives of the Flight 103 dead had come to Lockerbie over the years. Many came right after the bombing. Hundreds more came on the first anniversary. They came again for the dedication of two different Flight 103 memorials in town. Even when the official ceremonies stopped, relatives continued to come. A few made the trip as many as eight or ten times. Early on, a local "Friendship Group" formed to host relatives and show them around. Strong bonds between Scots and Americans formed.

I knew all of this, and I thought it was a nice enough thing, but I chose to show up in Lockerbie unannounced. The Friendship Group was not for me. Maybe because, back then, nothing felt as if it were for me. Maybe because, in the hierarchy of the Flight 103 bereaved, I felt that siblings didn't rank very highly. At the very top, it seemed, were the parents who had lost children, especially if they were younger or only children (basic evolutionary theory seemed to be at work here, with the greatest loss accruing to those with the least chance of perpetuating themselves into the next generation). On the next rung down were the widows and widowers. Among the younger people, children who lost parents ranked highest. Those who lost brothers and sisters, it seemed to me, were well below this, lumped in with a grab bag of other relations: aunts, uncles, in-laws, grandparents, cousins, etc., just one notch above the final catchall category of "friends and others." I told myself I didn't want any special treatment from the Lockerbie locals, but maybe that's because, as a sibling, I wasn't sure I fully merited it. Or maybe I kept myself separate for a different reason altogether: Maybe when someone you love dies among a mass of other people, you want some experience that feels singular, even if you have to manufacture it yourself.

I didn't stay in Lockerbie, at least not initially. I took a room in nearby Dumfries, at the Torbay Lodge, on Lover's Lane, near the train station. I put myself in the care of James and Helen, the Torbay innkeepers. James showed me to a room in the attic that reminded me of the room I'd grown up in. I thought this was a sign of some kind. I thought everything in Scotland was some kind of sign that I was on David's trail. I fell asleep with the attic window open, and something awakened me before dawn. I went to the window thinking the wind carried in its gusts the supernatural force of a clue. I expected to see an apparition, a billowing brother ghost in otherworldly vestments. Instead: just an empty traffic plaza built around a memorial to Scottish war dead, and a lone figure hunched against the cold.

At breakfast, James and Helen made a good-natured effort to tease out some details of my trip. *Will you be visiting any of the castles? Do you know the poet Robert Burns lived in Dumfries?* I don't remember what I told them about why I had come to Scotland, but the truth seemed out of the question. I thought my silence on the matter was noble, sparing them the burden of responding to a story so sorry and sad as a young man chasing after his dead brother's ghost. Now I suspect I said nothing for my own sake. To have exposed my story to daylight would have been to spoil it. I needed a special sense of mission.

For several days this was my routine: I'd leave the Torbay in the morning and head off to the Dumfries public library, the home of the "Official Archive of the Lockerbie Air Disaster." I had high hopes for a place with so grand a name, but most of what I found there proved unhelpful. Boxes of paperwork generated by the local government; scientific studies of long-term soil contamination from jet fuel; pamphlets from social service groups ("Grief—Dealing with a Major Personal Crisis," "Sleep Problems in Children"). I worked through a small mountain of press clippings, so many numbing variations on the same few sensational themes and images:

> FIREBALL OVER LOCKERBIE; JET INFERNO; FIRE-
> BALL FLIGHT; RAIN OF LIQUID FIRE; FLATTENED
> BY THE FIREBALL

So many overwrought glosses on the fate of the poor wrecked Scottish town:

> LOCKERBIE—A TOWN OF TEARS; TEA AND TEARS
> IN LOCKERBIE; RAIN OF DEATH RIPS TOWN
> APART; TOWN THAT TURNED INTO A BOMB SITE;
> THE CARNAGE OF LOCKERBIE

I was most drawn to those materials that let me glimpse some of the everyday details of the town coping after the disaster. A "Community Update" newsletter let local children know that their school had been taken over by the police, Scotland Yard, and the FBI. *January 3, 1989: Notice for all Lockerbie Academy students that Miss Wright's English class and Mr. Wilkie's biology class and Mr. Brockett's drama class will report to Assembly Hall, not the Annex Building, which is now the Lockerbie Incident Police Headquarters.* From the minutes of the Lockerbie town council, I found a proposal for a night of fun:

> After all the trauma of the past weeks the townsfolk badly
> need a night out to blow away the sadness following the disas-
> ter, and who better to do this than the Glasgow Wind Band
> playing the themes from 007, ye Band and Braies, and
> O'Bonny Doon.

I was most interested in the archive's unique collection of video- and audiotape news reports documenting the bombing from the very first hour. A librarian found me a TV/VCR with headphones and set me up in a room by myself to watch and to listen to as much as I could stand.

I listened as a local radio reporter walked through town just minutes after the bombing, tramping through mud and pieces of wreckage, the air thick with the smell of jet fuel and fire. Television reports from the days and weeks that followed showed scruffy black-and-white border collies sniffing around in the rubble for bodies; soldiers walking arm in arm across fields, filling clear bags with plane parts and black bags with human parts; eyewitnesses telling what they knew (all very similar accounts of hearing the jet as it neared the ground, feeling the impact, seeing the flames—but I listened to them all). I watched as the story shifted from the town and the wreckage to the arrival of the American relatives, their every movement becoming news for a thousand or more reporters who needed a fresh angle each day. I watched as the politicians and dignitaries made their appearances on the scene and the terror experts hypothesized about who may have bombed the plane. After two days of total immersion at the Lockerbie archive, I finally boarded the 81 bus to the town itself.

On those first few walks through Lockerbie, I was alert to all the physical and sensual details with which I could build my own account of what had happened here. I walked to a defunct chemical factory, which had been used after the bombing as a temporary morgue and property warehouse. Now it was a corrugated-box factory where they made the packaging for Jim Beam whiskey. In another corner of town, I found the Lockerbie Academy, whose classrooms had been commandeered by police for more than a year after the bombing. Photos of the men working there had made me sad—the cut of their suits, all wide lapels and washed-out browns; the color of their computer monitors, the green ones with the yellow type—all of it reminding me of how long ago the bombing had taken place, and how much had changed since then, and how David knew nothing of it.

Just down the road from the academy buildings, I found the South of Scotland Skating Rink. WELC_ME TO LOCKERBIE was assembled in uneven letters on a sign across the front of the building. Victims' bodies, like my brother's, were put on the ice, autopsied, and X-rayed here after the temporary morgue at the town hall was filled. I had often imagined the morbid scene here, the surreal arrangement of corpses inside lines that had been drawn on the ice for a hockey game. So it was not until I walked through the front door that it occurred to me that the people inside might simply be skating.

I was always aware when it grew close to 7 P.M. in Lockerbie. That was when parts of the plane had begun to hit the town. Many people said they had been watching *This Is Your Life* when the ground began to shake. From the flickering bright light I could see through people's living room windows as I walked past, this was exactly what they were watching now. A man with a dog passed me on the opposite side of the street. Maybe he had just finished dinner. I tried to imagine the scream of a rapidly disintegrating 747 breaking the quiet of the scene. *The man ducking for cover? The dog bolting in fear? A part of the plane landing on this very sidewalk?* But it was impossible.

It didn't take long to exhaust sites significant to the disaster. *Now what?* I decided to go in the opposite direction, to pursue Lockerbie as it really was—the philosopher's elusive "thing in itself"— not the town as seen through the lens of a disaster. I took an ethnographic approach. I stood in front of the window of a real estate office and copied down the listings, thinking, *This is what a house costs in Lockerbie.* I spent time in the Global video store (note: an unusually large selection of martial arts movies). I inventoried the items for sale at the pharmacy. At the Presto supermarket, I prowled around with my notepad long enough to compile a disturbingly complete list of products for sale: *Corn Flakes, Weetabix, Special K, Batchelors Pasta 'n' Sauce, Uncle Ben's Thai Sweet & Sour Sauces.* . . . I was pursuing this town down to its last detail, even if the details themselves were meaningless. I was chipping away at the mystery of the place and loosening its hold on my imagination. I was defeating death with a grocery list.

One odd find: In the dairy section of the supermarket, I found a line of cheese and butter products marketed under the "Lockerbie" brand name. It struck me as black humor, like "Chernobyl" brand ice cream or "Hiroshima" soft drinks. I later learned that "Lockerbie" had been a popular regional brand of dairy products well before the bombing, and industry trade journals such as *Frozen and Chilled Foods Monthly* frequently touted the new Lockerbie Creamery as one of the largest and most modern in the world. For a brief period after the bombing, however, the future of the brand was in question. The dairy's owner wrote to the town leaders before proceeding with plans to expand the Lockerbie brand into the lucrative "pre-pack" and "slices" cheese markets:

> In view of last year's tragic air disaster, the Company felt it was important to discuss its plans for further use of the Lockerbie name with local people to ensure that the launch is handled sensitively and no offence is caused to those affected by the disaster.

The dairy convened a "Lockerbie Cheese Consultation Day." People came and listened and sampled the cheese, but no one objected. I could not really think of a good reason to object, either.

My walks in Lockerbie usually ended late in the evening. Often I would be the only passenger on the 81 bus back to Dumfries. On the ride, I'd sort through my pockets and examine the day's evidence: A brochure from the South of Scotland Skating Rink. A time-and-date-stamped bus ticket from the Western Scottish Stagecoach Company. A plastic wrapper from a block of Lockerbie cheddar. I was proving to myself that Lockerbie was a real place, where people lived and worked and watched videos and ate cheese. And if this was true, I began to allow some eight years after those first strange reports about a 747 bombed over Scotland, it might also be true that my brother was dead.

V

AT 6:04 P.M. ON DECEMBER 21, 1988, a Boeing 747 pushed back from the gate at Heathrow Airport's newly remodeled Terminal 3. Registered as N739PA, the plane was the fifteenth 747 ever manufactured, bought by Pan Am in 1970 for twenty-two million dollars. The plane that flew as Flight 103 that night was christened *Maid of the Seas.*

Juan Trippe, Pan Am's founder, had a nautical fetish. He dressed his pilots like ship captains and called his planes clipper ships, after the great nineteenth-century sailing vessels. Pan Am's early clippers featured oak-paneled walls and formal dining service. As propeller planes gave way to jets and commercial air travel opened up to the less well-off, airplanes became more functional (pared-down interiors, instant coffee). Juan Trippe initially envisioned the 747 as the corrective to all of this. He imagined it as a kind of luxury cruise ship in the sky—a double-decker plane with a spiral staircase leading from the main cabin to elegant staterooms, a cocktail bar, a first-run movie theater, a library, a reading room. Trippe's initial order of twenty-five 747s would get the plane off of Boeing's drawing table and into production, so he had a lot of say in its design.

The problem, from Boeing's standpoint, was that most of what Trippe wanted was out of the question. They scaled down the design from a double-decker to a wide-body, but the 747 was still enormous. Promotional literature reached for vivid ways to convey this to the general public: "At 225 feet long, the 747 is more than twice the distance of the Wright brothers' entire first flight." "If one were to lower a 747 into Yankee Stadium, the wings would span from home plate to short center field." Pan Am also promoted Trippe's original idea of a return to high style and comfort in the skies. The early menus for Pan Am's transatlantic flights were said to have been inspired by chefs at Maxim's, in Paris. Passengers would enjoy roast tenderloin of beef with truffle sauce, Maine lobster thermidor, curried lamb, potato fondantes, saffron rice, hearts of palm salad, a selection of cheeses, puff pastry and cream, Bavarian cake in rum sauce, and coffee with Cointreau.

Photographers were on board when Pan Am flew its first regularly scheduled 747 flight from New York to London, in 1970. Pictures show passengers in formal dress watching with smiling expectation as comely air hostesses served coffee from silver pitchers. Other passengers are pictured relaxing with mixed drinks in the cocktail lounge on the upper deck, atop Trippe's signature spiral staircase. Even the airport would be new and improved for the 747. In order for passengers to board through all five of the 747's cabin doors simultaneously (and for the prized "Clipper-class" passengers to avoid contact with the riffraff in steerage), Juan Trippe commissioned a new kind of terminal, the outsize Pan Am "Worldport," at New York's JFK Airport, models of which would have seemed right at home at the World's Fair grounds in nearby Flushing Meadow, Queens.

This, anyway, was the original vision. The 747 my brother boarded that night in London retained little of its early-seventies swank; by the late 1980s, Pan Am's brave new Worldport vision for the 747 had all but completely faded. The 747 was supposed to save Pan Am, as the airline lost its exclusive hold on lucrative international routes—but it didn't. Pan Am struggled, trying unsuccessfully to square its grand vision of itself with the new realities of the deregulated airline business. In the summer of 1986, the airline touted a new "Alert" security program to attract passengers in the wake of a wave of hijackings that had left every international carrier hurting. But the "Alert" plan was later shown to have been a fraud, focused more on collecting a five-dollar surcharge on every ticket sold than on actually "screening passengers, employees, airport facilities, baggage and aircraft with unrelenting thoroughness." By 1988, Pan Am was still in decline. No longer the gleaming future of commercial air travel, the *Maid of the Seas* had become a Clydesdale workhorse for a company too cash poor to reupholster worn seats or update outmoded bathrooms. On the afternoon of December 21, 1988, the company's "Alert" guards in Frankfurt let a suitcase with a bomb in it pass through an X-ray machine, on its way to London, where it was then loaded into the belly of Flight 103.

Flight 103 took off from London in bad weather. The plane climbed above intermittent showers, ascending through thick clouds into relatively clear skies. At 6:54, about a half hour after takeoff, the *Maid of the Seas* leveled at 31,000 feet, cruising at more than 550 miles per hour toward JFK, where it was projected to land on time, despite a twenty-minute delay out of London.

At 6:58, the crew of Flight 103 first communicated with Shanwick Oceanic Control, on the west coast of Scotland, the last checkpoint on land before the plane headed out over the Atlantic. At 7:02:44, Shanwick radioed route clearance for the transatlantic passage, but the cockpit of Flight 103 did not acknowledge the message. At 7:02:50, a loud sound ended transmission on the cockpit voice recorder, and less than a minute later seismic monitors on the ground near Lockerbie recorded an impact measuring 1.6 on the Richter scale. (The wings had hit the ground near the A74 highway, and some two hundred thousand pounds of jet fuel had exploded on impact.) Air traffic controllers at Shanwick watched their monitors as the diamond shape representing Flight 103 broke into three green dots. Then nine. Then twenty-three. Then more than any of the controllers could count.

Investigators took only a few days to confirm that Flight 103 had been brought down by a bomb. Within a few months, they filled in more details: One pound of Semtex, a Czech-made plastic explosive that can be molded like cookie dough, had been fitted inside a Toshiba radio-cassette player, which was then stuffed in a Samsonite suitcase and loaded into one of the plane's forward cargo holds. In its solid form, the block of Semtex inside the Toshiba radio could have fit in the palm of one's hand; once detonated, the Semtex gas violently expanded to fill a volume ten thousand times larger. A wave of superheated, high-pressure gas blasted through the Samsonite suitcase, and then through the luggage container, and then blew a twenty-inch-square starburst-shaped hole in the underbelly of the *Maid of the Seas,* just between the *A* and the *M* of the Pan Am logo.

Fractures in the aluminum skin radiated out from the blast site along the circumference of the plane, petalling, curling, and then tearing off most of the plane's outer shell. Within a second or two, great sections of the plane began to pull apart along rivet lines. The hot gas of the Semtex bomb found its way into the air-conditioning ducts, and then up from the cargo hold into the main cabin. Waves of the Semtex gas ricocheted wildly off what remained of the cabin walls. Every loose object in the plane became lethal. Passengers became lethal to one another as they were thrown about.

The booming noise that ended the voice and data transmissions from Flight 103 was not the sound of the bomb exploding, as I had first assumed. It was the unimaginably loud sound of the front part of the plane tearing off, taking with it the nose cone, the cockpit, most of the first-class and Clipper-class seats, and Juan Trippe's beloved spiral staircase. Accident investigators referred to this event as "unzipping." Once free, this unzipped forward end of the fuselage was blown back into the right wing, knocking off the first of the four Pratt and Whitney engines. The forward fuselage grazed the tail assembly before flying off on its own course through the night. With the forward fuselage gone, the main cabin on the *Maid of the Seas* was now completely open to the wind at thirty thousand feet; it ran into a wall of air that was too thin and too cold (sixty degrees below zero) for the people inside to breathe. All of this happened within the first two or three seconds after the explosion.

The *Maid of the Seas* came apart in discrete stages, a reverse of the order in which it had been confidently riveted together in Boeing's Everett, Washington, factory. It was a perfect choreography of ruination, starting with the wings that could have stretched from home plate to short center field inside Yankee Stadium, and then quickly moving on to the Pratt and Whitney JT9D engines that landed—one, two, three, four—in and around the streets of Lockerbie. The six-story-tall tail assembly that had been knocked off by the careening cockpit landed in the woods a few miles east of town. The "super jet" that initially had been longer than the Wright brothers' historic first flight was reduced to half its size within ten seconds of the blast.

What remained of Flight 103 was now a dumb aluminum tube carrying two dozen rows of economy-class seats with most of the passengers still buckled in. For a few moments the main cabin continued on its charted course toward JFK, as if nothing had happened. The sheared-off front of the fuselage was hopelessly non-aerodynamic in the face of one-hundred-mile-per-hour headwinds, however. The cabin began to vibrate, decelerate, and tip downward, dropping to nineteen thousand feet in less than forty seconds. As it neared the ground, the disintegrating cabin was stripped to approximately ten or fifteen rows of seats attached to a section of flooring, plummeting through the night sky.

When Flight 103 left London, the fuel, the freight, the fuselage, the four engines, and the passengers had brought the final takeoff weight of N739PA to more than 740,000 pounds. My brother David's body, thin from a long time abroad, amounted to about 160 pounds of this mass. The last of it—the last of them—took less than three minutes to fall six miles to the ground.

How to begin to imagine what went on inside the *Maid of the Seas* in the moments after the explosion, or just before? In the seat pocket in front of each passenger on Flight 103 was the December 1988 issue of Pan Am's *Clipper* magazine. I could not really imagine David reading any of the features: One was about a Greek master jeweler who "looks to the ancient myths for inspiration"; another was on the "tony boutiques and refined specialty shops" of modern Frankfurt. I couldn't see David putting on the complimentary headphones to listen to the motivational speaking of Allan Boress, author of *Accentuate the Negative,* a "contrarian approach to the art of negotiation, persuasion, and selling." I hate to imagine David reading the description of the in-flight movie, *Crocodile Dundee II,* and thinking, just at that moment before 7:02:50, that he might watch it. *Had this been someone's last thought?* Hard facts about what really went on in that cabin are so difficult to come by that even this feels significant.

So does this bit of history: In selling Pan Am on the design of the 747 as a wide-body plane and not the double-decker that Juan Trippe wanted, Boeing engineers argued that too big a plane would make the public nervous. There were real safety concerns, they said. But more than this there would be a perception problem, a squeamishness about getting into a plane two stories high. Not so with the wide-body, they argued, because the inside of a wide-body would not seem like a plane at all. "For all practical purposes, you are sitting in the middle of the 747 right now," a Boeing engineer explained to Juan Trippe in a key meeting at Pan Am's Park Avenue headquarters. "The walls of the airplane are almost vertical, because the cabin is so wide—twenty feet wide. And they are nine feet high. For the first time, you'll be in a room, not a tube." In effect, the interior of the 747 would disarm the nervous flyer with dullness; it would seem as familiar and utterly forgettable as a room at a Hilton hotel. (In fact, the industrial design of the 747's interior would become a model for a whole new era of corporate blandness in planes, hotels, airports, restaurants.) The wide-body concept brilliantly comprehended a simple fact of the jet age: Most people like plane travel best when they forget they are traveling in a plane at all. All the more so when they are aboard the biggest commercial jet in the world.

So this is how I picture the passengers on the *Maid of the Seas* in the moments before the bomb exploded: Not six miles high in the sky. Not traveling more than five hundred miles per hour. Not on a plane at all. They are *in a room, not a tube.* They are in a movie theater watching coming attractions. They are at the bar, ordering another Chivas Regal. They are at the office, poring over a spreadsheet. They are in their favorite easy chair at home, dozing. Which is to say: One moment there was life on board the *Maid of the Seas,* just like the life the passengers on board had known on the ground. And the next moment there was death. Total death. Not the romantic death of the *Titanic* slowly sinking into the sea, the string quartet still playing on the deck as the bow tipped up. Not at all. The air disaster is the opposite. It is quintessential twentieth-century death in an instant. The destruction of Flight 103 is two people asleep on each other's shoulders at 7:02 P.M., and those same two people dead on the ground three miles apart at 7:05. Maybe this is why a plane wreck is so universally upsetting: We are proceeding along in life, watching our movie, drinking our drink, eating our peanuts, dreaming our dreams. And then, suddenly, we are not doing any of these familiar things. And we never will again.

VI

OF THE ITEMS MY BROTHER CARRIED with him onto Flight 103, this is what Scottish police were able to recover:

1. a bent metal strut from a backpack
2. two small plastic Ziploc bags of currency (just over £4 British and 32¢ U.S.)
3. $1,230 in unused traveler's checks
4. four T-shirts
5. two pairs of shorts
6. one pair of pants
7. two socks that didn't match
8. one pair of Converse "Chuck Taylor" high-top sneakers
9. four pairs of underwear [the Scots called them "gents briefs"]
10. an international student identity card, obtained in early December 1988 under false pretenses [he had not been a student for years]
11. a crushed package of Dunhill menthol cigarettes [with six left]
12. a disposable lighter that no longer worked

13. one shoelace
14. one whistle
15. one blue stone [it had a hole through it as if it had come from a woman's necklace]
16. one nail clipper
17. twelve batteries
18. an almost completely used tube of Crest Tartar Control toothpaste
19. one pencil
20. nine books
21. one pen [marked "too damaged to return"]

The U.S. embassy in Edinburgh returned these shabby relics to my family in Philadelphia a few months after the bombing. My father put them in a dresser drawer in David's room, and on visits home, I never missed an opportunity to study them. I had read about the tremendous effort to bag, tag, and match belongings with bodies. Volunteers hand-washed and ironed the tattered remnants. Investigators developed the rolls of film they'd found, in order to familiarize themselves with a person's clothes and possessions. When items were positively linked to an individual passenger they were placed in a banker's box with an enlarged passport photo of that person on the front. A British tabloid paper referred to the rows of these boxes as the "Shelves of Sorrow." Police officers who worked in the property room reported an intense and sometimes disturbing attachment to the dead passengers, whom they felt they had come to know over the months it had taken to identify the passengers' things.

The odor in the property room reportedly made one victim's father collapse. It was still on the items that reached my house in Philadelphia—that smell of death thinly masked by something fresh and minty. There was also some mud that had dried on a number of David's things, and small stones and blades of grass in the Ziploc bags filled with items that David had carried in his pockets. All of this felt like a minor failure in a very efficient system, but I was grateful for it. Unlike the relatives who went to Lockerbie in the days or weeks after the bombing, my family had

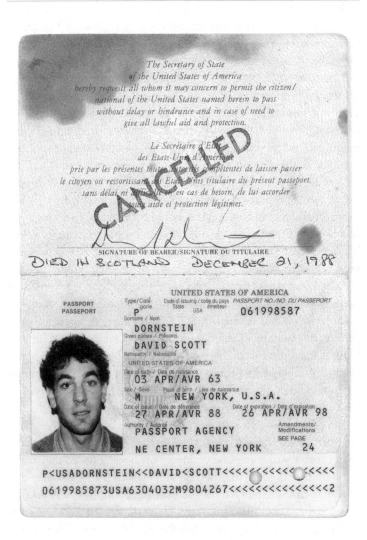

Passport returned from Lockerbie
along with a box of David's possessions

stayed home. For years, the dirt and grass and the odor were my only real, unfiltered facts about Lockerbie.

In response to repeated requests from families, a Lockerbie policeman reportedly had made a map of where every passenger had fallen. I went looking for it at the Lockerbie Police Station, but a constable there told me he knew nothing about it, and suggested I ask after it at the headquarters of the regional police force, in Dumfries. There, I met Detective Inspector Gordon, who said he was "the local officer in charge of the Lockerbie investigation." We talked for a bit before he said he was sorry, but he knew nothing about a map of where passengers had fallen.

I wasn't ready to leave Detective Inspector Gordon's office. I asked about property belonging to passengers of Flight 103, but Gordon said that everything that could be matched to a passenger had been returned long ago, unless it had some evidentiary value. Thinking that David might have boarded Flight 103 with some kind of manuscript, I asked about items that could not be matched to a passenger. Gordon said that the police had made a catalog of such things and showed it to relatives at meetings in New Jersey and Washington. Some items were claimed, he said, and the rest were incinerated. I got a sick feeling that something of David's had been lost in this process. I asked him if I could see the catalog, even if it was too late to save anything. I was surprised when he said no. It was part of the evidence, he said, and the evidence needed to be protected until trial.

Gordon spoke a lot about the "ongoing nature" of the investigation, and the need to protect the evidence until trial. The Scots were scrupulous, doing everything by the book, but did they really think there was going to be a trial? It had been five years since two Libyan men were indicted for the bombing, and there was no sign that they would ever be tried in a court outside of Libya. As for the "ongoing" investigation: Here I was, in the main office talking to the top guy, and it didn't feel like anything much was happening.

I don't mean to suggest that there was something wrong with this, or that the Scots should have been doing more. The investigation of the bombing of Flight 103 was unprecedented in scope and probably unrivaled in thoroughness. The bombed *Maid of the*

Seas had fallen across an 845-square-mile swath of Scotland and Northern England. Detective Inspector Gordon referred to this area as the "crime scene." From the very start, he said, the Scottish police were determined to search every inch of it—and by all accounts they did.

The search area was divided into ten main sectors, he explained. Sector A was the Sherwood Crescent housing development that went up in flames with the explosion of the wings. Sector B was the square of drab two-story buildings at Rosebank Crescent where many economy-class passengers had fallen—on rooftops, in backyards, along driveways. (More than sixty bodies were found in and around the home of a woman named Ella Ramsden, Gordon said. After the bombing, Ramsden moved away for good, but her rebuilt home became a place of pilgrimage for relatives, friends, and the occasional disaster tourist.) Sector C was centered on the Lockerbie Golf Course. This is where I believed David had fallen. I had slim evidence to go on, but I had once read an account of a Flight 103 passenger found on the golf course, and that person had been seated just one row in front of David, so it made sense that David might have fallen there as well. Another account seemed to confirm the golf course theory. I believed it described David himself, as a reporter for the London *Independent* had chanced upon him at 3 A.M. on the night of the bombing. The reporter wrote:

> On the steep hill rising from Lockerbie to the golf course lies the body of a man. He is not burnt beyond recognition. He is not crushed. The clichéd descriptions which spring to mind when you hear that a 747 has disintegrated at 31,000 feet cannot distance you from him. He is whole, strong and unmistakably human. . . . Around him are things which should not have survived when he did not. An unopened and unbroken quarter-bottle of Pan Am's claret. A green seat cushion with a gaudy cover.

There was not much here to suggest David in particular, but I liked the image of the man's body: peaceful, well-preserved, and surrounded by the everyday things of life. In the absence of real information, I could pick and choose the images I wanted to claim as my own.

Detective Inspector Gordon said he had to go. I asked again about the map showing where the passengers had fallen, and he instructed another investigator, Brian Sutton, to check into it for me. Sutton returned a few minutes later with what he assumed I'd really wanted to know when asking for the map. He said: "I just checked the file in the basement on your brother. David was found in Sector B . . . 71 Park Place . . . Ella Ramsden's yard."

After eight years of wondering, this information was a quantum leap forward in specificity, but I was more struck by hearing Sutton refer to my brother as "David." The intimacy caught me off guard—David seemed so incidental to the conversation about bombs and investigations and trials. I wondered what else was in his file in the basement. I asked if I could see it, but Sutton said this wasn't possible, and then he shifted the conversation to me. How long was I staying in Scotland? Did I know anyone in the area? Detective Inspector Gordon had called me "Mr. Dornstein," but Brian Sutton called me Ken. I didn't know how things had become so familiar. Maybe it was Sutton's sweet nature, but I felt like it had something to do with what he had just seen while looking through David's file. Police photographs of my brother being removed from Ella Ramsden's yard? The autopsy report? Maybe Sutton felt sorry to see me chasing after my brother in death, apparently not really knowing just how dead he really was.

That night, I found my way to Sutton's home. He had invited me to dinner in such a sincere way I couldn't turn him down. He lived in a new development on the edge of Lockerbie—a nice, neat complex of ranch houses built off the Dumfries road leading into town. Brian introduced me to his wife, Irene, who was fixing dinner. She said she was trying out a new recipe from a cooking class she was taking at the local high school. I helped her peel carrots. Emma, their teenage daughter, had just returned from a driving lesson. Brian turned on the television in the living room. He sat back in a recliner and we all watched together. For a moment I felt as if I had grown up in this house, as if we were a family, and that nothing could be more normal than living in Lockerbie. (I remember a line from a book about modern-day Dachau: "With its good schools and tight-knit community, Dachau was the perfect place to bring up a family.")

After dinner, we watched a popular British game show. Then Brian and his son showed me some of their golf equipment, and we took some practice swings in the garage. This was completely unexpected: I spent an entire evening in Lockerbie, and the subject of the bombing never crossed my mind.

VII

THINGS TO DO IN LOCKERBIE when you've budgeted two weeks to be there:

1. Walk past Ella Ramsden's old house and try to imagine what it looked like on the night of the bombing. *Note:* You will linger there just long enough to pique the interest of a man with heavily tattooed arms, who will lean out his door to say that there are bigger monuments to see elsewhere in the town and would you mind going off to see them now? You will notice that the South of Scotland meatpacking plant is just down the way from Ella Ramsden's, and the defunct Lockerbie Creamery is down the street, and you will wonder why none of the newspaper articles about the town ever mentioned gritty details like this.

2. Hike the two main "wreckage trails," where most of the remains of Flight 103 were found. As you tramp through the woods and streams miles west of the town, you will hope, however ghoulishly, to find your very own piece of the *Maid of the Seas* to take home.

3. Spend an afternoon looking for the main memorial to the Lockerbie dead, only to find that you've passed it a half dozen times on the bus without knowing it was there. The understated signage will strike you as the deliberate choice of a town that does not want to advertise its wounds.

4. Walk to Tundergarth, the heart of Sector D, where the nose cone of the *Maid of the Seas* came down. You will find Tundergarth idyllic, with its ancient low stone walls and its hills so lush, soft, and rolling green you will want to drop onto them yourself. You will wish your relative had landed here and not near the meatpacking plant and the defunct creamery. You will learn that, through an absurd accident of physics, most first-class passengers fell here at Tundergarth, on a first-class site, and most economy-class passengers got peanuts and soda at Ella Ramsden's.

5. Visit the "Remembrance Room" at Tundergarth. You will find a thick volume of biographical sketches of the victims of Flight 103, called *On Eagle's Wings*. With its photos of the passengers, favorite quotes, bits of poetry, and statements about career goals, *On Eagle's Wings* will strike you as the yearbook of a particularly doomed graduating class. You will also find a fat red album marked *A Book of Remembrance*. The words and phrases visitors have written inside it will not be hard to imagine: "missing you," "forever yours," "will not forget," "until together again." You will spend eight hours reading the words other relatives have written there, hoping that they will give you some insight into how they are managing their loss. When it comes time to go, you will wonder if you should leave a message of your own, but the gesture will have come to seem meaningless after so many hours of clinical study.

6. Play golf at the Lockerbie Golf Course, or at least watch as your policeman friend, Brian Sutton, and his policeman pals play golf on a Saturday morning. You will find

the camaraderie of Sutton and his friends endearing, as they rib one another about their shots from one hole to the next, but you will not forget for a second that bodies of Flight 103 passengers were found here. You will keep thinking about that perfectly preserved man whom the British journalist described. *He is whole, strong and unmistakably human.* This man will be just over every hill, just behind every tree.

7. Contact your girlfriend back in Boston. Send a fax from a photocopy shop in Dumfries because a phone call is too expensive, and because you want the chance to compose the perfect message, which says: *I'm here, I'm warm and dry and well fed. I'm doing what I came here to do and I'm missing you.* You both know why you've finally decided to make this trip: Because you've just quit your job; because of years of dreams about David still being alive out there somewhere if only you'd conduct a proper search; because you've been living together for three years and it seems as if you can't commit to anything with her until you've first made this trip.

A last thing to do before leaving Scotland: Review the entire transcript of the Scottish Fatal Accident Inquiry, an exhaustive set of hearings about the bombing that took place in Dumfries years earlier. One hundred and thirty-one witnesses testified over sixty-one days, with the transcript running to around fifteen thousand pages. "Hazel" at the procurator fiscal's office, in Dumfries, will lay out the first few volumes for you on a desk in a basement office. She will switch on a desk lamp and set a pen and a legal pad to one side. "You're planning on reading all of it, are you?" You are.

Hazel won't quite understand what you are doing. Neither will you, until you find the testimony of Davey Johnston, a police sergeant who gave evidence for two days about the recovery of Flight 103 passengers. Not every body was located or identified, but for each one that was, Johnston told the court exactly where and how. You will want to skip ahead to the entry about your brother, but you will force yourself to chart the details for each passenger, not leaving anyone out, as if there were something shameful about caring for one person more than others. You will feel nervous as you approach Johnston's testimony about David. When you turn to page 967 of the transcript it will be as if you had come upon him in Ella Ramsden's yard yourself.

Q: Now if we can turn then to Production No. 247, does this relate to David Scott Dornstein?

JOHNSTON: Yes.

Q: What was his date of birth?

JOHNSTON: 3rd April, 1963.

Q: What was his occupation?

JOHNSTON: Writer.

Q: Was he a passenger on Pan Am 103?

JOHNSTON: He was.

Q: What seat was allocated to him on the aircraft?

JOHNSTON: Seat number 40K, situated in the Economy Class area in the right hand side, window seat . . .

You will ask Hazel if you can photocopy the pages from the transcript. It will help you to see these words typewritten on the page when you get back home. David's death in black and white.

VIII

Eⁱᴀᴄʜ ʙᴏᴅʏ ʀᴇᴄᴏᴠᴇʀᴇᴅ from Flight 103 was photographed extensively where it fell. Not alone, but with a Scottish police official also in the frame who could later testify about it. According to Davey Johnston's testimony, Donald Black, a detective constable from Glasgow's Strathclyde Police, posed for the pictures with David. When I returned home, I found a phone number for him, and I called.

Black spoke with compassion and a deep desire to help me. He remembered finding David. He said David was largely clothed, not still attached to his seat, and not in an outwardly bad condition, at least not compared with other bodies he had removed from Ella Ramsden's yard. According to the Johnston testimony, David had been the last person removed from the yard—more than a day after the last of the others, the second-to-last person recovered overall. When I asked Black about this, he explained: "We had almost totally cleared the site, the bulldozers were ready to move in, when one of the dogs started barking. He'd sniffed someone out under a pile of bricks. A wall had collapsed on top of David, the side of Ella Ramsden's house. We removed the bricks one at a time until we reached your brother. I was relieved that we hadn't left anyone behind."

I momentarily shared some of Black's satisfaction in a job well done, and I was glad to have hunted down some information that set David apart from the economy-class crowd at Rosebank. But then I began to imagine the scene Black had described: David out there all those days, under a heap of bricks, with the crushed Dunhill cigarettes and thirty-six cents in his pocket, and the border collies barking when they picked up his scent. Details offer consolation, but only for a while.

I dug through my plastic bags of Lockerbie relics, looking for David's copy of Baudelaire's *The Flowers of Evil*. Judging by the mud on its cover, and the lack of mud on the covers of the other books returned from Lockerbie, I decided that David might have been reading *The Flowers of Evil* at the time of the explosion. I used to rub at the mud and try to picture where the book could have fallen to have gotten so dirty. Now I knew that this was mud from Ella Ramsden's backyard, but this did not much diminish my preoccupation with the last things of David's life.

For all the time I'd looked at the Baudelaire book over the years, I'd never bothered to read any of the poems. The corner was turned down at "The Voyage," so I decided to start there. The poem begins with an image of "children crazed with maps and prints and stamps," their "brains on fire" with all they don't know about a vast world they've never seen. The children, it becomes clear, are really the living, and what they can't comprehend is the experience of the dead. The children cry out: "Amazing travelers . . . / what have you seen?" And the dead reply: "We have seen stars and waves / We have seen sands and shores and oceans too / In spite of shocks and unexpected graves / We have been bored, at times, the same as you." Then the dead explain how their journey began:

> *The solar glories on the violet ocean*
> *And those of spires that in the sunset rise,*
> *Lit, in our hearts, a yearning, fierce emotion*
> *To plunge into those ever-luring skies.*

I might come closer to the experience of those who died on Flight 103, but I will never arrive. I know that my brother boarded the plane at Heathrow and I know that he was found by DC Donald Black five days later. But what happened in between? There are so few full-blown descriptions of death in a midair explosion of a commercial jet, even when you're prepared to search for them. The hardcore pornography of the cabin pulling apart in subzero winds and the people going, gone, in free fall with it—this is an underground thing.

The cabin of a passenger jet is like a big balloon that is blown up and deflated every time a plane takes off and lands, sealing the passengers inside an environment that is safe and comfortable, while the plane cruises at thirty thousand feet, an altitude that human beings can't tolerate for long. When the fuselage is ruptured, the pressurization balloon pops and the cabin begins to rapidly decompress. Gases in the sinuses, ears, lungs, stomach, and gastrointestinal system rapidly expand to reach equilibrium with the much lighter outside air, swelling the abdomen and bulging the eyes, forcing air out of the lungs. What does this feel like? One woman who experienced a rapid decompression on a 747 a few months after Lockerbie described the sudden drop in pressure as "a knife through my head." Another woman talked of a wind so howling loud that she couldn't hear herself scream. The survivor of a different rapid decompression wrote a shaky-handed note to his family on the back of the in-flight magazine: "Overhead blown out. Rows 1–9. Many missing pieces. Can see sky and clouds . . . Fiberglass insulation throughout cabin. Terrible noise . . . No time left. Love Dad."

The passengers aboard Flight 103 did not have time to write notes, but did they know what was happening to them? This is the question that waits at the end of the long road of investigation into last things. Look closer and you'll find several questions bound up together. Were the passengers conscious, and if so, for how long? If not conscious, were the passengers still alive? Could any of them have been saved if they'd been found right away?

The Scottish Fatal Accident Inquiry in Dumfries took up these questions, concluding that survival was "highly unlikely," even in the case of two passengers found on the ground outside of Lockerbie with relatively minor injuries. But investigators left open the question of consciousness during the three minutes or so it took to reach the ground. A jury in Brooklyn would take up this question a few years later, after Pan Am was found guilty of willful misconduct in allowing the bomb onto Flight 103. The jury was asked to determine whether any of the passengers on Flight 103 qualified for "pre-death pain and suffering"—compensation for the horror of realizing that they were about to die—with the most money to be awarded to those who suffered this knowledge the longest.

Experts on both sides testified about "useful conscious time," "occupant kinematics," "human terminal velocities"—a body in free fall can reach a speed no higher than 120 miles per hour— "flail phenomena," the tendency of the human body to spread out like a bird in free fall. Both sides agreed that passengers aboard Flight 103 faced many extreme hazards—the cold, the wind, the altitude, people and objects loose in the cabin. The passengers' lawyer, looking to prove consciousness, said that none of these things alone meant instantaneous death, but Pan Am's lawyer claimed that the combination was unsurvivable. He went on to argue that even if it could be proved that a given passenger survived for a time in the air, it would never be possible to prove that that same person had also been conscious. The lawyer told the jury: "We don't know what happened to any individual person on that airplane. Isn't that really a blessing? Your verdict should send a comforting message to the families. It should tell them that there is not evidence that your loved one suffered in this accident. Give them that peace of mind with your verdict."

The jury sided with Pan Am's lawyer, but I wasn't much comforted. Their judgment was a legal one, about standards of proof and degrees of certainty, not a scientific or medical conclusion. The jury had looked at the bombing from the ground up, so to speak, starting from the fact of the passengers dead on the ground, but I was still considering the matter in the other direction—*from the plane down*. I was imagining David sitting in his seat in row 40 at 7:02:50 on the night of the twenty-first, reading his Baudelaire, maybe, and I was still wondering precisely what had happened to him in the seconds and minutes before he landed in Ella Ramsden's yard.

I obtained a copy of the Lockerbie coroner's official "Report of the Death of an American Citizen Abroad." The report told me what David was wearing when he boarded the *Maid of the Seas:* a gray sweatshirt pulled over a checked button-down, black leather boots (size ten), Levi's blue jeans, a brown leather belt, white underpants, and a mismatched pair of socks, one white and one green. The report also said that his stomach was filled with a partially digested meal. *Had he eaten his last lunch at Heathrow before boarding the plane?*

There was a lot of horrible detail in the coroner's report, things I wished I hadn't read. Even a fairly simple line near the top proved horrible upon reflection. It read: "David Dornstein is six feet three inches tall and his eyes are brown." My eye skipped over this sentence a dozen times before I really took it in. In its simple wrongness, it shocked me like none of the other details I had found. David measured not quite six feet tall, and his eyes were an intense, luminous shade of blue. What might have happened to him after 7:02:50 on the night of the bombing to alter such essential qualities? I don't know why I continued to pursue the details, but I did.

The chief coroner from Lockerbie spoke to the Royal Medical Society in London years after the bombing, and I tracked down the transcript. The coroner was excited to report "something extremely puzzling and extremely interesting and unusual" that he and his staff had found in tissue samples from the Flight 103 passengers: traces of fat embolism typically released by the body after a trauma. This was a telltale sign of life, he said: "It suggests that [some 209 passengers] survived for a short, perhaps infinitesimal period after the initial incident took place after they sustained some of their injuries. This is difficult to interpret, but there you are."

It took just a few seconds after the bomb blast for the cockpit to "unzipper" from the main cabin—wasn't this enough time for people on board to register that something had gone very wrong? When the space shuttle *Challenger* suffered an explosive decompression at forty-eight thousand feet, Pilot Michael J. Smith was shown to have survived for a brief time. His last recorded words were just "Uh oh." If David or any of the others on Flight 103 had anything like a last thought or feeling, I imagine it to have been something like that.

A few months after my trip to Lockerbie, I returned to the cemetery where David was buried and found his headstone: DAVID SCOTT DORNSTEIN. APRIL 3, 1963–DECEMBER 21, 1988. It was a low grave marker, and moss had already covered over parts of David's name. I stood there and tried to think about him, to remember him, but I felt strangely out of practice. Over the years, I had found a less painful way to miss my brother, by not missing him at all, just trying to document what happened to his body after a bomb exploded on his flight home. It was possible to occupy myself for years with the last things of David's life without ever having to think much about David himself.

I wasn't sure why I had made this trip to the cemetery. Maybe it was like the trip to Lockerbie, an effort to conjure David's spirit, an attempt to find someplace where it felt right to say something to him where he might hear. Elie Wiesel once wrote, "Sometimes it happens that we travel for a long time without knowing that we have made the long journey solely to pronounce a certain word, a certain phrase, in a certain place. The meeting of the place and the word is a rare accomplishment."

I had done this now. I had stood in the Lockerbie woods and said, "David Dornstein is not destroyed." I had stood at his grave site on Long Island and said, "I am still here." I had crossed these things off my list, but on the drive back to Boston, where I now lived with a woman who had once been the love of David's life—the "girlfriend" I had faxed from Dumfries—I didn't feel that anything had been resolved.

PRIVATE INVESTIGATIONS

———

Time may be a fairly reliable physician for
human grief, but the first surgeon is
curiosity.

Compton MacKenzie, *Extraordinary Women*

I

I HAVE NOT YET SAID ANYTHING about Rina, the woman my brother lived with in Tel Aviv during the last months of his life. What I knew of her came almost entirely from David's letters to me. For all I knew, she'd been entirely his creation.

> August 2, 1988
> Dear Ken,
>   I've been in Israel just a week, but I've already got a thing for someone named Rina. She paints silk scarves, which she sells to tourists and to boutiques, and she's lived in New York. She seems pretty free for a twenty-seven-year-old. How can I get her to like me enough to keep me in her picture?

By the time I got David's next letter, he and Rina were living together, although neither of them wanted to put it so directly. They each needed to maintain a distance, to keep from rushing headlong into something so serious with a stranger. David sublet a room a few blocks away from Rina's apartment: a mattress on the floor, a bare bulb, a few of his books, a telephone. "Great for reading many books, writing many things, and thinking many thoughts," David wrote. "It's over the kitchen of a kosher Chinese restaurant. I look down on the men washing huge tin crates of fish and carrots. The sound of Chinese spoken in a Hebrew accent is one of the rarest language treats on this whole yapping planet!" I remember this scene striking me as very exotic, a bold adventure in a strange land, down and out in North Tel Aviv, but the reality was that David and Rina spent almost all of their waking, and non-waking, hours together at Rina's quiet, comfortable apartment ten minutes away.

Initially I think David imagined his time abroad in terms of the places he would see, the words he would write, the questions he would finally answer about himself. But then came Rina. After a trip the two made to the Greek Islands, David wrote to me: "Rina is very playful. She's originally from Turkey—a city named Izmir—and she knows her way around the Mediterranean. I am loving Rina, that's why I'm staying in Israel, and not going to Italy or a thousand other places I thought I might go."

I didn't hear much about what David was writing in Israel, but I heard about Rina. How she was Turkish and also a Jew ("thousands of years of ancestry!"); how she liked to talk long into the night with him; how she was "a dedicated and eager explorer of the human condition." In short order, David had completely revised his plans around Rina. He wrote: "In truth, I am sure I could make a life out of devotion to Rina. Painting scarves gives her satisfaction and money, and were I to make money too by concocting things in the adjoining room, it could be satisfying for some time. The days can be sweetly intimate for us both." For a time, David and Rina were simply happy.

Then the tone of David's letters changed significantly. His major theme shifted from love to leaving, and his mood turned to borderline panic. David announced to Rina that he had to go, but the only reason he could cite was an invitation he had received from my father to join a family ski trip in Colorado. The question was a relatively small one, as my father put it to David: "Would you like to join us for some skiing in December?" My father even seemed to understand that David might not be able to make it: "If your personal life is getting complex and you are not planning to return to the USA, except for purposes of joining us for skiing, that hardly seems to be worth the expense and effort involved, much as we would enjoy your company."

But David didn't see anything small in the question about the ski trip. By the time he wrote to me about it, he was already worrying about the next question: If I go on the ski trip, what will become of Rina and me? He wrote to me at length about this, signing one letter "Perplexed in the Holy Land." In another letter, he dressed up his dilemma in the language of Middle East peace negotiation:

November 4, 1988

In talks with Prime Minister Rina over the fate of our relationship held this week in her room, the emotions have RUN HIGH as it became clear that I was not planning to return to her in January. The Press is left wondering what the real issues are: Love? Work? Money? Marriage? I tell them, No comment. . . . I don't know why I can't say more. Rina is never mean to me, and nearly always tries to like what I say. Her bed is a large square of quilted comfort. Her bravery in the face of my cavalierly leaving is almost too much for me to bear. Yet for the vaguest impulses do I plan not to return.

In his letters, David had a habit of enclosing artifacts from his life, found objects, things lying around at the time he sealed the envelope: a box of cigarettes to show what he was smoking, clippings from the local newspapers to show what he was reading, condom wrappers, manufacturers' inserts from spermicidal jellies. He was especially forthcoming with the details of his contraception. He wrote: "Rina and I have used German condoms, Israeli condoms, and condoms by Dunlop. Did you know that Delek diaphragms are made in Israel on Arlozorov Street? Arlozorov, by the way, was a Zionist killed by other Zionists." In one letter, David went on about various sexual boundaries that he and Rina had crossed, but then seemed to have had second thoughts about sharing such intimacies. "PS," he wrote. "Promise me if you ever meet Rina, you won't let on I told you all this private stuff."

I remember talking to Rina on the phone that first time the

week that David died. I revealed all of the private stuff from David's letters right up front. I handed over the details as if they were the passwords to secret parts of Rina's heart. Instinctively, I wanted entry for myself.

Rina and I talked several times during those first few weeks after the bombing. We shared an instant, easy familiarity on the phone—nothing mawkish, nothing maudlin. To the contrary, I tried to make Rina laugh, probably too hard. I started off trying to say things that David might have said, and in just the way that David might have said them. This was a dangerous strategy for dealing with his absence, identifying with him so strongly—all the more dangerous because I did not realize it was a strategy. I thought I was being myself with Rina when I actually was trying to be David. I did not want to be the blindly admiring little brother with Rina, or the little brother at all. I tried to act bravely unsentimental about David. I told Rina that I thought David could be a pain in the ass at times, especially when he tried to bully me into writing more, or reading more, or caring more about the things that he cared about. I wanted Rina to side with me against David for all of his excesses and flaws, as if he hadn't so much died as been replaced with a better model—me. Chopping away at the pedestal I'd put David on was pretty easy, now that I think about it, even in the early days after he'd died. Hard would have been for me to tell Rina that I missed him.

After those first phone calls, Rina and I struck up a correspondence. Rina wrote first.

> January 10, 1989
> Dear Ken,
>   I start again and again. It is difficult. If you were here I
> would show you where David and I lived, and how. But I
> don't know how you are these days, or, really, who you are,
> except through David's eyes and heart. I am very reluctant

to assume things about you knowing how David told stories. . . . The way you answered "How are you?" that first night on the phone made it easy to recognize you. I suppose that you can tell that I miss David very much and I am full of grief places inside that nobody can see.

At the time that David died, I hadn't seen him in six months. I last spoke to him a month or so before the bombing. The delay on the transatlantic phone line, and the crackling quality of the connection, made it seem as if David were not only in a faraway place but also in another era in time. Rina's experience was much more recent and immediate. David's books were still on her shelves, some stray pieces of his clothing were still under her bed. "I still have so many things David left behind," she wrote.

An umbrella, jeans, books, some papers, Vitamin C tablets, the *National Geographic*s that he cut up and taped all over the apartment for reasons I don't fully understand. . . . There is an ugly green couch here where we would sit for formal discussions and not get up until there had been a resolution. We discussed many things on that couch, among them the future for him and me, if we would get married, and so on. And here I am left with uncertainty. He needed to go home for some reason, but don't ask me if I really understood why this was so necessary, so deeply crucial. . . .

I miss him. I had spent almost every day and night with him from August until he left. I can't remember life before David. Never had a person seen so deeply into the most hidden parts of my heart as he did. He stuck his nose into every possible corner, digging for things better left alone, questioning, questioning, and questioning until I would suggest that he volunteer for the Mossad's interrogation unit. Then he would start playing the part. I was "Ahmed the Terrorist" up against the wall, with him citing his methods for making me talk. There was no escaping his perception. I found him somewhat strange, at first, too loud for my taste, but I fell for him.

I must admit that sometimes he was too much. Some-

times I wanted to have breakfast without worrying about the
state of affairs in Bangladesh or listening to quotations from
whatever he was reading. I never understood what the hell he
was so worked up about so much of the time. And why did he
have to hurt so in the name of all the pages he read and wrote
each day? . . . Do you recognize this person, Ken? Are you
and I talking about the same fellow? I think probably we are.

How David and Rina had left things interested me. Would they
marry? Was she pregnant? (No, but "if I had been," Rina wrote
back, "you would have been Uncle Ken from America.") But I
shied from comparable questions about how David and I had left
things. Rina wrote in one of her letters, "You were a puzzle to me.
I did not manage to understand what David wanted from you, or
why he wanted it so intensely, or what the nature of your brotherhood was. I am not sure there was something specific, but somehow it seemed he wanted something from you, and you had your
own terms." *My terms?*

A good letter from Rina, I decided, was one filled with her
longing for David and with the details of their life together. A bad
letter from Rina was one in which she pushed me to reveal something of myself, to help her solve the puzzle of who I was to
David and who he was to me. She asked questions, and I answered
in complicated, wordy ways that boiled down to very little. I
closed off discussion, tying things up in knots, but Rina kept trying to sort it out.

April 11, 1989
Ken,
    There is much feeling for you here and much curiosity
about you for all the obvious reasons. For me, there is little
proof of David except in my mind, and some music he gave
me, and some things he left. The very fact of a Ken assures
me that "Dave" was not just an invention of my imagination,
or his. . . .
    I don't know what to say to you, or why say anything at
all, but somehow I must, and you are about the only person

who it feels relevant for me to say anything about this
to. . . . I wish there was a third party who could give me a
clue as to what you are like. . . . I hope you won't disappear,
and that I might be able to persuade you to say something
about yourself. *Maybe sometime we could meet.*

The summer was approaching, and I finally got the idea to plan a
trip overseas.

A digression: In the world of the Old Testament, if an older
brother died without leaving a son, the next-oldest brother was
supposed to take up with his widow. The practice was known as
"levirate marriage"—*levir* being Latin for "brother-in-law"—and
the primary levir's duty was to produce a son with the widow in
order to carry on the dead older brother's line. The younger
brother and the widow could marry and live happily ever after, if
they chose, but the arrangement was not contingent on their happiness. The younger brother and the widow had a job to do, plain
and simple. According to Deuteronomy 25:6: "The first son that
the widow bears shall be accounted to the dead brother, that his
name may not be blotted out in Israel."

There are a lot of reasons why a younger brother may not
want to procreate with his older brother's widow: simple prefer-
ence, for one, but also revulsion for an act that is dealt with elsewhere in the Old Testament, in a section on incest taboos.
Leviticus 18:16 says: "Do not uncover the nakedness of your
brother's wife, it is the nakedness of your brother." The younger
brother can find himself in a bind, then—caught, roughly speaking, between Deuteronomy and Leviticus.

A younger brother's refusal to take up with his older brother's
widow was a serious matter, but not unforeseen. The patriarchs
built into the concept of levirate marriage a way out. Deuteronomy 25:7–10 explains: "If the levir does not want to marry his
brother's widow, the widow shall appear before the elders and
declare, 'My husband's brother refuses to establish a name in
Israel for his brother; he will not perform the duty.' " The elders

of the town then summon the levir and talk to him. "If the levir insists, saying, 'I do not want to marry her,' the widow shall go up to him in the presence of the elders, pull the sandal off his foot, spit in his face, and make this declaration: 'Thus shall be done to the man who will not build up his brother's house!'" The younger brother's line is stigmatized for good, henceforth known in Israel as "the family of the unsandaled one."

It's not the letter of the Deuteronomic law that strikes me as significant here; it in no way applies. But the ancient rite, and thousands of years of rabbinical commentary about it, make clear one thing that I found to be true: When an oldest son dies without leaving a son of his own, there's a problem, and it's the duty of the next-oldest son to fix it, or to explain why not. The bond between the younger brother and the widow either must be cemented in some way, or it must be formally and publicly dissolved. That is: The widow and the younger brother cannot remain indifferent to each other. Even if only once, even if only to decide that this is how it should end, the two of them will need to meet.

II

THIS WAS THE PLAN: I would finish my sophomore year at college, and then, under the pretense of a summer semester of study abroad—brushing up on my French in Paris, say—I would arrange to meet Rina. I hadn't worked out all the details, or accounted for any of the costs of travel between Israel, Paris, and Scotland, where I imagined we'd make a pilgrimage. But once out of the country, I felt that everything would be possible. Abroad was abroad. The key was to get away.

Why the cover story about French? Why not just fly to Israel and meet Rina? I can't remember the particular chain of logic, but I imagine it had something to do with needing my father to approve of the trip, and to pay for it, and with suspecting that he would do neither if he thought it was about my traveling around the world chasing David's ghost, or his "widow."

Study was significant, I thought, and sentiment was not. So this is what I argued for: a semester in Paris studying French. I came on strong with reasons why I needed a second language— "Americans are such an insular people," "a second language is broadening," etc.—and I concluded that only total immersion in French would do. But my father was not an easy sell. If it was total immersion in French I wanted, he asked, couldn't I get that at a program in the United States? A friend of his had just sent his child to the summer language school at Middlebury College, in Vermont, and thought the program there was first-rate. "So why not Middlebury? It's total immersion."

I balked at this—Vermont?—but my father drew the line at Europe, and I had gone too far with my rhetoric about the need for a second language to back off the idea. So it was Middlebury or bust.

> June 25, 1989
> Dear Rina,
>
> I write to you from the Middlebury College campus where I will be living for the next seven weeks. I thought I might spend the summer in France, maybe somehow to arrange to meet you. But what with the perils of transatlantic air travel—have you heard there was a bombing of a Pan Am plane?—it was suggested that I stay on this side of the Atlantic.
>
> I am upset with myself for being so muddle-headed about my summer plans, letting them just slip away, and more upset about what I have said and done these last six months since David died. Or, rather, what I have NOT said or done. I am talking about David's writing. There is so much there and it is crying to be read. I am not sure if I'm the proper editor, the right man for the job. I feel like I've failed David by not speeding something into publication. I am sadly lost for cues to action. . . .

Rina and I exchanged letters for another year. The next summer, we made a real plan to meet. I was working in New York City, at Rockefeller Center, as an intern at NBC News. My unstated aim for this summer, like the previous one, was Lockerbie-related. I got myself assigned to the NBC News Archives and had the run of the place. I plugged key words into the video database—LOCKERBIE, FLIGHT 103, PAN AM—and pulled tapes from shelves and watched them. I had not seen many television pictures of the bombing—I had avoided them that first year—but now I was curious. I dug deep, but found little of interest, just the same few shots of the nose cone at Tundergarth, the crater at Sherwood Crescent, the bodies being removed from Ella Ramsden's yard.

Rina wrote that she would be in New York in July. We agreed to meet in front of the skating rink at Rockefeller Center. This was not the smartest place for strangers to rendezvous. With hundreds of people of every nationality hustling through, I saw a dozen Rinas walk past. Each time, I prepared myself for the Big Greeting, rehearsing variations on "So, we meet at last" and "So, you're Rina. . . ." And then the real Rina came up from my blind side and tapped me on the shoulder, apparently with no doubt that I was David's brother. My Big Greeting boiled down to just a dumb "Rina?"

I remember a lull while we decided what to do. For a year and a half, the subtext of our letters and calls had been that we had a lot to say to each other, but now I asked myself just how true this was.

We went to lunch at the restaurant in the lobby of Rockefeller Center and ate ridiculously overpriced deli sandwiches named after show business legends (a $13.95 "Sid Caesar" with pastrami piled high; a double-decker "Rosemary Clooney"). Then I took Rina on my own off-the-beaten-track tour of NBC. We walked through the *Nightly News* set and got shooed away because they were filming an afternoon "News Break." We took turns sitting in Bryant Gumbel's chair on the *Today* show. We looked at the bizarre Eddie Murphy "Gumby" exhibit in the glass case overlooking the *Saturday Night Live* soundstage. It was fun for me, but a little beside the point for Rina, who didn't know American television and who, anyway, had come, at long last, to meet David's brother.

I don't think it much mattered what Rina and I did together. We both seemed determined to have the least weird time together that was possible under the circumstances. We laughed a lot that afternoon—Rina had a ready laugh—but I don't remember what we said. I know we didn't talk in any significant way about David. To have made our meeting primarily about David—all dirge and reminiscence—would have been a kind of defeat for us, I think.

We walked around New York City—Midtown, Uptown, crosstown. Rina's walk was unique: slightly bent over, a little duck-toed. She had a funny way of running into doors—pushing, maybe, when she should have pulled—as if she were unfamiliar with the way things worked in the physical world. She had dark curly hair that recalled David's. What had they looked like walking together? There were no photos of David and Rina as a couple.

The few times our conversation turned to David, however tentatively and briefly, I remember trying to close off the discussion by sounding wiser than my years. I adopted the perspective of an old man looking back on the loss of an important figure from my childhood. I tried to say supremely sage, evenhanded things about David, like "He was just finding his way in the world." Or, "He had so much life still ahead of him," as if I had long ago settled in my life all of the questions about love and work and family that David had left unresolved in his. I spoke often as if being David's little brother were something ill-considered I had done in my youth, and now I knew better.

The old-man pose was at the opposite pole from where I really stood—still very much David's little brother (never feeling littler, really, up against the enormity of him in death), but feeling foolish about it, conspicuously alone in the old space of our relationship, as if David had just stepped out for a moment and everyone but I understood that he was never coming back. I also felt exposed for all the ways I wanted to take David's place, especially among his great group of friends. Better to be the much older man, at a remove from things, than the usurper. I was campaigning to be taken seriously as someone more than David's little brother. In Rina's case, I thought maybe we'd even have a romance.

I stayed overnight with Rina at her cousin Heymi's Midtown apartment. I don't remember if this was by design—I had my own place to stay that summer—or if the day's events just led in that direction. Rina and I went to dinner. And then, maybe to put the most normal cap on our normal day together, we rented a video. Unbelievably, after a comically long search of the video store shelves, we settled on *The Dead*, John Huston's adaptation of the elegiac James Joyce short story in which a woman recalls the lost love of her youth, who died tragically before the two could marry. *Did I pick this film, or did she?*

I don't remember, but I can report this: For at least a few moments, while sitting on the couch watching the movie, I felt as if Rina and I were a couple. Not a new couple, and not two people who had just met at a bar, backing into a one-night stand, but a couple seasoned enough in our coupledom that we could pass a quiet evening at home in front of the television with one of us nodding off and the other one looking on lovingly. It felt wrong to think of us in romantic terms, but I convinced myself that Rina was thinking that way, too. Did I want something sexual to happen that night? Did she? What about Leviticus 18:16? *Do not uncover the nakedness of your brother's wife, it is the nakedness of your brother. . . .* What to do?

As it happened, nothing. We watched the movie and went to sleep, she in her cousin Heymi's bedroom and I on the couch. If the evening had seemed at all romantic, I decided it was my brotherly duty not to acknowledge it. The situation that had brought Rina and me together, and the long buildup to our meeting, clearly fed the desire. And yet it was that very situation, and the memory of our connection to David, that killed the desire, inflicting a death by a thousand compunctions. At least for me. I scarcely thought about Rina's side in all of this. *Was she dating anyone?* I had asked her so little about her life.

Rina and I met a second time that summer, this time in Boston, where she was spending some time with her cousin Ralf before flying home to Israel. In August, I drove up to see her. I met her at Ralf's apartment and slept there several nights, but now Rina and I felt more like old friends than like "levir" and widow.

One afternoon, Rina drove with me down to Providence to look for an apartment. My senior year at Brown was starting in just a few weeks, and I needed a place to live. David had gone to Brown before me, and had no doubt told Rina stories, so she had her own reasons for wanting to see the place. We walked around campus, and I showed sites significant to David's college career—

the buildings where he had lived, the campus newspaper where he'd been a popular columnist, the theaters where he'd acted in plays. I tried to think of the comparable places from my own years at Brown. The benches in remote places downtown where I'd find myself crying at 2 A.M. in the months after David died? The basement level of the university library where I hid out from sunny campus life? My life seemed less vivid than David's, even to me.

Near the end of the afternoon, Rina and I sat in a Providence park fronted by a massive statue of Roger Williams looking out over the city he'd founded. I remember having a big, intense discussion with Rina there. I don't remember what the conversation was about—me? David? the lives Rina and I were leading now that he was gone?—but I know that we drove back to Boston in total silence. I felt at the time that this was bad, but I had somehow talked myself into that silence, and I could not find my way out again.

I did not write to Rina for months after our summer visit. Something had changed, and I didn't want to acknowledge it. I had always liked knowing she was out there somewhere. I had liked writing to her, getting her letters, and talking to her every so often. I liked the way it felt that we were always working toward something, not wrapping up, not winding down. But now maybe we had given the lie to this idea. The romance of our pen-palship had run up against the reality of who we were, and now we were back on our separate shores. Once again, Rina wrote first.

October 13, 1990
Dear Ken,
    They have changed, the reasons and the framework of letter writing to you have changed. The tone from before the summer no longer fits. It is a strange shift. You were an image before, or a fabrication of my imagination from the available clues. Now you have an actual face. And then there is the nature of our meetings this summer, all that was understandable about them, and those things put aside for later.

I have been sort of anxious about what would happen to "it" after we met—whatever "it" was that we had established in our earlier letters. But clearly "it" cannot be fixed or frozen in time. "It" will have to flow on. "It" is both fragile and has significant roots. . . .

Do you remember that time by the statue in Providence? I had wanted very much to get in touch with some of your "closed rooms." Sometimes when I am driven to get at deeper emotions, knocking on locked doors, I don't see how sensitive a place it can be. I stop respecting the balance of forces that makes it necessary to keep those doors closed, and I am not patient enough, and for that I am sorry. But, still, the drive back to Boston was overwhelming to me—and outside my control—in a way that was at moments embarrassing to me. I believe this had to do with the circumstances that put us in touch, with how long I had to wait before we met, and something, certainly, about you. I hope you will not mis-read this as disappointment. I will stand here even if you need to walk away.

I didn't have any explanation for the silence in Providence. I felt as if I should apologize for something, but I knew the language of apology didn't interest Rina. She was urging something else, and she was demanding nothing. I tried to acknowledge the terms of her letter, even if I couldn't really satisfy them. "I am working on plans for next year," I wrote. "I try to be hopeful about life after graduation. I have yet to deal with David's memory, but I don't think I can get into any of this without someone in my life who can help me to these areas within myself. I haven't found such a person yet, but now at least I am aware that this might be desirable. Perhaps this is also new since we met this summer. And perhaps you had a hand in making me see it."

A few months later I wrote to Rina one last time. Just a short note to say: "A few days ago, I took a job as a private investigator. I graduate in June and then I'm gone. I'll write to you next from Los Angeles." This, I realized, required some explanation, but it would be years before I supplied it to her.

III

AGENCY INVESTIGATIONS was a small private investigation company based in Venice Beach, California. I got my job there as a result of one of the more unlikely on-campus interviews. Steve, a private investigator who co-owned the company, was dating a woman who worked at Brown, so he decided to recruit during his visits East. His job listing said he was looking for a different kind of PI, more of a curious soul than a hard-boiled one, so why not look for that person on a liberal arts campus? A guy I knew had signed up for an interview with Agency Investigations, but when I heard the pitch, I took my friend's place and did everything I could to convince Steve that I was the man for the job.

Private investigation felt right. I liked the private part, with its suggestions of secrecy and interiority. And the investigation part had taken on some new appeal for me as well. I'd recently come across a book called *Gumshoe: Reflections in a Private Eye,* and the jacket copy had hooked me immediately: "Unhappy in his marriage and career, college philosophy professor Josiah Thompson was looking for a distraction from his personal turmoil. He found instead, a whole new life—as a private eye." I thought: *I'm a philosophy major . . . I have personal turmoil . . . I want a whole new life.*

Thompson wrote about a number of missing-persons cases. None of the details stuck with me, just this one very attractive idea: that people might seem dead and gone, but with some perseverance, clever tricks, and simple luck they might be found alive somewhere. I liked this idea. From the early days after Lockerbie, I had evolved a view of David as not dead but rather disappeared somewhere, deliberately gone at a crossroads in his life, to appear later with that novel or play he had promised. I imagined him eating alone in restaurants, then leaving just before I arrived. He passed through revolving doors of public buildings, going one way as I went another. I kept one eye on the spy for David at bus stops and shopping malls and sports events, and a few times I tailed people who I thought looked like him. My phone would ring and click dead after I answered. *A clue?*

I knew there was no true mystery here. But reframing David's death as a detective drama reduced the matter to a scale where I could do something about it, at least theoretically. There were comforts in the detective fiction, and preoccupations, and maybe the preoccupations were the central point. If I wasn't yet ready to occupy myself with the matter of missing David, I could invest myself in a story of him gone missing.

I started work at Agency Investigations just a few weeks after graduation. The office was located on the second floor of an old bank building with a rickety wooden staircase leading up from a back alleyway. To pull your car into the back lot was to splash through a mix of rainwater, urine, and runoff from a hose at the Tommy Burger restaurant next door. This was now home. During the day I worked at a desk in the big open room where the other investigators had their desks, and by night I slept on the floor.

Agency Investigations turned out to be a big, ominous name for a pretty small operation. For the most part, they didn't handle "matrimonials" (divorce cases) and they didn't do much "sub rosa" (undercover) work. The bread-and-butter cases were accident frauds—staged car crashes, faked slip-and-falls. Our biggest client was an insurance company.

Steve and Larry, the co-owners of the agency, were each great investigators and they gave me some good on-the-job training, but I was not the sharpest investigator on the street. I'd shoot photos of a damaged car with no film in the camera; I'd fail to notice that the face on a driver's license was a man when it should have been a woman. Once, I drove over my briefcase. The first case I worked involved taking a statement from a woman who said that her ex-boyfriend was faking his auto accident claim and that she could prove it. Steve let me do the questioning. During the next hour and a half, I strayed radically from the point at hand, mainly because I didn't really know the point. I spent most of the week transcribing the interview. Larry praised me for a job well done, but the information I reported was of so little relevance to the case that he couldn't bill the insurance company for it.

Larry was patient with all of my screwups, and I appreciated this. When I was in the field, I thought of him sitting at his desk in his half-glasses reading my reports, and I wanted to do a good job for him. He was warm and welcoming and made me feel like I was part of something. So did the others at Agency Investigations. These were the first new people I had met in a while. It felt like a fresh start. But then we'd be having lunch or driving to a law office or walking down the Venice Boardwalk, and a question would catch me off guard. "Do you have any brothers or sisters?" I'd try to answer right in stride. "I have a sister." This felt a little legalistic and awkward. *I did have a sister. Susan. She was going to medical school in Philadelphia. But did I still have a brother?* I did not want to get into it, and "I have a sister" cut off any further questions. It quickly became my stock reply in Los Angeles. *I have a sister. . . .* The more I said it the more I forgot that it was only half true. Actually, it was much worse than only half true, and catching myself in this act of erasure could be mortifying and sad. But only at times, and only for a moment.

For the most part I didn't think about Lockerbie when I was in Los Angeles. I told no one I met there about David.

This was Southern California, after all. It seemed right not to have a history here. Even more so in Venice Beach, a city whose very design—the ersatz porticoes, the Italianate flourishes, the canals, and the rest—had been a wild and largely failed scheme to impose a history on a place that had none. People came to Venice Beach to buy cheapo Chinese-made sunglasses, stupid T-shirts, and Rolex watch knockoffs sold out of suitcases. They came to Rollerblade, to body-build at Muscle Beach, and to take in the street performances of Robot Man and Skateboarding Grandma. People came to Venice Beach to score drugs and to look at all of the big breasts stuffed into small tops, maybe to dress in that one outlandish outfit that they'd always been too self-conscious to wear anywhere else. People came just to say they'd come, and often to get a picture of themselves there. But no one in the entire history of Venice Beach had ever come to wallow, worry, or grieve. And I had no intention of being the first.

I had come to California for the full, fantastical Los Angeles experience, and I would not be denied. By the end of that first summer, I was living in the guesthouse of a movie producer in Beverly Hills, the stepfather of a friend of a friend from Brown. The producer was well-known to an earlier generation, but he now seemed to spend most of his time dealing with lawsuits of one kind or another. He was sweet to me, and the guesthouse was a better place than I had ever imagined living, certainly better than sleeping on the floor of Agency Investigations. But there was a catch: The producer was fanatical about the upkeep of his house. His wife was an interior designer to sheiks and sultans and stars, and she went heavy on the chintz and floral prints, placing billowy curtains and lacy pillow shams in all the rooms. The place looked like a bungalow at a resort hotel, but without the housekeeping staff. I would be the one in charge of keeping it just so.

When I left in the morning, there was to be no sign I'd ever been there, no personal effects left out in the bedroom, no tooth-paste tube on the bathroom sink, no butter knife on the kitchen countertop. Once, I got caught leaving a banana peel in the trash overnight and awoke to find the producer himself pulling it out, then walking it to the outside garbage. Another time, the pro-ducer's wife left me a pointed Post-it note about an unmade bed.

(Not really unmade, I argued unsuccessfully in my defense, just no pillow shams.) The worst offense? I came in late one night to find the producer on his knees working my footprints out of the thick pile carpet with his hands. I had never thought about this—it seemed as if every week I became aware of new rules—but from that day forward I made a habit of getting rid of the footprints myself. Each morning, I smoothed myself right out the front door, leaving no traces. And at night, I smoothed myself right into bed.

It might sound like a terrible way to live, too precious a space for a young man, too repressive a housekeeping regime, but the producer was nice about his fanatic tidiness, almost apologetic for his excesses. And a lot of the house rules suited me fine. My life in Beverly Hills fit with my investigation work in Venice. I took pride in leaving the scene with no fingerprints or footprints. The Spartan life in Beverly Hills also fit my mood at the time. If David had lived his life to be memorable, leaving behind all those volumes addressed to posterity, I had developed an opposite tendency to leave behind as little as possible. I was constantly cutting back. My closet contained just a few shirts, two pairs of pants, and a single pair of shoes. In the social realm, I was more likely to cut ties than to make new associations.

The fact of David's death instructed me: To leave behind a heavily marked trail was to burden someone else with the obligation to follow after, to stick someone with all of the stuff of your life. Each item pruned was one less for someone else to deal with when I was gone, and this, of course, could be any day. Another possible explanation: some kind of survivor's guilt. Here I was, alive and living in sunny California, while David was dead, and *not* living in sunny California. It was as if I were committing a crime each day by living after he had died, and all of the carpet smoothing and closet thinning helped hide the evidence.

IV

A N ADMISSION: I am leaving out important parts of this story. I have mentioned Rina, for example, and I have described the romance we did *not* have. But I have said nothing about "K," a woman my brother fell in love with during his first week at Brown and dated on and off for years. K was David's longest romance and, before Rina, his most significant.

I saw K twice in the month or so after David died. First, at David's memorial service. She sat through all forty-five minutes of My Awful Eulogy, then came back to our house. At one point, I took her upstairs to David's room and showed her all of the things of hers that he had kept over the years, including a blue blanket with her name sewn in it and her old sleeping bag, which David would still occasionally sleep in on visits home.

K came to a second memorial for David a month later, this one at Brown, where I was now in the middle of my sophomore year. After the memorial, K and some of David's other friends came to my off-campus apartment to talk. The next morning I had breakfast alone with K. I walked with her down Thayer Street, Brown's main drag. K was strikingly beautiful—a sculpted face surrounded by a sexy-wild mane of hair—and she was older, clearly a resident of the world outside the university gates. I remember hoping that people I knew would see me with her and mistake her for my girlfriend.

A few years passed before I saw her again. It was spring break, senior year, and I was taking the train to Philadelphia from Providence, with a stopover in Manhattan. I ran into K at Penn Station. We were both looking up at the big board for Amtrak's "Keystone" service to Philadelphia. I think K spotted me first. As she approached, I thought she looked familiar but I could not really say how I knew her.

We talked the whole way through New Jersey. Not about David, but about how she had been a first-grade teacher and was now going back to school for an advanced degree. I told her about the new life I hoped to start as a private investigator. In front of Thirtieth Street Station in Philadelphia, we left it at *Maybe I'll see you sometime. Take care of yourself*. . . . I was surprised when she called me a few days later at my father's house. She was staying with a friend in Philadelphia who had just started dating someone new, and the friend and her partner were engrossed in each other to K's exclusion. K said she felt uncomfortable there. I was the only other person she knew in town, so she thought, *Why not call?*

We met for dinner the next night, and then had drinks in the bar-nightclub of a nearby hotel. I don't drink, but this was not really the point of going for drinks. I didn't know what to expect, but I was surprised we had so many laughs. This didn't seem like the person I knew through David.

We stayed until the place closed; neither of us wanted the night to end. There was an art exhibition of some kind in the hotel lobby, so we started to browse. One painting, called *The Maestro*, showed a sad-faced clown playing a violin. Another, called *The Wood Carver*, showed a very similar sad-faced clown whittling ducks. There were a dozen or more portraits propped up on easels, all of them sad-faced clowns in different poses. K had been a painter, so I enjoyed listening to her talk about what was truly bad about this work.

The artist turned out to have been Red Skelton, the aging comedian. Skelton's father had been a circus clown, the brochure for the "Red Skelton Gallery" explained, and Skelton himself had played a lot of clowns on television and in movies. Original Skeltons routinely sold for well over one hundred thousand dollars, would-be collectors were told, and this, in turn, upped the value of the limited-edition "canvas transfer" prints on display in the hotel lobby. K and I were getting laughs out of the situation, so I called the 1-800 number for the Red Skelton Gallery and chatted up the operator about investing in a print—*The Wood Carver,* perhaps, or maybe *Clown With Cigar.*

I was back at Brown when an oversize envelope from the gallery arrived. I had already gotten a postcard from K, on the front of which she had glued an ad for a collection of sad-clown jewelry—"a three-ring circus of pins, earrings, and pendants, crafted in bright enamel and gleaming crystal." Across the top, she had written: "Red Skelton spin-offs? Much more affordable. . . ." I knew a running joke when I saw one. I sent her the Skelton Gallery catalog with a letter thanking her for her interest in Skelton's work and commending her on picking such a fine investment instrument, et cetera.

The letters led to a phone call, and the phone call led to a visit the week before my Brown graduation. I planned to stay just one night in K's Cambridge apartment, but I stayed for five. A key moment early in the visit: K and I were walking in Harvard Square after dinner at a nice seafood restaurant, and I took her hand. Another key moment: I moved from the couch into her bedroom.

We crossed a threshold of intimacy during those few days. Now we couldn't part without a plan. She was rooted in Cambridge, though, working on a doctorate in psychology, and I was on my way to Los Angeles to start work with Steve and Larry at Agency Investigations. So there were logistical problems, but also a conceptual one: How could I start a new life attached to someone who so strongly represented the old one?

We needed to keep the plan limited, I felt. Nothing long-term, just a scheme to get another stretch of days together. The idea was this: K's older brother, Peter, was living in Los Angeles. She had plans to spend a week with him, and I was going to be driving out there myself in a few weeks, so why not make the trip together? K would fly halfway and then break her ticket. I would drive from Philadelphia and meet her at the airport in Houston, and then we would drive the rest of the way to Los Angeles together.

I went home to Philadelphia to pack my bags. Back in my old house, sleeping in my old room, I remembered the first time I saw K: David had come in late one night after a long drive home from Brown. He flipped on the light to my room, pointed at me, and said to K, who was standing beside him, "That's my brother." I was thirteen and in a night brace; they were nineteen and in love. Now I was twenty-two, and K and I were the couple. And David was dead.

I made my usual rounds in David's room, examining the artifacts returned from Lockerbie, looking through the drawers. Then I came to the notebooks and I realized that my orientation toward them had changed. I was no longer David's disinterested biographer. I felt as if I had a stake in what was written on those pages, as if this record of David's past now somehow contained answers to my future. I leafed through, looking for K's name. After a few days, I had read just enough to disorient and frighten myself. Then I made the mistake of trying to make sense of it all in a letter to K.

> Dear K—
>   I wish "we" could speak over and above you and David in my mind. But it's hard. I feel squeamish just writing "Dear K—" knowing how many "Dear K—" letters you probably got from David.

> Dear K—
>   Do things have to be difficult between us just because of all the history?

On my last attempt, I got only as far as "Dear K." In the end, I didn't send a letter. I didn't call her, either. I thought if our Houston reunion did not happen for some reason, if I drove those last miles into Los Angeles by myself and started life there with a clean slate as I originally imagined, then maybe that would be okay.

I sped through Pennsylvania to Chicago and straight down to New Orleans. Strangely, once I was in the car, I never really doubted that I would show up at the airport in Houston—but would K? I cleared the front seat, but I couldn't imagine her actually sitting in it. She had always been a little less-than-real for me. For years, my image of her had come mainly from an eight-by-ten black-and-white photo of her that David kept on his desk at home. It seemed to have been taken professionally. K was in profile and looked perfectly lovely, but rarefied, as if you could never actually meet her. David had told me that she grew up near the Metropolitan Museum of Art in New York, and somehow I combined this with the way she looked in that picture to form a view of her as a kind of museum object. Look, but do not touch.

That was then. Now I had no other choice but to believe that K was real: I was in Houston carrying her suitcase out of the main terminal at George Bush International Airport. I was sitting with her in the front seat of my car. We were talking about dinner and sleep. When the conversation quieted, I thought about how close I had come to missing her at the airport. Our plan to meet had been so tentative, and then I was late, having nonsensically reversed the one-hour time difference as I crossed into Texas from Louisiana. K was already on her way to her connecting flight to Los Angeles when we ran into each other by the escalator. She smiled and said, "Just in time," but her body language said she'd already written me off. Maybe she thought I'd done the same. Maybe she thought that my lateness was a measure of my ambivalence. That's where I hoped that the strawberries and the caramel popcorn and the other things I had bought her would come in. I hoped she'd notice how much room I'd cleared for her in the car and how generally clean and free of fast-food containers it was. I wanted her to know what she never would have if she'd taken that plane to LA: that I'd been thinking about her a lot since our time in Cambridge, that I knew she was for real, not just some made-up creature from my brother's past, and that I would have been truly disappointed if she hadn't waited those few minutes longer to see if I was for real, too.

·   ·   ·

I drove K to the motel near the airport that I had already checked us into. It was a grim $31.99-a-night affair that would be distinguished from the next night's grim $31.99-a-night affair only by the number of cigarette burns on the bedding and the magnitude of the stains on the carpet. It is impossible to enter a motel room like that with a woman who is not your wife and not feel that you are doing something you should not be doing. You are likely breaking at least one Biblical injunction—you know this, the woman knows this, the guy at the front desk knows this. In my case, the feeling was intensified by what I now think of as Leviticus 18 problems. *Do not uncover the nakedness of your brother's wife, it is the nakedness of your brother. . . .*

No one knew that K and I were on the road together. I had been home for days with my father and stepmother and sister; why hadn't I told them about the time I'd spent with K in Boston? Why had I danced around the fact that she would be driving with me out West? I was on the phone with my father just before meeting K at the airport, but I said only that I was picking up "a friend from Brown." I pictured myself being judged for trying to hold on to David through his old girlfriend, and pitied for not realizing it. I couldn't imagine simply telling a story about this exciting woman I'd met without it becoming a story about David. I could not shake the idea that a relationship with K could be had only at a steep price in pain or regret somewhere down the road. It couldn't last, so why go through the trouble of trying to explain it?

A possible turning point: One night, in a southwestern motel, I had a dream that startled me awake. I woke K and tried to tell her what I could remember of it. I said: "You and I were driving to California, and your brother, Peter, was stuffed inside of a big, hard-shelled case in the back. Both of us were afraid to stop the car to look inside the case to see if he was still alive. We were pretty sure that he wasn't, so we kept driving." I went on for a while about her brother Peter, dead in the back of the car, and when I was done K said, "I don't think it was *my* brother you were dreaming about." The comment was precise and fast-acting. I started to cry—just a few tears at first, but then it turned into one of those guttural, gasping sobs, with the choking pressure in the chest, the constricting throat, and no tears left.

In the few years since David died, I had had romantic encounters with just two women, and at some point fairly early on with both of them, I suffered a similar bout of inconsolable crying. Both times I felt that this had opened up a gap in the relationship that then could not be bridged. The intensity of my crying, the suddenness, the way it seemed out of character with the rest of my public presentation and indicated the sort of trouble that might lie just beneath the surface—I think this scared these women off.

I was sure I had queered things with K as well. I searched her face for signs that I had lost her, but she didn't seem alarmed and she didn't seem to need an explanation. This was an unexpected comfort, the flip side to the complicated history behind our relationship: K knew everything about me that I couldn't bring myself to say, and she knew it intimately. She had suffered her own loss when David died and she had some insight into mine. That night in the southwestern motel, I cried with someone else after years of crying alone, and I felt understood. If this was what it meant to be with K, then why did our relationship have to be such a shameful secret? *Why so doomed?*

V

A CLARIFICATION: I do not refer to K as "K" in order to mask her identity. K's name is Kathryn. I call her K in order to differentiate her as a significant character in two different stories, mine and my brother's. It's a distinction I struggled to make as she and I became a couple that summer. David did not know K; he knew Kathryn. And it was Kathryn, not K, who figured prominently in hundreds of pages of his notebooks, dozens of his letters, and a handful of his short stories, thinly disguised under David's own made-up names for her. What, exactly, had David written about her in all of those pages? With my K/Kathryn distinction in hand, it now felt safe for me to read.

This is where the story of David and Kathryn begins: David's first friends at college were two exceptional Artists—Alex, a sculptor, and Kathryn, a painter—and together they formed a threesome. Three turns out to be an unstable configuration for intimate human relationships, however, and David and Alex both wanted to be more than friends with Kathryn. She was bright and pretty to look at; she was an Artist, and she lived on their freshman hall. Alex and David were nothing if not competitive with each other. In the end, I think destructively so.

David and Alex argued a lot about what it meant to be an

artist, how to become one, how to remain true in the face of commercial pressures, all the usual questions. Initially, David tended to defer to Alex because Alex actually made things—sculpture and paintings—that looked more like art than anything David made. Alex also kept an artist's notebook, a spiral pad he carried with him wherever he went, filling it with ideas and sketches. David admired this. Within a few months, he transformed the notebook he had been using for his class notes into an official artist's notebook of his own. David soon dropped class notes from the notebook altogether. Now, on those same college-ruled pages, he would keep a meticulous record of his artistic coming-to-be, a portrait of the artist as a young man, all the more interesting, he thought, for being written by the young man himself as his youth was actually unfolding.

David's first notebook entry began in a grand, formal, high style:

February 4, 1982—
Beginning this day, a gathering of ideas, of epigrams, of feuilletons. . . .

But, in just a few days of around-the-clock journalizing, this Enlightenment posture gave way to the more tortured Romantic one that would dominate his notebooks for years.

February 8, 1982—
My stomach is in turmoil, malaise, maelstrom, and unceasing spasm. The butter churns without solidifying. Short stories—I've got to learn how to write them. A novel, maybe. But about what? I am scared that posterity will not vindicate me, not even the few who supposedly "knew". . . . Achievement. I have got to achieve. I can't ever start from the bottom, I can't ever be equal, only better. Untutored potential is more desirable than grit and climbing, so why lower myself?

The notebook entries began day by day, but soon they became more hour by hour. Neat handwritten pages gave way to urgent scrawl, and then to emphatic pronouncements in huge block letters filling half the page. Dream accounts, faintly scribbled in the night's small hours, often trailed off the page.

David trusted that the ideas he set down in his notebooks would flower into stories he could hammer out on his typewriter. This was the way Alex worked, wasn't it? A sketch in the notebook became a painting on the canvas. So why was nothing like a finished story coming out of David's Smith Corona? This was the kind of thought that sent David back to the notebook for more panicked entries.

My father had given David the typewriter before he left for college, along with a card that read, "Here it is, your very own, upon which to type all of those grand ideas and, of course, the Great American Novel." David took this deeply to heart, not noticing perhaps that my father's oracular pronouncement about his future as a writer came inside a Peanuts greeting card. (Snoopy is on top of his doghouse pecking away at the keys, and Woodstock is looking on in consternation.) In that first notebook, David seemed to be straining to live up to the expectation he felt had come with the gift of that typewriter.

> *February 11, 1982*
> *I think that I am living the strangest days of my life. I am sleeping in my clothes, writing until I pass out. I can't understand my dreams. I keep thinking that some mystical force will take hold of me and propel my writing into the land of the enchanted. It never happens. I don't understand what is wrong with me. I need to see more, cut more deeply into things, to understand how everything relates to everything else. Expand, expand. . . .*

David was never sure how much of this writer's struggle to share with my father. He wanted to tell him the warts-and-all truth, and often did, but always within the frame of a largely upbeat story about his progress toward that Great American Novel.

> February 12, 1982
> Dear Dad,
> It is 2 A.M. and two degrees above zero in my room, the

window wide open to the frigid night air so I can stay awake.
I am spending all hours poring over my books and papers. I
feel as though I've been awake for days, but I am finally
getting somewhere. . . . I am feeling, thinking, and doing so
much that to chronicle it would require a book, which, not
incidentally, I am still very much considering writing.

My father heard the strain and tried to relieve the pressure on
David. He wrote back: "I have no goals for you, David. Your life
is yours to do with what you want, how you want."

David found my father's avowed neutrality frustrating, and he
spent a lot of his time with Kathryn and Alex trying to parse the
real meaning of my father's words. *Does he not think I'm talented
enough to be a writer? Does he not think I have enough ambition?* David
might have preferred open resistance from my father, blanket dis-
missals of his chances for success, cutting judgments about his
talent. He could have rallied in the face of cruel judgment or non-
comprehension—the artist is never understood at home. Instead,
he found a fair amount of support, even when I think my father
did not fully understand what David was writing. If something
was holding David back, he was forced to conclude that it was
inside of himself. He tore himself apart in the pages of his notebooks trying to find the heart of this problem and rip it out.

Kathryn's place in this increasingly volatile mix seemed always to
be changing. David had fallen for her in a major way, winning the
battle with Alex for her affections. What had David seen in her?
In many ways, himself: Both she and David had thick curly hair
that they liked to wear long. Their chins were both strong; their
eyebrows full and almost square; their noses were straight and
(unlike mine) could pass as non-Jewish. I felt a strong sense of K's
resemblance to David—it made her familiar to me—but I'm not
sure David and Kathryn would have noticed it themselves at the
time. I imagine theirs was more of an unconscious matching, a
reason to be drawn to one person over another, something basic
and physical pulling them together. In any event, it didn't take long
before they were inseparable.

David and Kathryn (1982)

Not long into his freshman year, David wrote to my father about the new depths of feeling Kathryn had touched off in him: "Though the term 'love' still does not resonate from my innards, Dad, it has peeked out from under my tongue. It took a catalytic reaction with some lightning and thunder thrown in to create the conditions for this breakthrough in feeling, but it happened. I hope to discuss it with you more over Spring Break."

This was David and Kathryn as couple in love. But when the frame shifted to David and Kathryn as fellow artists, the picture wasn't as rosy. They were often at odds. He envied her productivity: She was usually in her studio, painting one canvas after the next, while he struggled to type a single story. Worse, she was also writing stories, and completing them. A true nightmare ensued: Kathryn wrote a story that got her admitted to a writing class from which David had been rejected. This enraged him.

February 21, 1982
Goddammit, I can write! The instructor said I've got promise, and suggested a few self-improvement exercises. Now I'm supposed to be reasonable, kow-tow, and skip out of his class to begin my Algeresque climb to narrative glory, with his sagely visage appearing to comfort me in my moments of doubt, the timeless words of his "appraisal" a spur in my left buttock. . . . Kathryn knows how to play the game, I guess. . . . Alex is right when he says college is no place for an artist to do serious work.

A panic settled over David around this time, and it wouldn't leave. He kept to his room, mainly, and to Kathryn's room. In these more vulnerable moments, he was no longer enraged at her. She was no longer Kathryn the Artist or Kathryn the Starcrossed Lover or Kathryn the Muse. She was Kathryn the Licensed Social Worker. She was Kathryn the Mother David Had Never Really Had.

A friend wrote David a letter as she watched him crash and burn that semester. "What I see in you Dave is a man who is powerful with his ideas, his insight, and his sense of self, but I also see a little boy who is weak and fears he is unloved. As much as the boy constructs an impenetrable castle, an indestructible fortress,

the man fears the collapse. You would like Kathryn to be your castle when yours feels under siege, but you know in the end, this
doesn't work."

For a time, Kathryn was the only person David saw regularly.
She brought him food and listened to him and held him when he
was incapable of words. The only sleep David got was in
Kathryn's sleeping bag, under her blue blanket (that same sleeping
bag, that same blanket he would still use years later). The only
classes David attended were those Kathryn walked him to herself.

David was in real pain, but he convinced himself that this was
just the sort of material from which great art was made. He and
Alex discussed this. The artist's responsibility—to himself, to art,
to posterity—was to record every anxious moment, every shiver,
quiver, and crippling doubt. A future generation of writers would
read his notebooks and know that this is what young artists really
went through, that *even David Dornstein* suffered on his way to
becoming the great "David Dornstein" they admired.

Alex supported David in the view that in his pain lay the seeds
of great works, but my father, the physician, took the opposite
position. He urged David to treat pain as something to be allevi-
ated and, if possible, eliminated. He suggested that David see a
psychiatrist. One night, after speaking with both my father and
Alex, David tried on both perspectives, the artist's and the physician's, and then he made his decision about which course to follow.

March 3, 1982

*I'm going to see a psychiatrist tomorrow. . . . Sorry Alex,
maybe I'm not an emotional daredevil. Maybe I cannot live on
the edge of the abyss and continue to function. Total panic is not
productive for me. Hyperanxiety is not spiritual growth, it's
paralysis. On this point, Dad is surely correct.*

*I'm sorry Kathryn if you expected more from me. But I've
got to escape this panic, this clinging to things, to you. And not
just escape, but eliminate. I love you Kathryn, I really do, and I
don't think you want me clinging to you all the time. I don't
want to hold you in desperation. But this is where creative
writing is leading me right now: straight down. Maybe I'm not*

a natural Artist, or a naturally creative person. I'm too preten-
tious, too polemical, too audience-conscious. This is all forgiv-
able, maybe to be expected. The trouble is that once I sort
through all of the bullshit, I find I've got nothing left to say.
And this is the most devastating blow to ego and ambition. . . .
     YOU NEED TO STOP WRITING IN THIS
NOTEBOOK, DAVID. . . . Your life is not the biography of
your life that you imagine. You can't live a book. You can only
live a life and if you're lucky one day you will write the book of
your life. But it needs to be done in that order. . . .

David stopped writing in his journal, abruptly, right here, in the middle of the page, as if he had just kicked out the ladder from underneath himself and now had nowhere to stand. He began to see the psychiatrist, but he didn't tell Alex about it and he didn't tell Kathryn. He had cut off contact with both of them. He seemed afraid that his future stability would be incompatible with having either of his artist friends remain in his life.

The next writing I found of David's was not in a notebook. It was a thick pile of letters, many dozens of pages, all addressed to Kathryn. It was months later, and he was working in the Poconos, at a camp for city kids who couldn't afford anything like the camp in the Poconos that he and my sister and I had gone to just a few miles away. He spent his days running around with a pack of eleven-year-olds, and he spent his nights in his bunk under a flash-light, trying to write his way back into Kathryn's life. He told her how awfully he missed her, and how much he felt he had grown and changed in just a short few months. He said that things would be different once school started again in the fall. He knew the difference between art and life now, he wrote, and he credited Kathryn with making both possible for him.

     David kept sending his letters, even when Kathryn expressed wariness about resuming their relationship. He worked and reworked his letters, numbering his drafts as they piled up; each one seemed to boil down to the same message.

June 19, 1982 "Attempt #1"
Dear Kathryn,

On the phone, you intimated that "Us" was a "was" and
not a "will be." But this time apart has allowed me to appreciate the depth of my feeling for you. I'll be brief. I love you.

June 19, 1982 "Attempt #2"
Dear Kathryn,

I will surrender to my feelings, now, Kathryn. I will
submit to the Romantic in me. I love you.

June 19, 1982 "Attempt #3"
Dear Kathryn,

I began this letter several times before I realized that all I
wanted to say was that I love you. I love you with an intensity
that does not compare with anything else in my life. How's
that? Goddamit, I love you.

By the end of the summer, David had scratched and clawed his
way back into Kathryn's life, and subsequently back into his own.
He thought again about writing stories. He bought a new artist's
notebook, opened it to the first blank page, and picked up right
where he had left off, making no comment on the period of
silence after he began seeing the psychiatrist. Those first few
entries read like a postscript to the year of struggle he had just
come through:

August 20, 1982

*Back at home in Philadelphia. Alex is here, visiting.
Bearded, exhausted from his summer travels. Looks like a
youthful Van Gogh, or a mountain man. . . . Alex says he's not
coming back to school in September and urged me to do the
same, if I really wanted to get somewhere as an Artist. I cannot
do that. . . . Goodbye Alex. It's a real shame how things turned
out. . . .*

August 22, 1982

DREAM: Kathryn and I are married. . . .

VI

WHAT DID THIS HISTORY between David and Kathryn have to do with me? Everything, it seemed, since K and I were now together. And nothing, since K didn't talk about David, and I never really knew them as a couple. If I hadn't dug it up, the history might have just remained in the background—indistinct, inert. But I couldn't help reading.

I should admit that I did not read every word David wrote about Kathryn. I often found their relationship exasperating, with the same conflicts played out time and again. Their sophomore year, like the end of their freshman year, was a nightmare of hurt and disappointment, tumultuous scenes at 3 A.M., frequent breakups and reconciliations, breakdowns and betrayals, and plenty of grand romantic gestures from David. A favorite: During one of their separations, David wrote about Kathryn on the wall of a campus men's room: IT'S A BAD THING TO FALL OUT OF LOVE WITH A GIRL WHOSE FEELINGS YOU STILL REALLY CARE ABOUT. Kathryn wasn't charmed—what woman is flattered by having her name on a men's room wall?—but the two found their way back into coupledom again not long after this. And they continued this way for years.

I skipped a lot of the explicit sexual descriptions in David's notebooks as well. (One of David's major inspirations as a journal keeper was Anaïs Nin.) I was the one with K now, and there were some things that the new boyfriend never wants to know about the old boyfriend, especially if that old boyfriend is his dead brother.

K worried about what I'd find in David's notebooks. I worried as well: Would I learn to see her through David's eyes and never see her clearly myself again? The fear was understandable, but it missed the point of why I was reading the notebooks. Looking for K's name gave me a focus, a way through all of the words, a reason to read at a time when I wasn't reading at all. But the true subject of that reading was not K; it was David. I had to read a lot of pages to find the key passages about K, and then I had to read more pages to figure out the references to other people and events. And after a while it was all of this other reading, the context of David's life, that kept me coming back.

I was enjoying David's company. I was learning things about him, adding new scenes to my highlight reel of his life. For a final project in a studio art class, for example, David showed up naked, clumsily covered in gold paint, and posed as Rodin's *The Thinker.* He sat on his pedestal until people grew uncomfortable—then read a manifesto about art, which he later burned. ("I'm obsessed by reactions," he wrote in his notebook afterward. "The reactions are the Art. It's better to be infamous than to be ignored.") David played John the Baptist in a campus production of *Salomé* (a plaster-of-Paris likeness of David's head was made for the beheading scene, and David fought with several people to keep the head after the show closed). David began writing a column for the campus newspaper called "Tortured Ravings" (later "My Reality"). The column was often a miscellany, short takes on campus happenings or world events broken up by asterisks, frequently capped with an apology for his not settling on one topic. He published these early columns under the name "Kristian Santini," a name that was never fully explained.

David made himself a whirlwind of creative activity on campus—in addition to the column and acting in plays, he wrote for the campus humor magazine—but he was no longer much of a student. In the sweep of his artistic ambitions, classes had

become a kind of nuisance, an irrelevance. He stopped completing most assignments, and made a stock-in-trade of the fevered
note of apology and explanation written to the professor the day a
paper was due, saying, essentially, that he cared too much about
what he'd read, been affected by it too deeply, to reduce his
impressions to mere argument for a grade. In the case of an
assignment to write on Samuel Beckett and Harold Pinter, he
claimed that his mute response to the midterm exam was "the
only honest encounter with the Absurd." To the professor who
ran his Civil War history seminar, he said simply, "I could not write
the paper that I intended to write so I will not write any paper, but
instead will give you some evidence here in this letter that I have
engaged the assigned reading and been changed for it. . . ."

David stopped taking classes for grades, an option made possible by Brown's wide-open "New Curriculum." He took all of his
classes pass/fail—Brown used the less damning language of "sat-
isfactory" and "no credit"—and, with his nonperformance on
major assignments and his classroom antics, he basically dared his
professors to give him no credit.

David waited at the end of each semester for a professor's
narrative "Course Evaluation Report." Even those professors
who passed him would often fill in some of the blanks here. One
professor wrote: "David's aggressive classroom behavior I believe
is often a child-like demand for attention and is more destructive
of self and less annoying to others than he thinks it is." David's
Art 10 professor tried to appraise his work after the semester of
the naked *Thinker* performance, writing that "David struggled
throughout the course, trying to accept or reject a definition of
art." The course evaluation form also left space for the student's
self-evaluation, and for Art 10, David wrote:

> I am groping intellectually. Art is for gropers. I am very origi-
> nal. I think independently. Or, at least, I delude myself into
> thinking that I am terribly original and intellectually bold. I
> grow a little every day. It's hard work. I grasp basic concepts
> and I think I even grasp abstract concepts. But I have no
> coherent educational program. My only background for the

course is that my two friends are artists. And my mother is an artist. *Was* an artist. But that's complicated. Please don't mistake these responses for sarcasm. I am nothing if not sincere.

Immersing myself in David's notebooks, it was easy for me to forget how little I really knew of his life back when he was living it. His academic misadventures, his artistic pursuits, his life with Kathryn—what did I know of it at the time?

I've got in front of me a journal that my eighth-grade English teacher made us keep. There are references to David throughout—"David is coming home from college today"; "David and I played basketball"—but not much curiosity about his life. My thoughts were mainly about math tests and French quizzes. ("I hope I get an A.") I organized a week's worth of entries around getting a new pair of sneakers.

My father was a significant character in my eighth-grade journal: I chronicled the things he did around the house (milestones in gardening and recreation), things he said, things we did together. My mother was a significant character as well, but mainly for the ways in which she wasn't around. I would wait for her to come for visits on the weekends, and then on Monday in English class, I would record my disappointment at her frequent last-minute cancellations. Sometimes she'd make the trip from New York, and I would write something about the visit: how we'd stay at the Marriott hotel on City Line Avenue; how she'd "hit the whirlpool" and feed me quarters for the video game arcade across the hall; how, sometimes, we'd play tennis. My journal accounts usually dropped off before my mother and I got to the Firehouse Tavern for an early happy hour; before she got a little tipsy and the men started hitting on her and she told them I was her husband; before she slept half of the next day away while I watched TV with the sound turned down low.

This is where I should probably say something more about the family. About my parents' divorce. About how it wasn't a question that my sister, brother, and I would live with my father and not my mother, who was in a private mental hospital at the time. About what my parents did for work—my father was a doctor, an internist with a growing practice, and my mother was an artist, or tried to be, making prints at the local arts center. I should say something about where we lived: in a working-class neighborhood on the Philadelphia border when I was born, but in a more affluent suburb at the time of the divorce.

I need to try to say something about my mother's mental state. David was haunted by the possibility that she was crazy and that her craziness lived somewhere inside of him. My own view of her is limited. I was just three or four when she had the breakdown that landed her in the mental hospital. I don't know what the diagnosis was or how she was treated. There is a story about her before this breakdown, before the divorce—she was a bright, vivacious, artistic beauty (Miss Boston University 1960-something)—but I really knew her only *after*.

Should I say something about the way it felt inside our house growing up? Should I try to draw the map of the family, who was who to whom? From where I stood, looking up at everyone else, I saw my brother and my father first, and then my sister and my stepmother, Dorothy, who worked for the lawyer who'd helped with my parents' divorce and was living with us a year later. As younger children, David and I were paired up for purposes of visiting our mother in New York City on the occasional weekend. Our sister, Susan, was old enough to go alone. These divisions were laid down early—while the divorce was being finalized, David and I were sent to relatives in Florida, while Susan went by herself to my aunt's place in California. David and I were a pair. Susan and David weren't close until his last few months, and I really didn't get to know her until after David died.

Growing up, David and I had rooms across from each other, the only bedrooms on the second floor of our split-level ranch house in our comfortable suburban subdivision. My sister, father, and stepmother lived downstairs. They rarely came up. David and I spent a lot of time in our rooms, and in the big, open den in between. This was our world.

When David wasn't around, I made a regular habit of snooping around his room, especially after he left for college. I knew

David and Ken in Florida (1974)

what was in his drawers and in the closet, and each time he came and went, I noted the changes. For the most part, I did not exercise the younger brother's right to claim whatever the older brother had not taken to college. There was very little rank scavenging; I mainly surveyed things and studied them, and in some cases puzzled over their uses and origins. A condom with a "receptacle end"? Rolling papers? Spiral notebooks filled with David's writing. (What were all of these words about?) Copies of *Mother Jones* magazine. I remember an eight-track tape of Kahlil Gibran's *The Prophet.* I associated it with the Mahavishnu Orchestra record albums on David's shelf, the covers of which hinted at heightened states of perception, higher orders of knowledge, and hallucinogenic drugs. My father had bestowed *The Prophet* and the Mahavishnu Orchestra albums on David, and I imagined that, one day, these things would be given to me, a rite of passage.

I looked up at David and my father for years, and they looked down on me with a shared interest in bringing me along. One thing that concerned them both: my total lack of interest in books. They made earnest and slightly desperate efforts to stimulate my reading impulse. My father gave me *The Ox-Bow Incident,* a story of rough justice in the West, and I slogged through it. David gave me *Goodbye, Columbus,* but I mainly skimmed the racier parts that he had been kind enough to underline for me.

I preferred television. I watched it before dinner and after dinner and just before sleep, weekdays and weekends. I watched all manner of game show, cooking show, talk show, variety show, sports event, and special event. On weekends, my father watched Louis Rukeyser's *Wall Street Week* and boxing from Atlantic City or Las Vegas, and I used to watch with him. But for the most part, I watched by myself. Books, I had no real use for. Television shows were my texts, and I knew the characters and the plots the way classicists knew Homer.

When David came home from Brown, I did not watch much television. I was afraid of his judgment and his lectures about the poisonous effects of TV on my brain. This is also true: I spent a lot of time with him during his visits home, and television seemed beside the point. He and I enjoyed each other and found a lot of different ways to have fun.

A case in point: One winter break from Brown, David joined the rest of the family on a vacation to Grossinger's, the old Borscht Belt resort in the Catskills. I remember the trip as a long string of jokes at the expense of kitschy American-Jewish culture. We got a lot of mileage out of a guy named Lou Goldstein, the hotel's longtime, full-time, "internationally renowned" Simon Sez master. Lou Goldstein ran his Simon Sez games with an iron hand, lording his decades of experience at the game over everyone who played against him, and he was not above using a technicality to dismiss a particularly tenacious contestant. ("You've been a great player, sir. You've really got me beat this time. . . . Put her there . . . uh-uh-uh . . . Simon didn't say!") Lou's wife, Jackie Horner, offered samba lessons every morning in the Pink Elephant Lounge. We looked for the two of them at meals— Lou in his official Simon Sez sweatsuit, and Jackie in her tights. They were Grossinger's royalty.

Our favorite character at Grossinger's was "Mr. Murray," a makeup expert who gave motivational talks and beauty tips to a standing-room-only crowd. At one point in his presentation, he would lower his voice to a hush, framing his central message with a dramatic pause. "I tell people time and again, don't be afraid of eye shadow!" Then he would repeat it in a booming full voice, "DON'T BE AFRAID OF EYE SHADOW!" David and I sat in on as many of Mr. Murray's talks as we could.

One morning at Grossinger's, David and I skied for the first time. We were required to submit to a brief session of instruction, which bored us for its emphasis on stopping, by way of the "snowplow" stance, and disappointed us for its lack of emphasis on going really fast, which was our intention. Once free of the class, David led me to the chairlift, which took us to the top of "Mount Grossinger." We locked hands, pointed our skis straight ahead, then pushed off with our poles, downhill-racer style. We were surprised at how quickly we picked up speed, considering that Mount Grossinger was such a turd of a hill. We were alarmed when we blew through a group of middle-aged Borscht Belters lined up with the ski school. And we were downright scared when we saw that only a dense patch of woods stood between us and Route 17. I tried to let go of David's hand to save myself, but he kept me in his grip. We wiped out before hitting a tree. It was exhilarating. We took the lift to the top and did it again.

In this way, David and I passed a pretty carefree, often joy-filled week. And yet I sensed at the time that this was an exception to some rule of strictness, seriousness, and torment that governed most of his time away from home. I didn't understand why it had to be this way. But what did I really know about it? I was living at home and saw his struggles mainly from my father's perspective. I knew that David was calling a lot from school, having long con-versations that left my father looking pained. My father and I would go for walks around the neighborhood and he would say something elliptical, such as "Your brother is making life so diffi-cult for himself" or "Your brother never knows when to let up" or something more direct, such as "Your brother is going to send me to an early grave." But that's usually about as far as it went. From my father's end, David's behavior seemed needlessly, inex-plicably, dangerously self-destructive. To the extent that I had an opinion of my own, I imagine it was some version of this.

David mostly shielded me from his troubles. I loved it when he visited home, and I loved it when he was in an upbeat mood; but when he was not at home, and when he was downcast, it was not really my business. I don't even remember wondering much about it. I assumed, as with the skiing, that however it looked to the people around him, David had things under control.

An exception: A few months after the trip to Grossinger's, David came home for spring break, and I finally saw him at his worst, in full psychological crisis, laid out for hours on the floor of the upstairs bathroom in some kind of pain. The heat lamp was on full blast, but he was fully dressed and wearing a woolen hat and scarf. This is how he spent most of the week: writhing around like a fish on land, then, in more settled moments, trying to record it all in his notebooks. *Was he a troubled artist? Was he just troubled?* It was frightening.

VII

DAVID'S DEBILITATING PSYCHOLOGICAL CRISIS of his sophomore year was almost an exact replay of his debilitating psychological crisis of his freshman year, only much worse. Once more, it had to do with art and with Kathryn, but these just seemed to be the triggers for a larger existential emergency. The year had started off well. He had finally gotten into an advanced fiction writing class and had rededicated himself to the creation of great stories. He copied Norman Mailer's Brooklyn address into the front of his notebook—he got the address a year earlier from Mailer's daughter, a fellow Brown student and friend of Kathryn's—and he believed that he might soon write something worth sending to him.

He began a number of stories—one in which his occasional alter ego, "poor little Kristian Santini," is sent off to summer camp with no clean underwear, and with a flashlight that doesn't work (he gets killed walking at night in a minefield on the grounds of an abandoned army training ground near the camp). Another story is about a little boy whose forgetful mother puts him in the clothes dryer. Both stories give out after a few pages. The more David pressed to finish, the more scattered his efforts. After months of work, he'd written nothing he liked, nothing to send to Mailer.

Time passed slowly. David's room was a classic writer's Spartan cell—a desk, a chair, a mattress on the floor, books stacked all around. He survived on a diet of Sociables crackers, peanut butter, orange soda, and Marshmallow Fluff spread. He described his life in a letter to a friend who was spending the semester abroad: "I have an electric typewriter, a chrome lamp, a mattress that I don't sleep on, and changes of clothes I don't wear. I stay mostly in my room traversing the postmodernistical literary geography, playing the hunger artist, talking in front of the mirror like I'm being interviewed by the *Paris Review* about my collected works. I'm using Burroughs's 'cut-up' method, scissoring through newspapers and magazines, pasting words down on the page hoping they trigger stories, but the results are mixed so far. What will I really do with my life? There are many options arrayed in front of me but all, I am afraid, with nooses to match."

David seemed always to be counting the hours—how long until the sun came up, how long before he needed to have his column done for the newspaper, how long before he needed to photocopy one of his stories for class, how long before he might see Kathryn again. The calendar and the clock seemed allied against him. When the time came to complete a work for his fiction class, he found himself unable to revise or finish anything. He started to wonder if he really had great books in him, or great stories, or any stories. These questions multiplied and intensified in his mind, crowding out everything in his head but doubt and fear. He felt himself shrinking from his own grand plans. On the front of his notebook he printed in big letters: "THIS IS NOT AN ARTIST'S JOURNAL OR ANYTHING REMOTELY SIMILAR TO IT."

By mid-semester, his life was in precarious balance, and it did not take much to tip it over. The trigger seemed to be the return of Alex, the sculptor, who had been "Kerouac-ing" around the country since dropping out after freshman year. Alex found out where David lived and left a cryptic note on the door of his room: "Meet me at your bench at 5 p.m." Their long conversations over several days set David on a downward spiral of self-examination.

March 18, 1983—

Alex just here, then he steals away, semi-calculated enigma. He asks if I am staying in college? Yes, I have no choice. We're different, Alex. You've cut loose, Alex. You may be finding IT, Alex, and I may not. That hurts, that's painful. But what right do you have to come here and wreck me?

March 19, 1983—

Alex, are you really on to IT, whatever IT is? Will I ever dare to find out? I will succeed, yes, but I will always pay the price of never knowing if where I am is where I should be. I could live in the wilderness, as well, I am sure. And I will. But not now.

March 20, 1983—

So many people doing things. I'm scared they're onto IT and I'm not. I do things simply to get a response, I don't have the necessary vision. I need the vision. I live only to write, I tell myself, and then I don't write, so maybe I'm not really living. I hate myself for wanting fame, for wanting to appeal. I hate the performer in me. I hate that I can't even suffer genuinely. There is no madness in these pages. I cannot even retreat from too-high expectation under the noble banner of madness.

"Madness" was good, it was clear from David's writing. Madness was nineteenth-century poets and painters touched by fire (Lord Byron says, "We of the craft are all crazy"). Alex was mad, David felt, and this meant he was a real Artist. By comparison, "mental illness" was dull—sessions with counselors, prescription drugs. Madness fueled the Artist's acts of creation. Mental illness was decidedly unproductive. How to tell them apart?

As it happened, Alex was more mentally ill than mad. Soon after seeing David, he was hospitalized and heavily medicated—lithium treatments, I believe—for some kind of a psychotic break. But that wasn't the way David saw him at the time. Alex walked away from campus to find a truth somewhere out in the country that only an Artist could see; next to this, David judged himself a fake, too painfully sane ever to amount to anything.

March 23, 1983

You are not an Artist, David. You are not a deep thinker.
What you do not know will always torture you—this you
must live with. You must not terrify yourself, or terrorize your-
self. Even if you are an Artist, you realize, it is making you
unhappy. Is this what you really want? Your constitution is not
suited for failure.

FOLLOW DAD'S ADVICE: HAVE FUN.
RELAX A BIT. GET PERSPECTIVE. GET
EXERCISE. DAD'S KEY WORD IS "HEALTHY"
AND THIS WAY I AM LIVING IS NOT HEALTHY.
STOP WRITING IN THE NOTEBOOK. TRY TO
BE MODERATE, DAVID, JUST PLEASE TRY
TO BE MODERATE.

DO NOT DESTROY YOURSELF.

CONCENTRATE
CONCENTRATE
CONCENTRATE . . .

YOU ARE NOT EZRA POUND
YOU ARE NOT SOREN KIERKEGAARD
YOU ARE NOT HART CRANE
YOU ARE NOT JACKSON POLLOCK

THESE WERE UNHAPPY MEN. YOU ARE
PERFECTLY HEALTHY. NO REASON TO BE A
MISFIT EXCEPT THE REASONS THAT YOU
MANUFACTURE. YOU ARE OF THIS WORLD,
DAVID, NOT HIGH ABOVE IT.

David hoped to spend that summer in New York City. He was
determined to get an internship at a magazine or a newspaper or
a publishing house. "Damn it!" he wrote. "I will serve sweet buns
to sub-assistant editors if I must, but I will work in the city for
some word-oriented concern. I will get there." But he sent only

one letter of inquiry, and when no one responded, he dropped the whole idea.

Faced with a summer at home, he hit on the idea of going to Los Angeles. I remember driving with him to the Greyhound bus terminal in Philadelphia, and then waiting with him until he was ready to board. He and I joked about all the Greyhound bus trips we had taken from this same terminal to see our mother in New York on weekends. I remembered watching the often sad procession of broken people come and go, some disembarking alone at Philadelphia, others bound for second- and third-tier cities in the South and Midwest. I remember the world through the windows of those buses, during all those years of weekends crossing New Jersey into New York. The mysterious lights in the dark distance, the exits to Rahway, Teaneck, and the Oranges, the strange change of driver in a parking lot outside of Elizabeth. Time with our mother was confusing, but David made those trips all right for me.

What did David think about those bus rides? We never talked about them in any serious way, but I see now that they were on his mind during the first leg of his trip out to California.

June 30, 1983

> *I'm somewhere near Pittsburgh still thinking about Greyhound rides to New York as a kid. . . . Thinking about staying in mom's apartment in Philadelphia after she left the house that first time. "Why don't you cry, David? You're just like your father." I was tearless. I felt strong. Mom was hysterical with rage. I don't know why I didn't cry. Now I cry all the time. Sometimes I'm desperate for a reason to cry and, finding none, I'll cry anyway. . . . But this is no way to start an adventure. I am finally off!*

David would be spending the summer with my father's sister, Greta. She lived in a nice house in the San Fernando Valley, at the top of a hill. Her husband, my uncle Jack, produced Johnny Mathis's records—everything after the earliest "Chances Are" period, I think—so David called Aunt Greta's place "the house that Johnny Mathis built." My uncle was no longer around. He'd moved out, or maybe he was kicked out. I think he'd been fooling around on the side, and he and Aunt Greta were talking divorce. It was a good moment for David to be there, as far as my aunt was concerned. She and David each liked to stay up late and talk.

David was supposed to stay in one of my cousins' rooms, but he slept mostly on my aunt's living room floor. He hadn't packed much in the way of clothes, and he'd taken only one book with him, Thomas Wolfe's *You Can't Go Home Again*. A few days after he arrived, David wrote home to Philadelphia for help.

> June 20, 1983
> Dear Family,
>
> I need clothes. Get help from Kenny on what clothes in my drawers I wear and don't wear. He knows everything that's there I'm sure. I need the jeans, the T-shirts, some white work shirts from the closet, some tennis shirts from the drawer, the BROWN sweatshirt, Adidas sneakers, white buck shoes (for dancing), the BLUE and BLACK chino pants from the drawer. Shorts! Underwear! Sweatjacket! Books! many paperbacks in boxes in the den. Send *The Sound and the Fury,* Bergson's *The Meaning of Laughter* (hardback in my room), and *Look Homeward Angel.* Send the *Norton Anthology of Short Fiction.* Send the poetry of Theodore Roethke, and the poetry of: TS Eliot, WC Williams, Ezra Pound. Send the drama of Bertolt Brecht, Pinter. Send *Life with Picasso* and Thoreau's *Walden.* Send any others you would like to send as well. I will read EVERYTHING this summer. . . . I'm not sure what else I need, but if it looks like I might need it, send it. Ask Kenny. He knows. Typewriter? Yes, if possible. I miss those keys.

David planned to write something great in Los Angeles, maybe that elusive piece of fiction good enough to send to Norman Mailer. He was free to stay home all day and do his work—no niggling course requirements, no interruptions, no financial responsibilities. But he didn't do this. He took a minimum-wage job as a cashier at the SavOn discount drugstore a few miles away and spent the better part of several days a week there. It was boring work, so he started writing a story called "The Lonesome Cashier by David Savon." It began: "Putting price stickers on soap and soda, moving diapers and heavy-flow tampons wrapped in a nauseating red-orange plastic, the lonesome cashier arranged for himself to be fired that afternoon, his slovenly appearance and his bald thefts from the register being more than enough to do the job. Later that night, he would be on his way back to her. . . . He had taken the job to distract himself from how much he missed his love across the country, but it wasn't working and he knew it."

David quickly grew to hate being a cashier, but he kept at it. He spent his off-hours lying facedown on a raft in my aunt's pool. He watched a lot of television. He read, but he did not write stories. Instead, he wrote long letters to Kathryn.

June 22, 1983—
Kathryn,

 We are apart. I wish that it were not so. I wish that you could feel the profound change inside of me that makes this separation different from the others.

June 28, 1983—
Kathryn,

 I miss you furiously. Is this a summertime phenomenon? I pray that somehow we will spend some time together before the Interrogation begins again in the Fall. I want to travel with you, Kathryn. I want to see the Grand Canyon with you. I love you Canyon deep.

David wrote me a letter that summer as well. I was at camp in the Poconos. I had never received a letter from him addressed specifically to me; this was not a postcard and not something sent generically to the "family," but a real letter to me. He seemed to be trying to open up a new line of communication between us.

 . . . I'm writing a lot of letters and working my cash register. Got caught stealing $300 dollars the other day. Was going to

buy you a life supply of those new contraceptive sponges. . . .
In all seriousness, Sprout, I miss you and wish we could do
some truckin' together. But I'm not worried. Eventually, you
and me, *and maybe Kathryn too,* we'll do some serious ramblin'
together. Enjoy camp! Next summer you'll have to start a
lemonade stand and look like a jerk. Write to me.

Love,
Your brother Dave

PS. SAVE THIS LETTER. You'll be sorry if you don't.

I remember thinking, David, me . . . *and Kathryn?* Who was
Kathryn to be included in *our* plans?

VIII

W E TOOK THAT ROAD TRIP through the Southwest, Kathryn and I, but without David. On our drive from Houston to Los Angeles, she and I carved a winding, tourist's path right through all of the major sites on David's imagined itinerary—Carlsbad Caverns, Monument Valley, the Painted Desert. David thought the Grand Canyon would be a transcendent experience; he wrote about it in the "I love you Canyon deep" letters to Kathryn. But K and I barely gave the place a chance. We were in that early, solipsistic stage of romance, focused tightly on each other, pushing even one of the Seven Natural Wonders of the World to the margins of the frame as we sped toward Los Angeles.

K's brother, Peter, made us dinner that first night in L.A. Peter would be the first person K and I presented ourselves to as a couple. I remember feeling the tension of the new boyfriend being brought home to meet the family, with the added weight of history: Peter had known Kathryn when she was with David, and he probably understood that Kathryn was not happy during those years. I imagined pointed questions about what we were doing together, but they never came. It was just a nice dinner.

K and I slept at Agency Investigations for a few days, in one of the back apartments where Larry and Steve lived, and then she needed to get back to Cambridge and I needed to start my job as a private investigator. I drove her to the airport. A teary good-bye was redeemed from complete morbidity only by a promise to stay connected by phone and by letters, and to think about how we could get together again soon. It had been a special time with K— I bought us a trophy at the end and had it inscribed with the dates of our travels and some mock language of commendation. But the more I reviewed our situation in the days and weeks that followed, the more uncomfortable I grew. K felt some strain as well.

> Dear Ken,
>
> I feel a little stilted and stiff every time I try to write to you. Maybe this is because you told me that you read my letters to Dave so recently. I don't mean this in an accusatory way at all—I can understand why you might have wanted to read them. It's just that I don't want all of that old stuff to undermine whatever we try to make together. I know that you are in a wonderful situation out in LA and should explore and be free of things that have weighed you down in the past. What I really would like is for you to be in that wonderful situation, feeling free, and we could still be a "we."

My response to K was long on the details of my new life in Venice Beach—the routines of the various performers on the boardwalk, the noise on the weekends that drove me wild, my daily rounds as a private investigator—but conspicuously short on hopeful talk about our future. Toward the end of the letter, I said that I did not think we had enough "data" to make a judgment about "us." I explained in my next letter that I had arranged a trip to Boston to do some more fieldwork on us: "I want to see you. I want to know what it is that we have together, and this will only be clear from looks in the eyes, and words spoken before sleep, and the way we say goodbye."

K met me at the Boston airport in a friend's car. She explained that we would be house-sitting for this friend, who was headed off on a two-week trip to Bali with her husband.

We drove through a tunnel, along the Charles River, and out to one of the nicer suburbs. We stopped in a driveway on a leafy street a few blocks from a high school. At the back door, we were greeted warmly and a little frenetically by two greyhounds that the couple had rescued from a dog track. The dogs would be our responsibility for the week, along with a fat cat who, we were told, would throw up whatever food we gave him. *"He's bulimic."* One of the greyhounds had horrible breath, and we were shown a toothbrush we could use if we wanted to give her a cleaning. Also, the husband said, the front lawn needed to be mowed and watered, and I could find the hose and sprinkler on the side of the house.

Once the friend and her husband left for vacation, K and I made what felt like a giant leap forward in our relationship. No longer a couple of strangers in and out of cheap southwestern motels on an uncertain course, we were now the Man and Woman of a very respectable house in suburban Boston.

I can't recall many details of that week together. My clearest images have to do with the greyhounds: running with them on the high school football field, trying to brush the teeth of the dog with the bad breath—me holding the dog at the chest and K trying to pry its mouth open to work in some toothpaste. Beyond this, I remember nights of take-out food and watching television and just reading quietly opposite each other in the living room.

A notable exception: One night, K and I fought bitterly for hours. I'd never fought like that with anyone. At one point, I asked her if she wanted me to leave, just take my things and go. I think I slept on the floor of the living room that night. What started it? I gather it was about David. I've got a letter from K written just after I returned to Los Angeles in which she writes, "I don't know how much our being together has to do with David, and I don't know how much that should really matter. I don't know if you will be able to find clarity, or to see me apart from the painful unknowns around David. . . . I have found myself thinking I should step back or aside (I am not clear on the direction), because whatever it is that we have, it seems to be adding pain and confusion to your life. That night when we fought, you kept asking me to step outside of our relationship in order to see the inherent 'craziness' of 'Ken and Kathryn,' but I can't look at us from the outside. I'm a part of it and I want to make it work."

The full version of this story involved both of David's big loves, Kathryn and Rina—the latter of whom happened to be in Boston for the month taking some classes. She'd written to me about this from Israel, and I'd written back to say I might be in Boston myself for a week and that we should get together. Once I got to Boston and was staying in that house with K, I felt strange about following through on the meeting with Rina. I did not call her for days after I arrived, and then when I called, I was unnecessarily cagey about why I was in Boston, probably giving her my line about visiting "a friend from Brown."

Rina figured heavily into my sense of the "craziness" of that night. She and I planned to meet for dinner at an Italian restaurant near her cousin Ralf's apartment, where she was staying. Late in the afternoon, I called to push back the time. When I finally left to meet her, it was after 9 P.M. I remember leaving K at our ranch house in the suburbs that night. I told her that I was meeting Rina, but as I drove her friend's Honda Wagovan out of the driveway, I felt like a cheating husband.

So here I was, driving from David's first love to his last love. I was distracted behind the wheel and, not knowing Boston that well, had only a vague idea how to get to the restaurant. I thought I could figure it out along the way, but nothing looked familiar and all of the streets conspired one-way against me. Time was ticking away, and I had no way to reach Rina to tell her I would be even later than I'd said I'd be. I banged the steering wheel and *Shit! Shit! Shit!*ed my way around the Boston Common until I finally saw the restaurant. Then I *Shit! Shit! Shit!*ed my way around the Common once more, trying to find a place to park. I was more than an hour late, so I settled for a less-than-ideal one-hour parking spot in front of a supermarket. One hour—that's what Rina and I had been reduced to. By the time I reached the Italian restaurant I was down to fifty-five minutes.

I would not have faulted Rina if she had left, but she was there when I walked in, seated at a table near the back. The big greeting this time? A flurry of *sorry*s for being late, and then a long-winded explanation for my lateness that mentioned everything but the fact that I had been coming from another dinner with another one of David's old girlfriends that went later than I had expected. I remember trying to tell Rina the short version of my moving out West, becoming a private investigator, starting a new life, etc., but my heart was not in it. I remember trying to listen to her tell me about her work and about her own new life in Israel after David's death, but I could not help but think about K at home waiting for me and the time on my parking meter elapsing. I can't imagine how Rina felt watching me rush out of the restaurant just forty-five minutes after I had arrived, too paranoid about the car to visit with her a minute longer. "So, I'll see you sometime? We'll write?"

I wish I had told her about my fledgling relationship with K, and how confused I was by it, and how meeting with her was intensifying all of this for me to the point of real panic. But I didn't know what I was feeling at the time. I was just running away from her and the Italian restaurant at full speed toward the supermarket parking lot, trying to beat the meter. Then I was back in the parking lot looking for the car, but not finding it, *Shit! Shit! Shit!*ing my way around, searching out something safe to kick in frustration. *Towed? How could I have been fucking towed? It hadn't even been an hour. . . .* A security guard approached me with a phone number to call to get my car back. Three hours and $71.25 later, I drove the Wagovan out of a lot somewhere in Boston and started trying to find my way back to K's friend's house.

It occurs to me now that the big blowup with K happened that night, or maybe the next. My insistence that K see the "craziness" of our situation must have had a lot to do with the way the night spun out of control. Something in me had broken at that tow yard in Boston. I sat in the driveway of the ranch house in the suburbs and thought about K sleeping inside. I thought about the look on Rina's face when I'd walked away, how disappointed she'd seemed, and how she'd tried to conceal it.

I didn't want to go inside. I could not shake the bedrock belief that I should not go on with K. My ability to live a life of my own depended on it. Los Angeles was the right place for me now, and private investigation might be right for me also. I wanted that new life I had so long imagined. To get it, I resolved that night, my relationship with K would have to end.

IX

In David's notebooks, I went looking for the story of how he and Kathryn finally ended. It began at the end of David's summer in Los Angeles. The "lonesome cashier" finally quit his job. He called Kathryn to say he was packing his things and hopping a Greyhound bus back to her, just like the lonesome cashier in his story.

David went out of his way to open himself to every possible experience on the bus ride home, striking up conversations with everyone who sat near him: Bob from Peoria, who had failed to find work in California; a wise-ass fifteen-year-old kid whose sentences were a breathless assault of "fuckin' this" and "fuckin' that"; "sweet Laura" and her not-sweet mother, whose buttocks were exposed when she reached up to the overhead storage.

In Flagstaff, Arizona, a Londoner boarded the bus and sat next to David. The two became fast friends. David wrote: "Glad to have adopted a companion to pass the time, a fine chap, a good bloke. I've been pretending to be a compatriot of his, a foreigner, to draw people out. Allows me to keep a fresh adventurous bearing, though I can't imagine it's not driving the poor Londoner crazy. I am showing him a memorable time, I think, a beautifully expansive time. I am a great host and showman and a gallant at heart. I would extend this trip forever, enjoying it so totally in fact and fantasy." The Londoner's name was Kevan Green. When I reached him by phone almost twenty years later, I was surprised to find that he not only remembered David but still had a lot to say about him:

> I met your brother in Flagstaff, I think. I was amazed we never stopped talking. David was fascinated by my accent. He seemed fixated on the fact that we Brits called cookies "biscuits." He kept repeating it: "Would you care for a biscuit?" "A biscuit would be jolly good about now. . . ." Then he started saying everything in a British accent. He would introduce us to new people on the bus as two "chaps" from London. He didn't fool that many people, but that did not stop him. He seemed to love not being himself. . . . At one point, he persuaded everyone to gather around as I stood in the middle of the bus with him and the two of us traded Britishisms. He said this was important because most of these people had never been outside the country, and probably would never have the chance to go. I asked him if he'd been out of the country himself and he said No, but he *could* and most people on a cross-country Greyhound bus probably could not.

I was amazed at Green's recall. So much of what he said could have been taken straight out of David's notebooks. He remembered getting off the bus with David in Philadelphia and staying one night at my parents' house. He remembered their farewell at the bus station the next day, more emotional than either of them could have predicted. Kevan said to me, "Saying good-bye to David was like saying good-bye to a brother. For some time I expected him to call and say he was in London and we should meet. It never happened."

Back home in Philadelphia, David tried to write the story of his summer. He sat at his typewriter to bang out the first of what he was sure would be "an explosion" of new stories inspired by his time on the road, but days passed with no explosion—and, maybe more upsetting, no word from Kathryn, either.

David grew more anxious. He tried to work, reviving his "cut-up" method of creating new stories. He sat at our kitchen table and began clipping newspaper headlines to paste into his notebook: SIGHTSEEING PLANE WRECKAGE IS FOUND NEAR GRAND CANYON. . . . HURRICANE MAULS TEXAS GULF COAST. That David's eye was drawn to the catastrophic and melodramatic turned out to be pitch-perfect for what would happen next. He and Kathryn were about to reunite.

David persuaded Kathryn to take the bus to Philadelphia. His mood couldn't have been more buoyant as he waited for her to arrive. "I am meeting her at the Greyhound Bus Terminal at 450 pm. I can think of nothing else. I feel in me that we will make it this year. I just feel different about myself, as I've told her. It has been a mythically handsome set of experiences this summer. I have not written very much this summer but have loved much in my heart. . . . Wait! Wait! She is here. She is here. She is here. . . ."

No sooner did David record his ecstasy at seeing Kathryn than the two were fighting again. They went to the Philadelphia Art Museum. David was irritated by little kids running around and paintings that didn't inspire him and by Kathryn, who just didn't seem to be responding to him the way he'd have liked. They separated in the museum. When David was alone again with his notebook, he tried to get clear on what had happened.

> I'm irritated, goddamn fucking irritated now, goddamn this, we are not, she and I, we are not in sync. I'm edgy but still but still but still. "Dave, don't forget you've got to compromise, give of yourself and SMILE when you do it, work at it, it is worth it, isn't this what you want?" How strange this life, the expectations, distortions, the way reality never measures up.

A week later, David and Kathryn were together again, at Kathryn's family's summer house on Long Island. They did not get along from the start. Every interaction was contentious: David wanted to go dancing; Kathryn wanted to stay at home with her family.

"The Writer at Work" (August 1983)

Kathryn's mother prepared a nice meal, but David refused to eat it. (He sat in the living room eating Marshmallow Fluff from the jar with his fingers.) That week, the weather was basic East Coast summer, hot and humid, and the summer house did not have air-conditioning, but I found this from David: "I wear my knit hat and scarf around the house all hours. I look like a cat burglar."

The final straw? At some point David and Kathryn read each other's journals and all of their rough judgments about each other were laid bare. The fight that followed was their most bitter yet. I don't know exactly how it came to be that David was back on a train to Philadelphia the next morning, but he later made an oblique reference to someone "flailing at me with a maga-zine." (Kathryn? Kathryn's mother?) And then he mentioned someone (maybe the same someone) saying, "I AM SERIOUS. I WANT YOU UP EARLY AND OUT OF HERE TOMOR-ROW MORNING."

David was back in Philadelphia the next day. I had just returned home from summer camp, so we spent the week together. David set an ambitious sightseeing agenda for us, trying to recapture the feeling of his cross-country travels. I have some photographs of a trip we took to the National Mushroom Museum, in Kennett Square, Pennsylvania. I'm standing in front of a display case that asks, WHAT IS A MUSHROOM? David is standing in front of a dio-rama labeled A MUSHROOM FARM—it's just a few silver sheds filled with pallets of dirt and mushrooms, but David mugs a look of awe. He insisted on posed shots all around the area—there's one of him buying an ice-cream cone at the Dairy Queen, another of him at the Brandywine Battlefield, where he's kneeling in front of a low wall with his shirt tied around his head pretending to dodge another barrage from the redcoats.

At home, David wanted to take more photos. He dressed me in a blue blazer, put headphones on me, and sat me at the piano as if we were in a studio recording session. He said this would be an important shot when I became a famous piano player. For his own Artist's shot, we moved a leather desk into the center of our den;

he piled it high with his papers and started writing in his note-book. He made me record on the back of the photo THE WRITER AT WORK, AUGUST 1983. David might have tried to talk to me about his breakup with Kathryn that week, but I don't remember it. I was glad his trip to Long Island had been cut short; he could spend more time at home with me.

Kathryn called later that week. She told David she was sorry it had to end the violent way it had. David told her that he understood. He had pushed things too far and he was sorry. He assured her that he felt their time on Long Island bore no consequence upon "our long love affair." But Kathryn hadn't called to patch things up. She'd called to say good-bye in a civil and final way.

Long, tense silences had become characteristic of their phone conversations, but the one that ended this call was surely the longest. David usually cracked first, saying something earnest and sentimental, but this time Kathryn cut it short by hanging up the phone. David turned immediately to his notebook to record his reaction:

> . . . as the phone clicked to dial tone I begin to mourn "us" then stopped myself. I wonder if there's not a better mate for me than Kathryn. I know there is certainly a better mate for her than me, one who can give more of himself to her. How will this read years and years from now? How will all of the questions be answered?

He took a walk to our local pharmacy and purchased a new spiral notebook. That night, he wrote about his first full day in the "post-Kathryn era":

> Now I am on the brown rug in the upstairs den playroom at home in Philadelphia. I have not slept in a bed in weeks, perhaps months. I sleep always on the floor or upon floor mattresses or couches, anything but beds, and I don't know why except that it readies me to write. And write this year I must! Now it is 915 pm on Saturday August 27. DORNSTEIN'S NEW JOURNAL STARTS TODAY! Please, dear reader, continue. . . .

For K and me, the Big Breakup came on our first anniversary. K flew out to Los Angeles for a visit, and we decided to take a drive up the California coast. We made it as far as Montecito before the heavy conversation began, with me making many now-familiar arguments about why we couldn't work as a couple. I could see the ways in which K and I were different from Kathryn and David—we laughed, for one thing—but we suffered from something that I couldn't exactly name, except to invoke David—and this affliction, I feared, could never be cured.

Over the course of a few days, K and I said everything we had ever thought of saying to each other. All of the extreme and terrible things couples say when they fight. All of the hard things that two people who genuinely care for each other say when the fighting ends. And then it was done.

I drove K to the airport, and we waited together at the gate. It was confusing. We'd gotten along so well on our drive back down the California coast that we weren't sure if we had actually broken up or just cleared the air. It was only when the plane began to board that the sense of finality set in. This was it. I kissed K on the cheek. It felt like the wrong gesture even as I did it, but what would have been right for good-bye?

K headed down the ramp and disappeared inside. It was sunset. I watched as the baggage and the meal carts were loaded into the belly of the big jet, and I imagined it all being recovered in a forest somewhere if the plane went down, the skin of the fuselage peeling back, the nose cone crushed in a field. . . . I stood at the window as the plane pushed back from the terminal and taxied out onto the runway. I watched as it took off and then banked out of view. This is how people exit my life, I thought. They take off on planes and don't come back. It was a little self-pitying, considering that I had precipitated the breakup and that K wasn't dead. But I felt that I was back on solid ground with thoughts like this. David and I would now be together again, old friends reunited by tragedy, and no one was left to bother us.

X

I took a leave from Agency Investigations. This was the language Steve and I found for it, but it felt like just one step from quitting. A friend of mine had dropped out of Brown and reenrolled at Berkeley. I decided to visit him. For several weeks, I slept on the floor of his apartment.

I had no master plan and no burning desires. Nothing keeping me in California, and nothing drawing me somewhere else. A mild panic set in about the future. *How had David passed all of those months at Rina's apartment just reading and smoking and writing?* I needed a goal, a focus. Something. I bought a copy of *Moby-Dick* and decided to make a project of reading it. This filled around ten days.

Then it was on to Joseph Conrad. During his last few months in Israel, David had made a project of reading everything by Conrad, so I settled into his works as well. I started with *Heart of Darkness*. Not too far into the book I found a passage that felt prophetic, as if David had put it in my path to read at that very moment in my life. Conrad's narrator says, "No, I don't like work . . . I had rather laze about and think of all the fine things that can be done. I don't like work. No man does. But I like what is in the work—the chance to find yourself. Your own reality, for yourself, not for others, what no man can ever know."

The words seemed more important for the fact that David may well have read them in the weeks before he died. Maybe he thought he was succeeding on Conrad's terms—finding himself in his work, not lazing about—but I wasn't. I needed to do something, but what?

My Berkeley friend pointed me toward the *California Journal,* a public affairs monthly for the Sacramento crowd that was edited by a man named A. G. Block, a friend of my friend's father. I sent a query letter to Mr. Block, proposing an article about the accident fakers I had come to know on the job at the agency. Block was lukewarm to the topic. *But,* he added at the end of the call, *but.* . . . if I wanted to write the article anyway, he would look at it. This was pretty slight encouragement. It was no encouragement at all, really, but it was more than enough for me.

Question: What was I going to do with my life? Answer: I was going to write an article about auto insurance reform for the *California Journal,* and Mr. A. G. Block was going to publish it. I started making calls to state legislators and trial lawyers and experts from universities and think tanks. I felt important telling people I was working on an article for the *California Journal.* I borrowed a button-down shirt from my Berkeley friend and scheduled meetings every day for a week.

I wrote my article and sent it to A. G. Block. I heard nothing for more than a week, so I phoned. Block was brief. He said something about the magazine "changing its direction." My story wouldn't be right for them at this time. I got the point. Sort of. Not really. I didn't drop the story altogether. I didn't drop it at all. Instead, I decided to return to Los Angeles to make it better.

I needed to make a small story seem bigger, and the best way to do that, it seemed, was to give that story a history. I began my research at the Beverly Hills Public Library, just up the street from the producer's house, where I still lived. The library had a printed index of the last hundred-plus years of *The New York Times,* so I started combing it for accident-faking stories like the ones I had been investigating. Those first few finds were exhilarating: an ex–circus performer sentenced to five years in Sing-Sing in 1905 for "flopping" in front of cars and pretending to be hit; an "accident gang" in the 1920s that had staged dozens of accidents with horse-drawn laundry wagons. . . .

I stood at that wall of newspaper indexes most hours of the day, most days of the week. I filled out call slips for microfilm reels and delighted in each article found and photocopied. This was not a pipe dream, I needed to convince myself. David had never crossed the line from the great things he had imagined to something he could actually point to—but I would. Forget Mr. A. G. Block. This was bigger than the *California Journal,* more than a magazine article. *Much more.* Question: What are you doing with your life? Answer: I am writing a book about the history of accident faking in America.

I felt that I had made big changes in my life, and K was the only person I really cared to tell. She had a way of making me feel that my choices were good ones, that they were getting me closer to realizing some vision I had for myself that was separate from David's. But I had lost her. It took a few months, but I realized I had made a mistake going through with the breakup on our drive up the coast. In all of the calculations that led to our split, I had not factored in one essential part of the equation: My relationship with K had been going pretty well before I ended it.

I wrote her a letter. I told her that I had left Agency Investigations and was now working on a book. "I don't expect you to write back. . . . Maybe I'm just sending my wish to stay a part of your life while I'm trying to build one of my own." She didn't reply right away, so I wrote more letters, little notes in a bottle like the ones David had sent to Kathryn from my aunt Greta's place in the Valley, just a few miles away.

K finally wrote back. She said that she was really happy for the changes I'd made in my life. And then we talked on the phone. It was all very comfortable and natural, as it had once been, except that K had started dating someone else.

I kept writing to her anyway. My life had narrowed mostly to my accident-faking research, but K had a way of framing what I was doing that felt larger. We wrote letters and talked on the phone for months. Then she came to Los Angeles to visit her brother. I saw her briefly outside a ceramics store in Venice. It was exciting to see her again. I watched as she sorted through the store's clearance table for bargain coffee mugs and dessert plates. She was dressed in a short, black silk dress, looking young and desirable, but her nose and eyes were scrunched up like an old lady's as she looked for cracks and defects and price markdowns. I thought: *I know this woman.* I used to refer to her jokingly as "Sadie" for the way she delighted in saving twenty cents on a roll of paper towels. I found this terribly endearing, the bohemian who liked a bargain. It was a side of K that David had never seen.

We made a plan for dinner. K was doing some house-sitting for a cousin who was out of town, so we decided to meet there. We ate outside, on a patio—me sitting with my back against the side of the house and K sitting cross-legged opposite me. I remember us talking for hours in the late-summer light and thinking I hadn't had such a deep and honest conversation with anyone since the last time she and I had spoken.

After that visit, our letters grew more frequent and intimate. It was an old-fashioned kind of courtship, through the mails, but it was effective. I made a plan to come east for an extended stay with K. I told her that I thought it was time I stopped keeping us a secret. She wrote back to say that she had broken it off with the man who'd been pursuing her, but she still had questions about us:

> I was thinking today about you telling your Dad about me. My great fear is that he will see us as being about Dave. Is it possible for people to see us on our own terms? This led to my next fear which is that somewhere in the back of your mind or your heart you feel that we are about Dave too. You still talk about the need to "continue" Dave. . . . I get the sense that there is this burden that you carry and I really don't want to be part of that burden, to add to it. I see you as so separate from David—you are both so different—and I'd hope that

you could feel that way too if we were together. . . . Do you think you can?

A few months later I smoothed myself out of the producer's house in Beverly Hills for the last time. I packed all of my things back into my Honda Civic and retraced my steps across the country: through the Southwest, across Texas, north into Chicago, and then up into New England.

K and I had decided to give it one more try.

DREAMS

There's nothing beautiful and excellent
left, dear brother. You must dream up
beauty and goodness and justice. Tell me,
do you know how to dream?

Robert Walser, *Jakob Von Gunten*

I

I WOULD STAY WITH K at her apartment in Cambridge for one month. Not two months, not indefinitely, and not without helping with the rent. We would live together, yes, but this should not be confused with the story of a man and a woman taking that first step on their way to . . . *who knows what? Marriage?* No. I was not making a commitment to forever.

I arrived at K's apartment with one suitcase full of clothes and a cactus that was alive when I left Los Angeles but was now almost dead. (I had mistakenly watered it with windshield washer fluid on the drive east.) I had no job, and no prospects for a job, not even a firm sense that I needed a job. My savings had dipped to a few hundred dollars.

I was going to be living with K, but I still found a way not to tell my father and stepmother that we were a couple. I said I was going to Boston to do some library research for a book I was going to write about accident fakers. I was worried that it was going to be too expensive to stay in Boston while I did my research . . . *then I remembered that David's old girlfriend, Kathryn, lived in the Boston area. Do you remember Kathryn? She and I have kept up over the years, and Kathryn offered to let me stay at her apartment while I did my research. I thought this was really nice of her—she's a really nice person—and I thought this made a*

*lot of sense, very cost-effective. So that's what I think I might do. Stay with
Kathryn awhile in Boston. . . .*

K's apartment was a treasure, a rent-controlled haven on the
top two floors of a Victorian house. The apartment overlooked a
beautiful yard ringed by an English garden that seemed always in
bloom. K's landlords lived next door; she watched their two children some afternoons in exchange for a rent reduction. The neighborhood had a thick canopy of green leaves and old sidewalks of
hand-laid brick; when we made the turn onto our street, the change
from concrete to brick subtly conveyed a sense of history, warmth,
and seclusion. K said this felt like a real home for her. She imagined
buying her apartment from the landlords and living there for years.

At one end of our street was the Harvard-Radcliffe campus. K
and I used to walk to the main green late in the afternoon and
throw a baseball around. We got pretty serious about it. We
bought baseball gloves and tried to keep a regular time for our
catches. A steady stream of people walking by probably saw us as
one of those annoying couples on campus always laughing and
having fun. In those moments, we *were* that couple; these were our
college years. This is the way it felt, anyway: that gradually, by
increments, Kathryn and David's experience together in college
would be overwritten by afternoons like these.

K's apartment was big—two full floors connected by a wrap-
around wooden staircase. K had an office where she did her doc-
toral work. I had a room of my own just down the hall. I filled it
with books and papers about accident fakers, which I had brought
back from California. There was a time when I first moved to
Cambridge when I might have stopped to consider why I was
spending so much time on research that didn't much interest me. I
might have decided to make a break with everything that I had
been doing in Beverly Hills. Agency Investigations had been fun
for a time—total immersion in a world I knew nothing about—
but what did I really care about accident fakers or insurance fraud?
Why was I spending so much time ferreting out this history? There
was a time to ask these questions, that is, but I never did. I plowed
ahead. I set up a desk and arranged my plastic crates of papers

around me in a semicircle. I closed my door and got back to work. I needed to write a book, to start it and, more important, finish it.

After a trial month together, K and I started making a home on a more permanent basis. I remember considering our first piece of joint property—a magazine rack on sale for twenty-nine dollars. Should we buy it? *Who would get it if we split?*

I remember our first domestic disagreement: K told me that she didn't like the way she'd arranged the kitchen, or its disorder, and she suggested that I might be able to help improve it. I took this as my cue to rearrange it completely when K left the apartment. I listened from upstairs as she surveyed what I had done, and I waited for her praise. Instead, I heard cursing and the sound of pots being banged around and bookcases being moved (presumably back to where they were before). I came downstairs to find her in a fit of activity. She looked up only long enough to ask, "What the hell did you think you were doing?" *Fixing your life,* was the answer that came to mind, but I stayed silent. She said, "If you want to move things you've got to ask me first. We've got to talk about it. *It's a relationship.*" The time for fantasies about who we might be for each other was over, I gathered from this. I was not going to fix her life, and she was not going to fix mine. And David needn't have anything to do with it, either. It was about what K and I could make together.

Those first few months in Cambridge had been a late-summer idyll—regular catches on the Radcliffe Green, long walks, trips to K's parents' house on Long Island. (Did her mother remember David eating the Marshmallow Fluff on her living room floor?) But K and I spent a lot less time together when the school year began. She was busy with teaching and coursework; she also had a wide circle of friends whom she met for dinner many nights of the week. She left early in the morning and often didn't come home until after dark. During the eight or ten or twelve hours in between, I mainly stayed at my desk, trying to see something truly epic in all of my papers and photocopied sheets on accident fakers.

My days usually began guiltily, with me still in bed as I heard K close the front door on her way out; and they ended for me, often shamefacedly, when I heard K come back through the door at night. I had busied myself with one thing or another since she left—searching out books on library shelves, taking notes, underlining, sorting papers into manila files. But when I heard her enter the apartment I often felt, in a sudden rush of blood to my head, that another day had passed without my accomplishing anything. "How did it go today?" she'd say, and I'd respond with a long list of minor accomplishments, weighing in heavy with details about accident frauds that I knew didn't matter to either of us, except insofar as they assured us both that I was working toward something significant.

K believed I was writing a book, and that helped me to believe it, too. She also believed me when I said I was pushing so hard on the project as a kind of memorial to David. This was his dream, after all—writing a book and getting it published—and I would see it done for both of us, the Dornstein boys finally making good. It was an ennobling vision, implying a life of self-sacrifice on my part, but it was mainly practical: Nothing propelled me through life like David's drive to write a book, so why not save his dream from the fire while I learned to dream a dream of my own?

The subject of the book didn't matter. I needed to get something published, and fast. The clock was ticking. I was twenty-four. That felt old at the time. Terribly old. David died when he was twenty-five. For years I'd thought about the idea of being older than my older brother, and now that day was approaching. Twenty-five should have been a hopeful thing for me, but I experienced it, instead, as an approaching danger, something speeding toward me faster than I wanted. The buzzers went off at twenty-five. It was pencils down and please pass your papers to the front. *What had David accomplished by age twenty-five? What would I?*

I worked single-mindedly on my book, trying to manufacture a publishable thing. A part-time research job at Harvard Law School kept me afloat financially. More significantly, the job gave me borrowing privileges in the Harvard University library system, and it was there, in the sub-basement storage areas, where I would go looking for my book. Before work, during work, and after work I prowled from one Harvard library to another. I spent days going through stacks of old issues of *Railway Surgeon* magazine and *The Weekly Underwriter,* digging out stories about "banana peel artists," who staged falls on trains for money around the turn of the century. I proceeded page by page through twenty-three years of *The Bulletin of the American Railway Claims Association.*

I took a special pride in the fact that most of the books I checked out of the library had never circulated: Dr. Hector Gavin's *On Feigned and Factitious Diseases* (1843), for example; Smith R. Brittingham's *The Claim Agent and His Work* (1927). I saw myself on an almost messianic mission to rescue these abandoned books—the more obscure, the less interesting the titles, the better. I was saving these long-dead-and-gone souls from the ranks of the totally forgotten.

I would like to say I realized that my interest in these books may have been misplaced, that I knew that this really was about the most important forgotten writer on my shelf—David—but I never stopped to think about it this deeply. I was locked in a battle with the calendar. I was ruled by fear, mainly—fear of failure, and equally of success—and fear, like guilt, crowds out most other feelings.

I turned twenty-five in February of 1994. Seven months later, I reached the age David was when he died. (I had calculated it down to the day.) I had pushed myself to be published before I passed David in age, and strictly speaking, I had failed. I still had not completed a manuscript. I had written a number of chapters, however, and I forced myself to send them off to publishers. I was surprised when editors from two major publishers phoned to express interest. One said he really wanted to publish the book; he offered one thousand dollars for all rights. I took it.

Starting *Accidentally, On Purpose* and working on it to the exclusion of everything else for years would be the easy part, it turned out. Finishing that book and letting it go out in the world—doing that thing that David had never lived to do—was where I would get stuck.

II

I F I HAD TO POINT TO A MOMENT when things fell apart for me, I would say, without question: Christmas of 1995. My delivery date with the publisher was the end of December, but as the week approached, I knew I wouldn't make it. I had completed most of the book, grinding out hundreds of pages in a workman-like way during regular shifts at my desk, but now I found myself unable to write a word, or even to look through the pages I had written.

This was bad, and it quickly grew worse. K and I were headed to Los Angeles for the holidays, along with the rest of her family, to spend time with her brother, Peter, and his wife before she delivered their first baby. I decided to use the trip to renew my flagging sense of purpose about the book. I would do some inter-views and visit Steve and Larry at Agency Investigations and drive the mean streets of L.A.'s personal injury underworld one more time. I hoped that this would get me writing again, but it didn't. Once I checked everything off my list, the writing still wouldn't come. I didn't know what else to do.

A story: One afternoon, K's family left to go shopping, and I stayed behind in Peter's apartment. I said I had work to do, but as the day passed, I accomplished nothing. I found the late afternoon the hardest time not to be working when I was supposed to be. There was still time to open to a fresh page and start writing, to make the phone calls that I'd put off since the morning. I picked up the phone and dialed. I reached one person—an undercover officer at the Fraud Division of the Department of Insurance—but I was delighted to find that most of the other people I phoned had gone for the day. For a moment, I felt free, released back into the world on my own recognizance—free from calls, from the book—but then I realized that I was not free of anything, that the clock was still ticking and the calendar was still against me.

I had invited failure into the room, and now it would not leave. I paced. I showered. I tried and again failed to write. K and her family returned home. Her mother asked how the day had gone, and I said, *Fine, not too bad. The work is coming along. . . .* But when I was alone with K, I said I wasn't feeling well. I said I didn't know what was wrong, but I felt that I might be having some kind of nervous breakdown. K asked again what the problem was, but it felt indescribable.

A photograph from that night survives: I am at dinner with K and her family, seated around a big table at a kitschy Mexican restaurant, a strolling violin trio working the room in the background. We are toasting K's brother and wife, holding aloft our margarita glasses. I am trying to look joyful, but not succeeding. My eyes are slightly downcast, fixed on the salt shaker maybe, or on the faux–Mission-era murals, but not on Peter, his wife, or anyone else at the table. My look seems empty. Vacant, maybe, is a better word, as if the person who used to live inside of me had skipped town. I felt nauseated, but it had come on too soon for me to blame the Mexican food. Another anniversary of the Lockerbie bombing had just passed. Pictures of the *Maid of the Seas* nose cone were back on the news, relatives were interviewed, the president spoke at Arlington Cemetery, vowing not to forget and promising to press for a trial of the two Libyan suspects. Maybe this played a part in my mood as well. December felt like the season for trouble.

The next night, K and I were on a red-eye flight back to Boston. K fell asleep early. My reading light was on, but I couldn't read. I was a shaky, defeated mess. I was not quite twenty-seven. I carried my not-quite-finished manuscript of a book that was not quite what I had hoped it might be, and I was seated next to a woman who was not quite mine, and maybe never would be. It had been not quite a year since I passed David in age, and I was no longer on solid ground. I was the cartoon character who speeds off the cliff and just keeps going forward—feet moving, pedals turning, doing fine until, some distance out, he looks down.

My fall, like David's, began at thirty-one thousand feet. It started on that plane ride from Los Angeles, but once back at the apartment in Boston, I kept falling. I was unable to pass an untroubled waking moment. Panic came on first thing in the morning, filling me up one limb at a time, as if someone had unscrewed my head and poured bad feeling into my body from a pitcher. Just before bedtime, I found, the bad feeling drained away, the burden of expectation lifted, and I slept. In the morning, my gains were erased and the cycle began all over again.

I started keeping a journal of my falling apart, a record of every shiver, quiver, and crippling doubt, written first in daily installments, then hourly, then minute by minute. The pages could have come from David's notebooks, complete with references to K, who administered to my couch-bound self just as she'd done for David at Brown. I was experiencing the full-blown torture of a breakdown about a book. It was horrible, but in a way horrible helped. I felt closer to David than I had in years.

David had gone for counseling at a few of his lowest moments, but I resisted. I had an idea of the therapist as a kind of con man who robbed you of your stories. You weren't healed by therapy; you were just emptied of all of the valuables that you had been keeping for years in a safe place.

I struggled for almost two weeks, surviving mainly on Xanax, which my sister (who was finishing medical school) had prescribed for me. And then I had no choice but to get some kind of help. K urged me to go; she demanded it, really. She was scared for me, and exhausted by me. She found me a psychologist and walked me to the office, and she sat with me on the couch during that first visit as I tried to explain myself.

The psychologist was a smart, kind man with a reassuringly rumpled manner, a deep listener who, crucially for me, had a thick beard just like I thought psychologists should. He sat silent and waited for me to talk. I didn't know where to start. I began with my missed book deadline. I tried to describe my morning panic, because it was the most immediate and worrisome of my present troubles, and because it seemed like a bona fide clinical problem. I mentioned David—*my brother died on that Pan Am plane bombed over Scotland; do you remember Lockerbie?*—but I didn't see it as the beginning of a conversation, just the reporting of a fact about my life. I told the psychologist that K was David's old girlfriend and that this history often got in the way of my being able to see a future for us. Again, just the facts.

I agreed to meet the therapist ten times. My insurance plan covered twenty sessions, but I couldn't imagine how we would fill ten fifty-minute hours, much less twenty. I didn't really understand psychotherapeutic practice. I thought it would be like going to the doctor: I would give a history, submit to some examination, and get a diagnosis. Over the first few sessions, I laid out in as clear a way as possible all of the elements that I thought the psychologist would need to make his assessment, beginning with my mother's spotty mental health and my parents' divorce. I was too young to recall much about either of these things, I told him. I remembered my mother standing by the U-Haul truck outside our house before driving away for good. I remembered the divorce as a good time, actually: David and I spent time together with relatives in Florida while everything got sorted out. There was a picture somewhere of him and me clowning at the pool in my grandmother's building. David remembered that time as tragic, a rupture, but what I remembered, mainly, was David and how he made things all right. The psychologist asked, "So, David was like another parent for you?" Very few of the psychologist's suggestions stuck with me once I left his office, but I wrote this one down when I got home.

At the end of each therapy session, I waited for an evaluation, a clinical judgment, some kind of pronouncement on "my condition." I hoped I suffered from something serious, a clear syndrome, maybe requiring heavy medication and hospitalization. I pictured myself wearing a robe and paper slippers and looking out of a window with bars on it. I wanted to be relieved of the responsibility of taking any action to help myself.

The psychologist did not seem to be in the business of diagnosis, however. He wanted to talk, and he seemed to take his cues from me about what our subject should be. This approach seemed risky; what did I know about what I was feeling? But I continued to go to his office every Thursday evening.

At the end of our tenth session, still no diagnosis. Instead, the psychologist told me a story. It was about a man who awakens one night to find his house on fire. The man rushes out of the house and runs down the street. He runs until he can no longer see the smoke or smell the ash or even remember why he began to run in the first place. He runs until he is lost. And then he stops. Now the fearful scene inside the house hits him with full force. The sorrow at what he's lost, the panic about which way to head now—he experiences it all as if it were happening right then, as if he could still be engulfed by the flames. Only now, from a standpoint of relative safety, does the man fear for his life. The psychologist said that the man's fear and panic are a measure of his resistance to the one idea that he finds most terrible of all: that he's survived the conflagration, even though others haven't, and that it was all right to go on living.

I agreed to ten more sessions with the psychologist, and when these were done we just kept going. I knew I needed to talk more about David, but it was hard. I was unaccustomed to the sound of David in the past tense. *David was six years older than me. . . . David and I went to the same university. . . . David had curly hair. . . .* The words felt wrong, the memories inconsequential. None of it seemed to add up to the David I had known, the one who may once have actually lived, as opposed to the one I felt I was inventing right there on the spot to explain my present troubles. I often felt as if I were handing over pieces of David in exchange for compassion and understanding. The more memories and stories that came out, the more I felt that I was losing something that I could never get back.

I needed to do something. The therapist was keeping a set of notes after each session, so I decided to keep a record of my own. I sat at my desk and began to list everything I could remember about David.

He liked orange soda.

He took long showers. (He once told me that he would like to live in the shower if he could.)

He worked as a golf caddy at a country club one summer and lost a wad of tip money he'd been stashing in his sock.

He used to try to get me to slap fight or wrestle, and I'd always get pummeled.

He crashed my dad's Plymouth Champ hatchback into a telephone pole coming home from a party one night during high school.

He liked starches—noodles, bread, rice—and hated red sauce, spices, ketchup, and mustard.

He used to argue politics with my father at the dinner table, point-counterpoint style, a real clash of worldviews.

He was driving me to an orthodontist appointment when we heard that John Lennon had been shot. We listened to the radio in silence all the way home.

He lost his virginity in the summer of 1979 during our family's first trip to Grossinger's, in the Catskills. He slipped out of the room he shared with my sister and me, and met an older waitress who initiated him into the ways of sex.

I was sorry I hadn't thought of the idea sooner—so many memories already gone. But this only made me more determined not to lose any more. I kept at it.

David didn't carry a wallet, stashing his money, driver's license, etc., loose in his pockets.

He had a deep voice and liked to hear himself talk and read aloud from books.

When I was eleven or twelve, I went to Florida with my mother and came back with a shirt for David that said I GOT JUICED IN FLORIDA. He wore it a lot more than I imagined he would.

He stopped using a toothbrush for a time after college. (He brushed with his index finger.)

He sometimes told people that he played the drums, but he didn't.

He became oddly emotional at a screening of the Pink Floyd movie *The Wall*. Afterward, he said the song "Comfortably Numb" was one of his favorites of all time.

He acted in plays in college and afterward, but I never saw any of them. Not one.

He said there was a guy in his high school class named Joe Slaughter who wanted to kill him. (There was.)

He said he once won a fistfight with a boy in the neighborhood, one strong punch to the boy's gut knocked him out.

He often slept fully clothed, with a book over his face (he called it "learning by osmosis").

He once took me to an art house theater to see a film called *Liquid Sky,* and I tripped on the way to our seats and spilled popcorn on everyone around us.

He and I once dressed up like Joe Six-Packs to get into a bowling alley on League Night.

He used to get his hair cut by a man named Ernesto.

The summer before he left for Israel, he asked me to go into a 7-Eleven and buy him a pack of Kool cigarettes. I refused, but I don't remember why.

When inspiration failed, I tried to proceed systematically through the different eras of David's life, one by one, to see if something new came to me. I was always pleased to be able to add something, but after not too long, the idea ran its course. This is when I decided to tell the therapist about it. I thought that he would let me off the hook for my apparent shortcomings of memory, maybe congratulate me on a noble effort at recovery, but his response surprised me. He asked, "Do you think it's your responsibility to save your brother?" I suspected that the right answer was no. *It's wrong and vain to think you can save someone, isn't it?* I waved off the suggestion like a bad smell in the air, but the idea of saving David lingered.

A few months later, in the summer of 1996, I made a trip to the house in Philadelphia. I went to David's room and gathered up all of the notebooks and manuscripts and piles of letters that I had organized into folders over the years. I loaded them all into two jumbo-size Rubbermaid containers I had bought at an office-supply store.

I probably should have asked my father if it was okay to take David's stuff out of the house, but I didn't want to open myself to questions. I think my father saw my various curatorial efforts over the years as a little mistaken. So I made it a cloak-and-dagger operation. I waited until the house was empty, and then I lugged the filled-up Rubbermaid chests out of David's room. I told myself the house was on fire, just like the therapist had said. I had escaped with my life, but now I needed to go back in and come out with David.

As I dragged the chests down the steps, I thought of the part in *Ulysses* when poor old drunken Paddy Dignam's coffin is being taken out of his house, and Dignam's son hears the *bump, bump, bump* of the coffin coming down the front stairs. I thought about how a writer's body of work is often called a corpus. Those chests were awkward and heavy as a man.

I maneuvered the Rubbermaids out the back door, down the driveway, and into my car. As I drove off, I felt good about finally doing something with David's writing. I was filled with a sense of the rightness of my intentions. I felt myself on the verge of doing something that was going to change both of our lives for the good.

I brought David with me back to Cambridge, to K's apartment, where, it now seemed, the three of us would be living. K helped me carry the Rubbermaids up to my office.

I was ready for the next thing. The book on accident faking was now basically finished. The publisher had accepted the manuscript and placed a listing for it in the fall catalog. By the end of the year it would be published, and I would get my first review, a few paragraphs in *Publishers Weekly,* the opening sentence of which would confirm my worst fears about what I'd done. It said: "At half the length this would have been twice as interesting, for Dornstein gets buried under the avalanche of material he amassed and seems to have lacked editorial help in digging out."

I didn't disagree with *Publishers Weekly;* my own review would have been much more cruel. I was stung by that image from the first line: "Dornstein gets buried under the avalanche of material he amassed. . . ." Was that the function that the book had served in my life all those years: to bury me alive in an avalanche of paper? I looked again at those Rubbermaid chests filled with David's writings. Had I simply found new boxes to bury myself in? I opened the lids of the plastic chests and arranged David's notebooks in chronological order. I lined up the tops of the files so I could see them at a glance. I tried to leave all of this material alone for a while, to enjoy the freedom I had won from years of work on a book, maybe to actually engage K on the topic of marriage and children instead of sidestepping it. But I didn't do this. Instead, I opened David's notebooks and began, once again, to read.

III

I FOUND DAVID back at Brown after the summer of SavOn and the split with Kathryn. It was the start of his junior year and he needed to get back to writing. He bought a new notebook and began, as he often did, by looking back at what he'd written in the previous one. Then he wrote his own review of what he'd done:

> We see many of the characteristics of Dornstein's later work emerging in these youthful journals. We see the self-consciousness the wit the vivacity of language the gaming the searing honesty the bald confession the compulsive neurotic notetaking and recording of every scrap of minutiae of his life. We see a young man very much taken with himself and with his observations with his style with his insights.
>
> Indeed we see a young artist goading himself to flower, aching away in flimsy whimsy. . . . We see a young artist in a perpetual drive to place himself in the world among the artists of greatness trying to place himself within his family within his own fantasy world, trying to go one two three even four up on any who might try to outstrip his wit, not realizing sometimes his own transparency. . . .

We see a great deal of ponderous wasteful muttering. We see bushes that need trimming and shaping. We see a boy staying out too late trying to collect fireflies and growing tired.

When it came to writing stories, David had no patience for revision. He said that his first draft was his rawest and most honest and that everything after that felt to him like compromise, a defense against the original truth of what he'd written. He also just liked to show people what he'd written, ending the loneliness of the process, and revision just meant delay. But now his hand had been forced. He was trying to get into an advanced writing class with the novelist Robert Coover, and he needed to submit something. He reworked a story called "Don't Analyze Me, I'm Just a Train Run Amok" and gave it to Coover. A few days later Coover let David into the class.

This was the big time. Coover and John Hawkes were the heavyweights of Brown's Creative Writing Department, and there was intense competition for spots in their advanced classes. There were a number of star students from these years who went on to publish novels, and a few—Rick Moody, Jeffrey Eugenides, Donald Antrim—who would enjoy the success that David fantasized for himself. Not just publication, but acclaim and prizes and movie adaptations and voice-of-a-generation status. No one planned for this kind of success more than David; among the chosen ones of the Creative Writing program David jockeyed hard for position.

A month or so after Lockerbie, Rick Moody wrote to my father:

Dear Dr. Dornstein,

I've done a lot of thinking about David since Christmas morning. I didn't know him the best among his friends from Brown, but I was kin in one way that was important to me, and I think to him, too, as writers. And I'm writing to you about that aspect of David in hopes that it will help somehow.

I was ahead of David in school, and so I was a little more

established on campus (for whatever that is worth now), you
know, writing with the heavy teachers and so forth, but I
became aware of his precocious presence, his enthusiasm
and volubility, pretty quickly. David was a wild agitator of the
arts at Brown. He and I would talk pretty often about what
we were reading, what he liked, and David was always challenging my preconceptions and lobbying for things that were
more immediate and urgent. Whenever I'd found something
new, an undiscovered talent, it seemed David was reading it
simultaneously. It was remarkable, really, how restless and
inquisitive his mind was.

This literary sparring went on after school, for my part
with a great fondness, though I wish now I had said so,
made it more clear. I would check in with his closer friends
to find out what was on his mind, how it was going with his
novel, whether he liked Cynthia Ozick or Stanley Elkin as
much as I liked them, always certain that it was only a few
years before his significant contribution—that whatever else
he was doing in the meantime, he was honing his sentences,
like Stephen Daedalus, who said it would take him ten
years to write the novel he had in mind. I'm going to miss
this colleague, and miss that novel, which I was looking
forward to a lot. He was a great presence, your son, a real
genius. . . .

David worked hard to win Professor Coover to his side. He wrote
more for him that semester than ever before. Not just short fiction of the sort he had been piling up for years, but a first draft of
what he thought of as his breakthrough extended work. A fictional autobiography. The idea? An unknown young writer dies in
a plane crash leaving behind lots of notebooks and bits of stories,
and the narrator sets out to piece it all together into a story of the
unknown writer's life.

THE STORY IN SUMMARY: Born, lives, dies, entirely
    through words. I am the book, the book is me. Bound up
    together, we become indomitable.

A BLURB FROM THE BOOK JACKET: "A thoroughly
spellbinding exploration of a young writer's fears and
nocturnal dreams, told with hilarity and sensitivity and
perspicacity and vivacious spiritual wisdom."

INTRODUCTION BY A FAMOUS WRITER?
MAILER? . . . I must write to Mailer in Brooklyn. . . .

David gave this fictional writer's notebook the same title as the
one he'd been keeping that semester: *The Fall Journal*. It wasn't
clear whether these were David's own entries or the unknown
writer's—David never really sorted it out. He slipped in and out of
different personae from one page to the next. Sometimes the narrator was a guy named Wells, who drove wildly around his suburban hometown with a sidekick named Jay P, the two of them
crying at "the sheer joy of movement." Then he was Kristian Santini, the unfortunate young boy whose "life history is a compila-
tion of every horrible conceivable story about a young life lived in
an orphanage." Then he was an effete French windbag named
Henri Bloviay, who voiced every pretentious thought about narrative art in David's head.

David wrote in *The Fall Journal* until dawn, then slept until the
early afternoon. For lunch and dinner, he ate two cups of white
rice mixed with peanut butter, and the occasional lemon-lime
water ice for dessert. Then he'd move to his typewriter. He
pounded on the keys so hard that he joked that it was his main
form of exercise. After a month of this, the letter *a* on the typewriter stopped functioning. He couldn't afford to fix it, so he
would handwrite all of his *a*'s from then on. Another problem:
David's stereo speakers shorted out; he liked to listen to loud
music when he wrote. He couldn't afford this repair, either. He
took a job at the University Food Services. It was minimum-wage
labor—slicing roast beef and ladling au gratin potatoes—but he
liked that it took him away from his desk, at least for ten hours a
week.

Out of the blue, David received a letter from Alex, his Artist
friend from freshman year. The return address appeared to be a

psychiatric hospital. Alex said he was doing better now that he was on lithium and he might soon try to live on his own in New York. "I'd love to hear from you and get a glimpse of how you're doing and what you're doing. Though I feel you're crazy, my feelings towards you are warm ones." David wrote in *The Fall Journal,* "Alex says *I'm* crazy?"

Once more David was a little thrown by Alex. He wished he could write back about all that he'd accomplished, all that he'd written, but he was at a particularly low point in his work, so he didn't write back at all. He thought about going back to the psychiatrist from Health Services. He tried to write, but there was no music, and that damn broken *a* had become a true distraction, and now there was a guy who kept calling his apartment looking for "Don." It happened so many times that David found himself waiting for the phone to ring, trying to think up a smart-ass response. He finally got his chance. David wrote: "FUCKING PHONE RINGS AGAIN! I say in a pleasant voice, 'Yes, Don is here. Please hold.' I pause. Then I say, 'Hello, this is Don. WHY THE FUCK DO YOU KEEP CALLING ME?' And the guy hangs up."

It was mid-November, and the semester was more than half done. As his deadline for Coover's class approached, David tried to write some conventional short stories. He'd typewrite them on loose sheets then paste his favorite parts into *The Fall Journal* as if they were excerpts from the writings of the notebook's fictitious young author. The longest story was about a man named Gene Yuss (pronounced "genius"). When we meet him, Gene Yuss is in a tailspin. "He has stopped reading the newspaper. He has fled responsibility. He has donned a wool hat and scarf from his favorite college football team. His notebook, which had been continuous, has become disjointed. So Gene Yuss decides he'll write a story about his decline, hoping it will keep him from smashing up. It fails. Gene Yuss doesn't know what to do. He is hyperconcerned with the achievements and activities of others. He is an avid consumer of the front and back matter of books—'F. Scott Fitzgerald was this old when he wrote Gatsby; Thomas Wolfe was that old when he couldn't go home again. . . .' Gene Yuss feels tremendous pressure to produce, but he can't. He feels he should write to his father and his brother, but he does not. He should not be afraid to show his weakness. But he is."

The story of Gene Yuss ended abruptly with this from the narrator: "This is not a story, it is an anxiety attack. CONVULSIONS. SHIVERS. Poor isolated Gene Yuss doesn't want to burden anyone with his sufferings." David dropped Gene Yuss and began to draft a letter to my father:

> Dear Dad,
>
> I am writing stories, but what I am writing is making me sad. I am nowhere near a panic, but I do feel "bad" sometimes, maybe like everybody feels bad but probably a little worse than what most people feel when they say they're feeling bad. . . . I worry sometimes that if I sound less than spiffy to you over the telephone or in my notes you will become concerned or worried. . . . My health is good, so you should not fear now for my health.

But he never sent this letter.

By late November, David was out of time. He needed a manuscript to submit to Coover, so he assembled *The Fall Journal* from whatever he had at hand: photocopied selections from his own notebook entries; stories from his typewriter with the missing *a*'s filled in with black pen; clippings from *The New York Times* and from the *Weekly World News* ("DOWN-AND-OUT FAMILY LIVES IN A TOILET," "DENTAL EXAM KILLS GIRL"); an excerpt from the story about Gene Yuss. He also added an essentially straight autobiographical account of our mother telling "her sad story" to strange men in hotel bars: "I never listened closely enough to be able to tell exactly what my mother's story was. I picture myself at age fourteen, sitting at the bar poking my straw into Shirley Temples, eating pretzels or peanuts, watching the ball game, listening to the piano guy. But I will not dwell on the past. . . ."

Notebook cover (1983)

David stapled, pasted, and glued all of this together and then slipped the manuscript into Professor Coover's box in the Creative Writing Department. A week or so later, Coover returned *The Fall Journal* to David along with a page of typewritten remarks. The critique began in a promising way:

> David,
>   The strengths of this piece lie in its inventiveness, its audacity, its sometimes startling and provocative juxtapositions. Its energy, too, and its sense of humor. . . .

But the other shoe dropped quickly, as Coover found "a disaffecting lack of direction in the piece" . . . "flat, pointless, and silly" journal entries . . . "arbitrary and seemingly private linkages" between story fragments.

Coover's comments became more damning from there: "One of the problems with this text, encountered almost immediately, is that the narrator has almost nothing to say, except for a few indirect comments on narrative technique itself. He covers this lack, we feel, with melodramatic events and brash efforts at outrageous situations—gaudy clippings, casual violence, mom on the make at the bar, etc. When nothing else works, he throws in some old story fragments, hoping for the best. . . . The writing here, for all its variety of subject matter, culled from the popular press, dredged up from memory and fantasy, or borrowed from your diurnal rounds, has a tendency to sound somehow all the same, chewed up in your prodigious word-processing machine into a kind of even mash of hysteria and fatigue. What you look at, you turn away from. What you invent, you abandon or wreck. . . . It would seem to me, not that you have invented a new form, or are 'on to something,' but that you have here the germ for one good story . . . *one perhaps you're not quite ready to write. . . .*"

This is how David responded to Coover's critique: He revised *The Fall Journal* to include an oral history of the life of its author, "David Dorrance-Dean." Friends, family, associates, colleagues, and former teachers are all asked about Dorrance-Dean. One of the mock interviews is with a writing professor who failed to accurately grasp the merit of Dorrance-Dean's work way back before Dorrance-Dean made his great name in letters. The writing professor tells Dorrance-Dean's biographer: "I remember David showing me a volume of his diary notebook. He was rather grandiose about it, as though he were revealing one of the great literary treasures of his era to me. He was pompous and silly. I can honestly say I missed the boat on Dave. I didn't think that what he was doing at the time was of any great importance. Even now, I'm not sure I think his work is of great importance, although he certainly has garnered for himself something he has always craved: FAME, ATTENTION, RECOGNITION. He has what he's always wanted, I guess. And he has attained it remarkably early."

David submitted the mock interview to Coover, adding this note: "Dorrance-Dean was a master at absorbing unanticipated criticism and incorporating it into his work." He struck a cool pose here, defying Coover to mean what he had written about *The Fall Journal,* but at the same time, in his real notebook, David hyperventilated over the disappointment.

December 8, 1983
   . . . all man has ignored you or misconstrued you has wronged you has hurt you has sapped you has treated you unkindly and you are obsessed with changing their minds and you write you write you write, alone, you write the story of your life and then you pass on, you pass away, you are a dying man and your words are left, your story it lies on your desk and you are dead and they want to be cruel and they find your words and they use them only to dismiss you and you are gone you are dead and gone and so few really see until one day you become fashionable and then everybody thinks that they see and then you live you live but in your life you were beaten and you were cast out and there was nothing you could have done about it, you struggled against it, you told the story, you told the story of your life, and most everyone regarded you as vain and obnoxious and most did not return to you what you gave to them and

some went further and tried to hurt you and some tried to make
you sorry for the very fact of being the way you were. . . .

This is when David began having the dreams about planes
crashing and dying young and only his notebooks surviving.

December 11, 1983
  I am sorely greatly vastly mistaken to hope to be able to
support myself on my writing. What must I do? By no means
am I headed for prosperity or happiness. I need to write a single
extended work. I need to create a genuine world apart from the
world in which I flail and thrash and crash about. . . . Humor-
ously, tragically, I really am starting to believe that the only way
any of these notebooks will mean anything is if I die an early
death. . . .

December 13, 1983
  I have become faintly disturbed that I may become, and I
can't recall who like, but I may become someone who never
becomes great himself, the darling of the bunch but the one who
fades off in time. . . . I stay awake all night trying to figure out
why I want to be remembered, why I deem it so vital. To be re-
membered! Put back together from scattered parts. Organs, limbs
regathered. I want to hold together over time. . . .

December 15, 1983
  DREAM: Young brother Kenny has died and I am eulo-
gizing him. . . . No, it's me who's died and it's he who's taken
my place at the dinner table.

IV

I DON'T REMEMBER a particular moment when David turned his attention to me. What I do remember are the letters. One and then another and then another for weeks and months and years. After the semester of *The Fall Journal,* David came home to Philadelphia for Christmas break. He and I spent almost all of that time together. Then he went back to school. That's when the letters began.

Jan 13, 1984
Dear Ken,
    I'm only here a day now and I miss you real bad. I want you to know that I'm back up here almost against my own desire. I've still got myself some pretty grand and glorious dreams and fantasies. Trying to write and think and read is one of the only ways I know to force myself to be sensible about these fantasies. But it's hard and a fella can really start to question whether he really wants to be this or that.

January 25, 1984
Dearborn Kennel,
    Today was the first day that the classes were taken place.

I pledge that no dust will collect upon our communication.
Not an instant passes that I do not think of you, my brother.
How's by you? Did you make the basketball team, squirt?
Keep me postered.

Within a month or so, David's letters grew much longer and
his tone more searching and confessional. He asked me lots of
questions about my life that seemed to be equally about his own.
"Are you happy?" "Won't you ever tell me of your lovers? I
had one from the first week of school, Kathryn, but this has
changed. . . . Details. Can you share details? Anything you send
to me, anything you write to me, I will lap up like a dog. . . ." I
wasn't sure how to respond. My "lovers"? I was just about to turn
fifteen. My daily occupations felt ordinary; my crises were not
existential. I deflected David's questions back onto him, and he
gladly responded.

February 14, 1984
Dear Ken,
    You told me you wanted some more facts about what
I'm doing and what my life is like here. The facts are these: I
get up in the morning after having slept for a healthy number
of hours, and I write down as much as I can remember
about my dreams. Usually the dreams are boring, some are
worrisome. I usually take a shower. Most mornings I will
spend entirely by myself. In my room, I will sit at my typewriter typing the first things that come into my head. I will
never write anything that is sophisticated, or particularly
challenging, or especially beautiful. I will never write a poem.
I will never sustain anything of any length.
    Then the afternoon will darken into the night. Some-
times I will go to dinner and sometimes I will go to the
library and sometimes I will turn the music on and dance
around my room making pretend I'm on stage. And sometimes I will take a walk and sometimes I will just stay in my
room at my typewriter.
    This all does not change much on the weekends.

I stop at the mailroom every day. Most of my letters come from Dad. They are usually short, sometimes sentimental. Some will be terse reminders about stopping in to see people in the university, or about finding a summer job, or about the importance of not failing out of school. Some of his letters, as you know, will not be written letters at all, but will be clippings of various sorts. They are always interesting. Almost all of his letters will have one sentence of true profundity that I will think about for a while, and almost all of his letters will end with Love, Dad, although some of the letters with just clippings won't end with Love, Dad, and I will wish that they had. Mom doesn't write. She calls sometimes, but we struggle for something to say. You know how it is with Mom. Is it the same between you and her?

I wish that I could write to you about all of the charitable and fascinating and enjoyable things that I have been doing with all of my close friends and lovers and pals, but I can't. I could make up stories, but I feel like being honest with you and telling you how it is. If I tell you things you don't really want to know, please let me know, because I don't know just how much of this you can stand. I didn't have an older brother who confided in me, or seemed like he wanted to really pour his soul out to me, so I'm never sure if and when I should constrain myself with you. I don't have to tell you that long confessional letters like these are as much for me as they are for you, if not more. I don't recall spending much time brooding when I was fifteen, although I'm sure I did spend a lot of time constructing elaborate visions of future athletic triumphs or achievements with pretty girls. Am I being lucid? You will only get older. When you write to me next, tell me whether or not you understand things far better than I know so I don't have to be afraid of talking straight to you.

A typical letter from David consisted of ten or twelve sheets of paper stuffed into a standard envelope, then sealed tight with tape to keep it from busting at the seams. My father often seemed concerned when he saw these envelopes. I got the feeling that he thought there was something not quite right about David writing to me so often, at such length, so I tried to snatch the letters from the mail pile before my father saw them. I'd read through, skipping the long passages that David copied from books "for my edification," and then I'd stash them in a sock drawer.

David frequently complained about not hearing from me. He imagined a much more vital correspondence than I could muster. He often ended his letters with an exhortation to write more regularly and more honestly and at greater length. He wanted me to be a better reader of books—he sent lists—and a more thoughtful consumer of his own extraordinary output to me. In a P.S. to one letter, he wrote: "My letters to you get long and I think that you read them once and not again. No, they are not the great texts of lost Jerusalem, but they bear rescrutiny."

I often experienced the length of David's letters as a burden. What I took from his words mainly was the knowledge that there was a perspective on the world that was not my father's or my teachers' at school, and that knowledge was power. I carried around the photocopies he sent from *The New Yorker,* or a Henry Miller book, or Borges, and I would hold them in an ostentatious way so my teachers would see. I hoped they understood from this that I was operating on another plane. I was here in class because I had to be, but I had connections on the outside.

David sent me some of his own manuscript pages as well. He'd ask, "Do you have any ideas where the story could go from here? Your ideas are good, *mi hermano,* and always welcome." I was flattered that he'd ask. I'd wade right in with suggestions: "I think it needs more action. Nothing happens in this story." I made lists of what I thought were pertinent questions. ("Why does the guy masturbate into a fish tank?") I sometimes carried David's stories with me to school and made a show of working on them: cradling my head in my hands as if searching for the right word, staring intently at the pages as I'd seen David do with his notebooks. I waited for someone to ask what I was doing and then I'd say: "My brother's a writer and I help him out with his stories sometimes."

I didn't have any idea what the stories were about, or how to write a story at all, but it didn't matter to David. He treated me like a peer, a fellow traveler. He saw me as a younger version of himself who still had a chance to make it as a writer at a time when he had doubts about himself. He was grooming me to be the writer that Robert Coover had said he wasn't.

On David's next visit home, he said we needed to set aside time to write together. I imagined writing to be a solitary thing, but David made it seem like an activity best done in pairs or groups. He had me sit across from him for a half hour and do warm-up exercises in free association, starting from "apple pie," for example, and seeing how far each of us could stretch the chain of associations from there. David couldn't wait to share his list: "Apple pie, apple 'Brown Betty,' school lunch, second grade, coming home to an empty house. . . ." He insisted, at least for pedagogical purposes, that he'd turned up material for a dozen stories in just one page of free association. Then we tried to write one of these stories, trading off paragraphs for a few pages—not so much that we'd actually finish a story, but just enough to prove that it could be done.

David tried not to pester me about what I was reading, or whether I was reading at all, but he couldn't help himself, especially if he caught me watching television. "What's the matter, you've got nothing to read?" I told him I was reading just what I was assigned in school: *Twelfth Night, Jane Eyre, The Iliad.* . . . "Give it to me," he'd say. "I'll reread it tonight, and we can discuss it in the morning."

David didn't sleep in his room any longer. He set up shop in the den between our two rooms, surrounding himself with dozens of books he hoped to read. With each book, he moved closer to what appeared to be his goal: to read every significant book ever written, or at least to hold them in his hands for a while before sleep. I added my schoolbooks to David's pile and said good night. I had a vision of him working through the night like an elf in Santa's workshop, wrapping up all of his interpretations and challenges with a nice red ribbon, ready for me by the time I awakened.

I got up for school around 6:30 A.M. and peeked in on David.

He was asleep on the floor with books all around and his note-book spread open on his chest. He was bundled up in a woolen scarf and hat as if he'd just come in from outside. The books I'd given him were right where I'd left them, apparently untouched. As the week passed, David and I never got around to writing more stories together, either—another relief. I liked that he saw me as a writer, but I didn't want to have to prove it.

A story from that same spring break: One morning I left for school, and it was raining. It was still raining when I got home that afternoon. I found David pacing the floor in a rage. He told me that he had lost his notebook the night before while he was out with a friend. He'd left it on the table at a diner, he felt, but the hostess at the diner told him that no one had turned in a note-book. David didn't accept this, but he had to wait until 5 P.M. to speak to the night manager. In torment, he sat at the kitchen table for hours typing on my father's old manual Smith Corona.

> This is trauma, I am traumatized. I am frantic with desire to track down the notebook. . . .
>
> I have convinced myself that the notebook is not destroyed. I believe that it was found by a waitress who was intrigued by its contents, and took it home to examine it fur-ther, an intelligent person, probably a diary-keeper herself. I believe this waitress will be at the restaurant tonight, with the notebook, knowing that I will be returning to claim it. This waitress will ask the manager for a short break, and we will sit together, perhaps at the very same table at which I consumed a chocolate sundae with orange ice, where I carelessly and fatefully left the notebook behind. This waitress will be very excited, and will talk to me about the notebook, openly con-fessing to have read through it, in search of clues about its owner, about how the notebook reawakened feelings and desires within her that had lain dormant for decades. This will be an older woman, and she will give the notebook to me on the condition that I correspond with her. She will believe that

I am a very special boy, a magical boy, someone sent to her for mystical reasons she does not understand but also does not question. She will view the experiences as enchanted, perhaps divine. I will remind her of her grandson who died but a few years ago. . . .

I don't know how I'll wait until 5 P.M. to phone Mr. Knapp at the restaurant. Now it is 2:45 P.M. Father has just returned home. I shall confide in him this loss.

My father listened to the story of the lost notebook while he ate lunch. When David was finished, my father threw up his hands, smiled widely, and said, "Losing that notebook is the best thing that could have happened to you. Now you can get on to writing bigger things." David didn't want to hear this. My father left again for work, and David returned to the typewriter.

When I walked in, David told me the story of the lost notebook. I listened, but I should have stopped him right away. In the morning, when I left for school, I had seen a notebook in the street, but I was late for the bus and didn't have time to investigate. "I think I saw some notebook pages spread over the lawn," I said. David looked at me with astonishment and horror. "Are you fucking kidding?" David hadn't left the notebook at the diner; he'd dropped it in the street on the way into the house that night. I was a little embarrassed that I hadn't put two and two together sooner, but there was no time to apologize.

David tore past me, hitting the wet driveway in his socks, and I trailed behind. We spotted a notebook page by the curb, and then another some feet away, and a few others blown against the trunk of the cherry tree on the front lawn. We pursued some pages down the street, and others under a neighbor's bush. We fished some out of a storm drain. We brought the pages inside and laid them out all over the house to dry. Later, we attempted to press some of them flat with an iron. We saved maybe twenty pages, but most of the notebook was lost.

That night, David settled in on the floor of our den surrounded by the notebook sheets we had salvaged from the rain. He picked up the pages he had typed earlier in the day and wrote at the bottom: "NOTEBOOK DESTROYED." This didn't seem like a story with a silver lining, but I was surprised to find one in what David wrote that night. He decided that his loss would be my gain if the whole incident taught me the vital importance of the notebook to the young writer.

To start me on my way, David gave me one of his blank notebooks that night. I had been using a little notepad for my free-association sessions with him, but now I was getting the call-up to the Big Leagues. *My own notebook.* David said, "This will be notebook number one in a series that may well stretch the rest of your life. I can only imagine where I'd be now if I had started when I was your age."

David began a new notebook of his own that same night—"It is with painful plodding dedication, and re-dedication that I begin again"—but his real enthusiasm seemed to be reserved for me. "I gave Kenny one of my old blank notebooks tonight and he told me he will really begin to keep one now. He's already making free association lists. He said he will start jotting down notes and funny expressions people use and bits of dialogue and his own observations. Our correspondence will no doubt only grow richer. . . . I love that boy more fiercely than ever."

David's aspirations for me continued to grow. Before heading back to Brown, he officially made me curator of the "Dave Archives," the box of his manuscripts and finished notebooks that he kept in our den. He encouraged me to improve on anything he had written if I thought I saw a way. He seemed to have transferred something onto me during that trip and it made him feel lighter.

April 5, 1984
Dearest Kennel,

Time at home with you was pure moonshine. You still writing stuff in your notebook? Making lists? Reading anything? Finding anything you like in the Archives? You will be a terrific writer, *mi hermano.* The new and improved Dorrance-Dean. Keep at it.

V

THAT YEAR, David couldn't make it home for Passover. This felt like a big deal. Not because my family was religious; even by the lax standards of American Jewry we were not very observant. Our seder was seriously abridged to get the Israelites in and out of bondage in time to keep the turkey moist. But tradition was different from religion, and Thanksgiving and Passover felt inviolable. David needed to stay at Brown to finish some writing, he said, and he'd just been home a few weeks earlier, so he was excused.

I decided I needed to capture the full Passover experience and send it to David. I set up a tape recorder in our upstairs den and dangled a microphone over a balcony, pointing toward our dining room. My great-uncle Herman sat at the end of the table closest to the microphone, so I mainly recorded his running commentary about the best grapefruit he'd ever eaten (Indian River grapefruits, without doubt), the sweetest sweet potatoes, the most tender chicken, etc. Uncle Herman had worked as a produce buyer for big hotels and supermarkets, so his passion for produce and poultry was, perhaps, understandable. I thought it was entertaining and I knew David would, too.

Throughout dinner, I'd rush upstairs to switch the tape and add some commentary. I pretended our seder was a major breaking news story. "We are getting unconfirmed reports that three of the four questions have been asked.... According to sources close to the Patriarchs, we recline this night because we are free men." I gave the event its own tag line—"You've been listening to Seder '84: The Night That Truly Was *Not* Like All Other Nights"—and I repeated it to an annoying degree.

David wrote me the day he got the tapes in the mail. "I listened to the first part of Seder '84 and giggled audibly. It's hilarious." For some reason, though, David didn't send this letter right away. When he resumed writing a few days later, his mood had changed.

I'll tell you, as if you could not sense it yourself, it's hard for me to retain a purely upbeat comic outlook on life. You'll have to grant me my seriousness my gravity my earnest and sad hours and words. We as comic writers should not be afraid of that which might be more dismal in us. Not to say that you have much darkness in you. I'm not sure if you do or if you don't. . . .

These comments are by no means slyly intended to make you bleak. You are beautiful and your nature is a narcotic to me, my time is not ever so blissful and rich and fulfilling as when I am in contact with you. Life can only become more full and more complete between us. I have absolute trust and belief in you. Just keep growing. I am young I keep reminding myself. And you are even younger.

Caution: Warn me if I become overly pedantic, overly wise. This is a common occurrence in older brothers, fathers, philosophers, poets and scholars of every type, men of the cloth, old people on buses (you remind them of their grandchildren), immigrants who bear exotic tales of their hardship from across oceans and centuries, taxi drivers, old people in stadiums who wear hats. And veterans of foreign wars, who also wear hats. But especially older brothers, who feel surges of closeness to their younger brothers, and want to give them all that they are able, who are effusive older brothers anyway. You must realize that what I write to you are love letters.

In a separate padded envelope, David sent along an audiotape of his own. One side was marked "Essay on Genius." I started to listen to it but couldn't hear David's voice, or anyone else's. I turned up the volume and realized it was David at his desk typing. I thought this was clever. I kept listening and was surprised to find nothing else on that side of the tape, just forty-five minutes of David typing. In his letter David wrote that he spent much of his life at his typewriter hoping something great would come out:

> I keep fulminating to close friends about wanting to do something large, something magnificent. But I don't know what that might be. You know me. I'm your brother. I always want more significance out of life, and that's neither wonderful, nor execrable.

On the other side of the tape David wrote "Sunday Brunch." This was a more conventional recording, with David narrating right from the start. "I just left my room and I'm walking to the dining hall right now. I am walking across Charlesfield Street and soon will be entering the dining hall for Sunday Brunch." David runs into a good friend named Tim right off—or maybe he planned to run into Tim, since Tim was a great character, an actor from Oklahoma who could improvise and deliver sharp dialogue and generally raise the quality of a joke cassette quite considerably. David explains to Tim, "I'm making a tape for my brother, Ken. I want him to get the full Sunday Brunch experience." David explains this to everyone he meets that morning, always the exact same way, the repetition of the line now becoming a running gag for him.

This was the first big surprise for me on "Sunday Brunch": how many people David knew. In his letters, he'd always presented himself as terribly isolated, but during the short span of the tape, ten or twelve people greet him. The exchanges are so light and convivial and erudite. I couldn't follow it all, but I aspired to. I listened to the Sunday Brunch tape for months, usually before bed, with the tape still running as I fell asleep. I often dreamed I was there with them all, ready with witty, informed repartee of my own.

Listening to the tape now, I'm struck by how many times David finds a way to work me into the conversation. Several times he stops his taping so he can play sections of my "Seder '84" tape for different people. Then he reinserts his tape and prompts a reaction from them. "It's hilarious, don't you think? He's only fifteen." At the very end of the tape David leaves Tim and goes in search of other people he knows so he can introduce me to them.

DAVE: Oh, there's Mark Safire, son of the famous columnist William Safire . . . and Stephanie Factor . . . I'm making a tape of Sunday Brunch for my little brother. . . .

STEPHANIE: Hi bro. How are you?

MARK: What's your brother's name?

DAVE: Ken.

STEPHANIE: And how old is Ken?

DAVE: He's fifteen years old. . . . He just sent me 180 minutes of Passover seder [laughter]. He bugged Passover seder. . . .

STEPHANIE: That's a riot. Umm, David do you have an older brother?

DAVE: No, I'm the oldest.

STEPHANIE: Just you and Ken? That's it. Just you and Ken?

DAVE: No . . . and a sister, a middle sister. . . .

MARK: Ken, I'm sorry but your older brother who is famous for his improv talent doesn't have enough skill to entertain you for one hundred eighty minutes of his own but instead has to explain who you are to other people and it's supposed to be entertaining. . . .

STEPHANIE: Does Ken know where he is right now?

DAVE: Yes, he's intimately acquainted with that fact. I've narrated Sunday Brunch from the minute I walked out of my room.

STEPHANIE: What grade is Ken in?

DAVE: He's in the ninth grade.

MARK: It's a wonderful year. . . . How's puberty?

DAVE: The tape is almost done and on the other side is me typing an essay. Prototypical college experiences.

STEPHANIE: I feel like I know Ken, I've spoken to him for
so long.

DAVE: You *do* know him. You know him because he's *just
like me.*

STEPHANIE: Is he really?

DAVE: Yes. *Just . . . like . . . me.*

MARK: Literate, though, I hope.

DAVE: He's a writer *just . . . like . . . me.* Better than me one
day, no doubt.

STEPHANIE: Does he look like you?

DAVE: He even looks sort of like me.

I remember this theme with David—how we were so much alike.
He'd sound it every time he introduced me to someone. *Don't you
think we look alike?* I remember being flattered initially, but then
being irritated by it, and finally openly resisting. The part about us
looking alike seemed the most demonstrably wrong. My father
and I looked a lot more alike, and seemed a lot closer in tempera-
ment. But David seemed to have invested a lot in the story of our
similarity. He seemed to tell it with pride, as if I were a chip off
the old block, but also with some self-pity. The day he sent me his
Sunday Brunch tape, for example, he wrote in his notebook about
his fifteen-year-old brother, Kenny, surpassing him in everything
he attempted. "He'll be *the one*," David wrote. "I'll be the brother
who was mighty highly influential, but he'll be the one. Am I
skeered of this? Skeered of falling out of the picture? Yes. It
seems that falling is a major fear of human beings: falling in love,
falling into debt, falling into disrepair, falling apart, falling for a
joke, falling from grace. . . . But I will make my own way. That my
brother will do what I have done far better than I have done
excites me thoroughly."

Beneath this, David wrote a note to himself to pick up two
books from the library: W.N.P. Barbellion's *The Journal of a Disappointed Man,* a book that ends with the author pretending to have
died an early death in order to ensure more interest in his notebooks (and then actually dying an early death a few years later),
and a new edition of Vincent Van Gogh's letters to his younger
brother, Theo.

. . .

That summer, David stayed in Providence—to write, of course, but also to finish courses that he'd failed to complete during the year. He'd gotten a letter from a dean telling him that he'd been placed on serious academic warning. "We remind you that failure to improve your academic record during the coming semester may result in your being considered for dismissal from the university in January 1985."

A copy of the warning was also sent home. It came at the end of months of letters back and forth between David and my father about David's summer job search and his plans for what to do after graduation. My father urged David to get more concrete about pursuing a writing life if that's what he thought he wanted to do with his life. "You don't need to write a masterpiece every time out. There is some virtue in starting small, especially if it gives you the paychecks and experience that allow you to think bigger." David wrote back:

> Do you know what I want to do with the rest of my life, Dad? Exactly what I am doing this instant: I want to type what I think. Do you know that I actually believe that I can earn money doing this? I'll pen some feature articles about ferrets as pets and write a ripped-bodice Yukon adventure like *Lust in Manitoba,* and in this way I will satisfy the public and pay the bills while I toil away on that great big book I'm always rattling swords about. . . .
>
> I've got a lotta heart, Dad, and this heart might appear aimless and irresponsible but it's not. It might be a partially destructive heart, but it's a heart with gumption. It's a heart with moxie. There is nothing to worry about. I'm not worried.

Into this story came me, and the question of whether I would spend a stretch of time with David in Providence. I was going to be in Boston for six weeks, at a summer program my father had forced me into for fear that I might never get serious enough about schoolwork to get into the college of my choice. Boston was just an hour or so away from Providence by bus or train, so it made sense that I would see David. But when I asked my father if it was okay, he said, "David needs to buckle down this summer so he can graduate. . . . I'm not sure he has the funds to host you either." I wrote David to say I didn't think I could visit. He must have sensed the source of my concerns about the visit—my father's concerns—because he shot back a quick response:

> June 12, 1984
> Dear Ken,
>   Don't you worry about me and work and money. When and if I decide I need a lot of money I will work to acquire it. Right now, it's more important for me to sweat all day in the sun reading literature and waving to the many serious people who walk past me with places to go, wishing they could trade places with me I am certain. Dad has his hesitations about sending you to stay with me before or after you go to the Wellesley Work Farm, but if you yourself want to come I will lobby the Dad Legislature for a Bill of Permission.

One month later: I was standing on a street corner in Boston at night, near the end of a field trip from Wellesley to a disco roller rink of some kind, when I heard a guy doing a heavy rap about giving money to the homeless. He was haranguing someone. No, he was haranguing *me*. "Hey, buddy, can you spare a dime? Hey, you! Hey, buddy! I'm a little down on my luck. Can't you spare a dime?"

I was in a pack of teens and preteens headed back to a chartered bus, thinking maybe about who I was going to sit next to and whether or not that someone would be a girl. But the homeless guy persisted: "Hey, Dornstein! DORNSTEIN! You too busy to spare a dime for the homeless?" I turned my head to find David in shorts, a T-shirt, and flip-flops, with a deep suntan. Even after I realized it was David, and went to give him a hug, he stayed in character, stooped over, cantankerous, and yelling things as if he were truly homeless and I were the society that had ignored him for too long.

David's theatrics made it hard for me to embrace him, but he snapped out of it in a few minutes and was given permission to ride with us on the bus back to Wellesley. I was glad to see him, but I knew I would have to switch gears entirely to meet him at his same pitch of excitement about the visit. He loved to appear like this without warning; he dared you to find whatever it was you were doing more important than spending time with him. He always seemed prepared to be monumentally hurt if you couldn't get into the spirit of his visit. His surprise visits were a test, and I always wanted to pass.

David slept on the floor of my dorm room and he went with me the next morning to my classes. I was taking Economics and Fiction, a perfect mix of father and brother. David came with me to the fiction class. He said he would sit in the back and observe, but he ended up making a nuisance of himself, showing up the teacher, who happened to be someone he knew from Brown and didn't think much of as a writer.

The rest of the day, David and I walked around Wellesley. He thought we should make a tape together, one that was much better than my "Seder '84" or his "Sunday Brunch" for the fact that we would be doing it together. He wanted us to write stories together, too. When we ran into people I knew, he would always take the lead: *We look alike, don't we? Do you think we look alike?* It might have been annoying, but the general tenor of the day was sweet. He talked to me about his fears about life after college, and I got a truer picture of what his life was like. It was probably the most concentrated real time we had ever spent together. He left after dark. On the train back to Providence, he reached for his notebook.

1038 pm Wednesday July 11
  The night and long day spent with Brother Ken was more than beyond description: deserves a deep and loving description of a sort that I'm not that practiced at. He's a young man. I am a young man. We look alike? We don't. We are alike? We are

not really alike. But, oh, do we understand each other, oh the
world is ours, the world is ours.

David wrote a letter to my father the next day, assuring him
again about his academic standing and about his visit to see me as
well. ("I do not believe I disturbed his studies.") Next, he wrote a
letter to me. He started light—"We had a helluva time last
Wednesday didn't we?"—but then he turned fatalistic:

You will only get older, Kenny, this is the nature of time, and
as you get older, I can be more sure of who you are, what we
have together. Right now, to be honest with you, I'm wondering if a conflict will arise in you between essentially polar
natures: that is, Dad's nature, which it is clear you have inher-
ited yourself, and my own, which I don't think you could
comprehend so well if you didn't have a fair amount in you to
start. I believe you have the greatest chance of any of us to
reconcile these natures and make a feast of yourself. You
know the story: Two soldiers in a bunker and one of them is
shot real bad. . . .

> *I'm dying, Ernie.*
> No, Bob! No!
> *Yes, Ernie, I've had it . . . go on without me . . . I'll just keep you*
> *back . . . go on without me.*
> No! Bob! Bob! . . . Baaaaaaaaab. . . .

I don't know what you'll do in life, Kenan, who you'll be, what
you'll desire and not desire. My way with you is as a *pardner.*
My way with you is as brother and coconspirator. Maybe I'll
be the inspirational figure from somewhere in your past who
helps you to where you're going even if he doesn't make it
there himself. Pressure, however, is nonextant. Do what you
want, and do it as well as you can, as long as it doesn't hurt
people unnecessarily. And try not to be frightened of getting
hurt yourself.
    I'll just end here, mail it. I want to keep my letters shorter

to you so they don't get too overwhelming. I'm coming again to visit and I might already be there because today is Monday and I don't work again for Carr Caterers until Saturday. Look quick over your shoulder and I'll be there.

David never made it back to Wellesley, but I saw him one more time that summer. The day the Wellesley program ended, I took the train to Providence's old downtown station, and David met me there. He and my father had worked out the terms of the visit. My father's last letter was addressed to both David and me in Providence—"Dear Sons, I'm expecting you to arrive any day next week." He included some money for the train ride home.

I was tired when I got to David's apartment, having stayed up the whole last night of the Wellesley program. David borrowed a mattress for me to sleep on. When I awoke it was dark. David was sitting across the room, propped up against the wall reading a book. This was David's life, I thought. Here I was on the inside, in the room with the typewriter and the jar of peanut butter and the books stacked up all around. This was probably what it was like in David's room when no one else was around.

"Are you hungry? Do you want to get something to eat?" David was a supremely attentive host. Whatever his own sleeping or eating habits, he seemed wholly dedicated to making my stay as comfortable as possible. He loved to pay for things with a big wad of cash he kept in his back pocket. A book? Some music? A movie? An Italian water ice? *Whatever you want.* He had so much to show me, too: the places he'd lived; the theater where he'd played one of the rapists in Shakespeare's *Titus Andronicus* (I remember the publicity photo of him in a loincloth); the Health Services building where he'd holed up for a week with some terrible malady he didn't explain. We ran into people on the street, and David seemed just as eager to explain me to them as he'd been on the Sunday Brunch tape. It didn't matter if I was standing right there. He'd still say to them, "Do you think we look alike? He's *just like me.*"

The morning David and I were due to head back to Philadelphia, we overslept badly. It seemed to me that we had missed the train, but David wouldn't concede defeat. We had told our father that we'd be home that day, and nothing was more important to David than keeping to this plan, not failing on the terms he'd worked out with our father.

David didn't have that much to carry, but I had a whole summer's worth of stuff; clothes, tennis racquet, cassette player, and all the rest. My suitcase was a huge square of vinyl made to look like leather, balanced on two flimsy sets of hard rubber wheels. It was an awkward load, but David said he'd handle it if I carried his backpack full of books.

This image is clear in my mind: The two of us running toward the train station, with David pulling that big, square suitcase behind him. We made good time for a while, but as College Hill dropped steeply toward downtown Providence, the suitcase started to get away from him. His energies were now spent holding it back, not dragging it forward. We hit a bump in the road, and he lost his grip.

The suitcase took off down the hill like a go-cart. David and I stood and watched as it gained speed. It ran a red light at Benefit Street and fortunately didn't hit anyone. Then it hit a curb and spun out of control, bounding end over end, up onto the sidewalk and into the side of a building, where it came to a stop. The faux leather was pretty torn up—I could see clothes peeking out—and one of the sets of wheels had come dislodged from the base. Now the two of us needed to team up. We carried the suitcase between us, walking fast, then jogging, through a road construction zone, across the Providence River, and into the train station, where we boarded just before the train's doors closed. We were soaked in sweat and dirty from carrying the now-filthy bag, but David seemed ecstatic with the whole episode. This is the way he lived his life, he seemed to be saying. It wasn't pretty, but he knew how to get the job done in the end. He seemed pleased that I'd learned this about him: If he really needed to, he could make the impossible real.

We didn't call my father when we got to Thirtieth Street Station in Philadelphia. Always the fan of the surprise arrival, David insisted we take the commuter train to our local station and then walk home from there. I remember the two of us carrying that tattered suitcase through the streets of the town where we had grown up—past the elementary school and the houses of children we used to play with, and then onto our own street. We were like two soldiers home from the war. David's sense of himself as the brother who wouldn't survive and me as the brother who should leave him for dead—this was not the way it went. We had both made it home. Even the seriously wounded suitcase had made it home. My dad greeted us in the street with a big smile, a hug, and a kiss. "My boys are home." There were no losses that day.

VI

AFTER LONG STRETCHES with David's notebooks, I often felt a strong urge to call him on the phone. His number was always on the front cover inside a box that read, "If found, please call," so it seemed like a straightforward enough thing to do. And if it made sense to call my long-dead brother, why not try talking to the living?

On the inside covers of his notebooks, David wrote the names and phone numbers of people who were significant in his life: friends from Brown and from high school, people he'd met in his travels. For years I avoided contact with them. I was afraid that they knew about K and me, that they thought it was strange or wrong for us to be together, and that a call from me would seem similarly misguided—David's brother not giving up the ghost. But now I felt free to make those calls. It was the summer of 1997, and K and I had just split.

There is a long story to tell about this. Indeed, there is the whole history of my relationship with K, of which I have said little. Call it the real story of our relationship, the everyday ups and downs of two people trying to love each other as best they can. It's hard to tell this story—real life is never so neat as the stories we choose to tell about it—so, when pressed by K, say at the end of a long, draining talk about marriage, children, and the rest, I often reached for this *other* story, the one about us being crippled by our shared history with David. For all of its complication, I knew how this other story began (meeting K on a train), and I knew how it ended: with our inevitable separation. This went on for years, this telling and retelling of the David story every time K and I got stuck. It never helped. When K finished her doctorate and I finally published my accident-faking book, things came to a head: We looked up from our desks and papers and saw a relationship that wasn't moving.

Months later, I made the trip to Lockerbie. K and I were both invested in the same idea: namely, that grief was a place that I could visit for a time and then leave, having resolved something about David that would free me up in some essential way. She faxed me a week after I'd left, wishing me luck in finding what I needed to on the streets and hills of Lockerbie:

> I have had this image in my head of you that I know is probably inaccurate, but it is indelible nonetheless. I see you walking through the fields, by the side of the road. You are wearing your blue baseball jacket, your hiking boots, your knapsack. Your head is down a bit, watching where you are walking, but every so often you look around at the cows, the green, and the old stone walls. I'm not sure where you are going or where you have come from, but you are on your way to a place where you will learn more, and feel more of what you need to feel. There is such a sense of purpose and of important solitude in this image I have of you.

Things felt different for a while after I returned, but six months later we were having the old argument again, and this time we decided to go to separate corners. K was living in our old apartment, and I had moved to a rented room about two hundred yards away.

It was not yet what you'd call a final break. I left the bulk of my things behind at our old place. Most of what I took with me was

David's—his notebooks and papers, my entire Dave Archives. We were finally going to spend a summer together, David and I. Our big adventure.

It was hard to split from K—we had rooted into each other in a thousand small ways that I couldn't see until I pulled away—but I felt hopeful about what I was doing. I was living a dream that I had been having for years. David returns and I am the same person I was when he left: no attachments, no job, no plans I can't drop, ready to pick up where we left off.

I pulled names of David's friends from his notebooks and tried to develop current phone numbers for them. When I found a match, I'd pick up the phone to call. This is when nerves kicked in. I was afraid of creeping people out with the Dornstein name, a voice from the grave suddenly on the phone. I was equally afraid that the name would mean nothing to them. *David Dornstein? Do you remember him? Sorry to bother you.*

A guy named Rob was my first call, and he put me at ease right away. In fact, Rob one-upped me in possible weirdness: He said he had just finished recopying David's name and phone number into his new address book. "I just didn't like how it felt to leave out David's name." He said he'd done it every year since David died.

The next name I pulled from the notebooks, Ken Mingis, wasn't hard to link to a person. Mingis (that's what David called him) had been a reporter for *The Providence Journal,* and he was still there. I left him a rambling phone message about being David's brother and wanting to talk if this interested him, but also understanding that it might not interest him, and that was okay, *that was fine,* whatever he wanted. Mingis called back within the hour. "So you're Dornstein's little brother? I was wondering when you were going to call."

A few days later, I met Mingis in front of the *Providence Journal* building. He greeted me with a firm handshake and a slap on the back. He called me "buddy." It was the kind of instant familiarity I could attribute only to his having been so close to David. David mixed fact and fiction so thoroughly in his notebooks that I felt as if I had come to Providence initially just to confirm that Ken Mingis was real.

Mingis and I walked to a bar across from the newspaper. He asked a lot of questions. He liked hearing about David's life, and as we continued, I found that I liked talking about David with him. Something about the way I had come to him—through David's notebooks—made me trust in what we were doing together.

Mingis had known David mainly during the summer of 1984, the same time I visited David in Providence. He said he remembered my brother and father being in conflict over David's grades and his future. Mingis had been having troubles with his own father, so one night, over beers, he and David hatched a plan. "We'd put on paper all the mean things kids think about their parents, seal up the envelopes, and mail our letters to each other. . . . My dad would get his comeuppance from me, and Dornstein's would get blasted by him. And neither one of them would be hurt." Mingis said he wrote his letter, stuffing into it every raw feeling and recrimination he could muster, and then sent it to David according to plan. Weeks passed, but Mingis didn't get anything from David. This made him angry. "I never got his letter to his dad because I suspect he never wrote it. An hour after we talked he was probably on to something else. . . . Or maybe he just didn't know what he wanted to say about his father."

When the school year began again, campus life proved too much for David, and Ken let him crash at his apartment. David always seemed inordinately grateful for these small kindnesses, Mingis said. I showed him a line from David's notebooks in which David said he owed Mingis a great "debt of care." As I watched him read these words I felt as if we were closing a loop that David had wanted closed.

The meeting with Ken Mingis inspired me. I pulled more names from David's notebooks, made more phone calls, and wrote more letters. I told people I was working on the Dave Oral History Project, a name sufficiently grand to have satisfied David's wildest fantasies of posthumous fame.

I took the work seriously. I was in search of every name I could link to a flesh-and-bones person—the closest friends and lovers no more than the people who came and went from David's notebook in less than a page. David had worked hard at being memorable, and from the stories people shared with me, it seemed that his work had paid off.

David's sophomore-year writing instructor asked David about his other interests besides writing, and David answered: "I really like fucking."

David was the guest of honor at a formal dinner painstakingly prepared by a group of friends, but he balked at the main course. ("Could I get a grilled cheese sandwich instead?")

In a history seminar, David launched into a tirade that provoked the professor to say in his crusty New England accent, "DAWN-STEEN, I'm gonna run you up the flagpole!"

On a drive home from Brown, David and some friends showed up at my mother's building in Manhattan. He buzzed her to come down to the lobby, then pulled his jacket up over his head and zipped it closed as my mother approached. Everyone stood around as David started repeating, "I lost my head at college, Mom . . . I lost my head at college." One of the friends recalled: "Your mom was pretty perplexed. She tried to get David to show his face, but he wouldn't break character, he wouldn't drop it. I left at this point. Not sure what could have happened next."

In the name of the Dave Oral History Project, I made contact with dozens of people that summer, going hat in hand for whatever they had left of David to give me. People remembered David feverishly writing in his notebook and reading aloud to them against their will. They remembered him arguing, sometimes out of fierce conviction, other times just to get a reaction. This was a big theme: Dave as provocateur. (When David's name first came

David at Brown in 1984
(Photo given to me by a participant in the
Dave Oral History Project.)

up in reference to Lockerbie, several of his close friends con-
fessed to a fear that David had had something to do with it. One
said, "I thought he'd gone too far this time.") Another theme:
Dave as man on fire, a person with limitless energy, manic and creative. One more theme: Dave as a self-conscious promoter of his
own myth. Here, David clearly succeeded: Most people remembered him as "larger than life."

This was the person who many people wanted to remember:
David the Wild Agitator for the Arts; David the Tormented Intellectual; David of the Luminescent Blue Eyes and Flowing Dark
Curls; David Who Never Compromised. This was how I saw
David, too—call it my little brother's perspective—but one
woman who worked with David on the campus humor magazine
urged caution:

> I know you are kind of searching for the Dave as Mythic
> Campus Figure, but to be honest there were only a handful of
> us who were aware of his Presence. I'm sure if you surveyed
> the other 88% of the people who write into the alumni mag-
> azine about their third little girl, Tiffany, or their promotion at
> Large Conglomerate or their cure for World Hunger, they
> would go, "David who?"
>
> If your brother was larger than life, it was because we all
> allowed him to be, the way you let your suburban roommate
> think she's Sylvia Plath. He stood out, in part, because he
> wouldn't allow himself to fit in. . . .
>
> Ken, I know it must be terribly painful to have to recon-
> struct your brother from scratch. Knowing him as I did at
> Brown, and knowing what I did of his life in the "real world"
> afterwards, I'd just like to suggest that perhaps he is better off
> having lived the fast life he did. Better off not having to have
> compromised the mythic Dornstein for Dornstein the Neigh-
> bor, Dornstein the Editor, Dornstein Who Has to Answer to
> Someone Else.

Even this attempt at sobriety indirectly endorsed the very view of
David it tried to correct: Namely, that David stood for something

pure that no one wanted to see sullied by the messy business of life. If adolescence was a time to believe in ideas passionately, completely, and absolutely, David would become the boy who never had to grow up. It was a good story, and it seemed to mean more to David's friends as they grew older and settled into careers and families of their own. But where did it leave me that summer? I was Ken Who Had Quit His Job. Ken Who Had Left His Girlfriend. Ken Who Was Broke.

A break: An editor at a magazine had seen my accident-faking book and wanted me to report a story about it for him. The call came like a reprieve from the governor. I needed to get away from my basement room, from David's notebooks, and I needed the money. But the most attractive part of the offer was the free trip to Los Angeles, where the accident-faking story was supposed to be focused. My Dave Oral History Project research had turned up a dozen or so people who now lived in Los Angeles, and this was a way to meet them.

I called Rob, the friend who still copied David's name into his address book every year. He lived in West L.A. and seemed excited to meet me. He said he might be able to round up some others on my list for a bull session at his house. They were mostly actors and actresses, people David had known from plays he'd been in at Brown.

Seven or eight people were set to come to the L.A. meeting, but Rob and I had a miscommunication and he called it off at the last minute. The oral history session came down to just him and me and another actor from Brown having dinner at a hotel restaurant. The conversation was mainly about David the Actor. We talked about who had starred in what play when, which were the best productions, the most outstanding performances, the most interesting backstage stories. (Rob's friend said that David had relished his role as chief sadist in Shakespeare's *Titus Andronicus*.) At one point, I asked Rob, "Was David a good actor?" Rob found a nice but clear way of saying no: "David's acting suffered from too much Dave and not enough acting."

Then Rob remembered something. He called it "David's truest performance," a monologue that David had once performed in class that "blew everyone away." It was from a John Guare play called *Landscape of the Body*. David played a character named Donny. Later I found Donny's big monologue.

> DONNY: I'm not ever going to believe in dreams again. I dreamed the other night and the night before that, and once again about six months ago, that a yellow checker cab stopped, and a man got out and dragged me in, and when the cab stopped we were in a quiet warehouse so you could look down and see the river, and waiting in a line was all these men with drool coming out of their mouths, and my feet were in cement and the old man touched me only he wasn't old anymore and that dream came true just now. Bert was the old man. My feet were in cement. I am not going to end up my life in any dream. I stopped that dream. Anybody tells you dreams don't tell the future you send them to me.

Rob asked David how he came to give such a true reading of these lines, and David told him: "Because it happened to me."

It wasn't clear to me what this story meant. Rob thought for a moment, then said: "David told me he was nine or ten years old. He had a friend who lived on his street, and the friend's older brother used to hang around with them. Sometimes the older brother would seek David out on his own 'to play.' David said this guy molested him for years until your family finally moved away."

This was a bombshell story, but Rob didn't tell it that way. He assumed I'd known, for all of my closeness with David, and my readings of David's notebooks, and my extensive researches. But I hadn't. I approached the oral history project dutifully (*this is what David would have wanted*) and with tongue in cheek (*this is how David would have done it*), but I didn't think of it as an investigation, a search for secrets. If I was looking for answers, the questions were about my own life more than David's. But now here was this important story. What to do with it?

Rob told me the rest of what he remembered: "David said that he once went back to the old neighborhood looking for his friend's older brother. He said he went to their old house and found the older brother still living there. The guy now had a wife and kids. David said he insisted on meeting them. He wanted to make the guy uncomfortable in front of his family—this would be his revenge. David told the guy if he ever touched his own children or anyone else's, he would come back and kill the guy. Just like Donny in *Landscape* had done to his so-called friend Bert."

Back in my basement room in Cambridge, I read through David's notebooks for references to the neighbor, whom I'll call Bill Donoghue. Now that I was looking for them, I found some: One said, "Bill Donoghue. I remember his tongue. Conscious memory? Unconscious?" The next one said, "Must explore Bill Donoghue link, being molested as a small child, French kissing for payment. . . . How to write about this? People are uncomfortable with real facts, real emotions. They want it sugarcoated, slathered with FICTION FICTION FICTION. But I can't make fiction out of this."

It's hard to imagine my reading these things and not thinking anything of them, initially, but there was a lot of audacious material in David's notebooks, most of it framed as fiction, and a lot of sexual explicitness, too, which I tended to skip, especially where it involved Kathryn. This, in fact, is where most of the Bill Donoghue references were—mixed into pages about David and Kathryn. Had he ever said anything to her about Donoghue?

I needed to call K, even if it meant breaking the ground rules of our summer separation. I told her about Rob in Los Angeles and *Landscape of the Body,* but K was way ahead of me. "Donoghue," she said. "I think David said the neighbor's name was Donoghue. He said he was ten or eleven at the time. It went on for years." I didn't know what to think about her telling me this. *Why hadn't it come up before?* I might have been discouraged by this, but in a strange way, it made me feel close to her again, as if there were still so much for us to know about each other. We agreed to meet. K went looking through journals she'd kept at Brown until she found an entry about Donoghue from her freshman year. She felt awkward showing it to me—maybe this is why it had never come up—but she decided, in the end, that it was important for me to see it.

October 3, 1982

I finally asked Dave why he doesn't like to kiss. He kisses me less and less and I didn't understand it. It upsets me . . . after a while he told me this story. As a little nine-year-old boy he had a friend who had two older brothers. Bill was the oldest. Bill loved Dave and would take him places. In return for gifts and happy days, he would ask Dave for favors. Dave can only remember kissing, and knowing that he hated it. Now he says that he still doesn't like to kiss because all tongues feel the same. And now I feel like I can't kiss him. I feel such hatred towards Bill, confused hatred.

I checked the date against David's notebooks and found no mention of his telling Kathryn about Donoghue, but I could see that the six months around this revelation had been tumultuous for him. It was a time when David gave up sleeping in beds in favor of the floor, and invented the alter ego Kristian Santini, the ten-year-old boy from a broken home to whom terrible things were always happening. It's when David suffered another of the breakdowns that would send him to the university psychiatrist for little pink tranquilizers; recorded many lurid dreams about incest and gay men in public parks; wrote a story about a man named Kramer "who's had this stuff inside of him since he was a little boy, but he can't get it out."

Kramer threw things and the things broke. During the moments of throwing things and breaking things he felt stuff escaping him. He realized he couldn't keep throwing things, or he would break all of his stuff, but he couldn't stop. He threw and he broke all of his things. He broke his house. He felt empty.

Rereading David's *The Fall Journal,* my eye now stopped at the headlines he'd clipped from supermarket tabloids: "WAYS TO TELL IF YOUR CHILD HAS BEEN MOLESTED" ... "HOW TO SAVE YOUR KID FROM PERVERTS." These no longer seemed like the melodramatic distractions of a narrator with nothing to say, as Robert Coover had concluded. They seemed more like flags planted firmly in territory the narrator needed badly to explore, but couldn't successfully navigate yet.

Near the end of the Dorrance-Dean oral history that David wrote for Coover, an unnamed man speaks: "I used to molest Dave when he was eight years old and I lived down the road from him. He was the prettiest boy I have ever seen. I used to take him to the park and buy him things and then ask for tongue kisses for payment. Soon I asked for more. It went on until he was ten or eleven, and then I stopped. I didn't want him to figure it out. When I read his bestselling book about his prolonged battle with homophobia and his breakdowns, I felt sorry and stopped seeing that other little fellow down the street."

VII

I THOUGHT IT WOULD BE EASY to track down Bill Donoghue, but I found myself stuck with a private investigator's worst assignment: a long list of Donoghues from a Philadelphia phone directory and no reason to favor one over another. I made many more calls than I thought I'd need to before I reached a man who seemed to know *my* Donoghue. I said that I was a Dornstein, David's little brother, and the man said, "We all remember Dave fondly." The man launched right into recollections of David and the old neighborhood, as if he'd been expecting the call. "When David was little, he spent a lot of time over at our house and out in the street playing sports. Your dad worked a lot and wasn't around that much. I don't remember much about your mom. We didn't see a whole lot of her. She was a pretty lady, though. Real pretty. . . . Your brother was a real good-looking guy, too. I remember seeing his picture on the news after the plane went down. Lockerbie, right? It was terrible. We couldn't believe it."

Michael Donoghue was closest to David in age and had been his best friend. I thought it was Michael who had answered the phone—that's who I had dialed—but something about the man's tone, and his passing reference to being much older than David, made me question this. I asked him, "Is this Bill Donoghue?" And he said, "That's me."

Was this going to be my big confrontation? I wasn't prepared. The image in my head up to this point had come from David and his friends: Bill would confess, and then I'd decide how long he needed to be punished, and in what way. I thought the mere presence of a Dornstein would tell Bill that he had been found out. But Bill Donoghue seemed only happy about the contact from me. We talked for twenty minutes or so, and then he said, "Feel free to call anytime, day or night. I'm up all hours. . . . I really liked your brother. He was so bright. It's such a loss for the world. I still miss your brother very strongly. Just driving past the old house sometimes I think about him. If you ever come back, I'll give you a tour of the neighborhood."

A few months later, I was in Philly and called Bill Donoghue. We made a plan to meet at a deli around the corner from where our families used to live. I got there first and was standing outside when he pulled up in an old station wagon. From about five feet away, he said, "There's a Dornstein if ever I saw one!" He moved in to shake my hand, maybe even to clap me on the back or to hug, but I left it at a shake.

He was balding and not that tall; he had a gut and ruddy cheeks. He told me on the phone that he'd been an "Irish guy" growing up, by which he said he meant he'd been a heavy drinker. His hair was dyed. He pointed this out to me himself, saying, "It's something you have to do when you're in sales." He was wearing a long-sleeve white button-down shirt and blue slacks, a uniform a waiter might wear, although I think he said he sold cars. My overall impression was of a guy trying to make a neat appearance but not entirely succeeding. I thought of a slovenly boy whose parents made him dress up for church on Sundays.

We sat in the deli and talked. I told Bill that I was writing a book about David's life and was trying to talk to people who'd known him at every stage, and to revisit the places where he'd lived. I'd brought along my video camera—I told Bill that I worked for public television and might make a documentary about David's life someday. In short order, I told him everything I could think of about why I'd come, except the main reason: that I had amassed a lot of evidence that he had molested David when David was a young boy, and that David had suffered a lot over this, and that I was there to get from him whatever justice there was left to get.

Bill was an easy talker, with a quick wit. There was something doughy and youthful about him, despite the obvious signs of wear and tear. At the same time, I thought I saw something predatory in his face. His eyes were small and deeply set and darted from side to side as he listened. I felt that he was appraising me, trying to gauge what kind of jokes I thought were funny, what interested me about the old neighborhood, about him.

After an hour or so of conversation, he looked at his watch and said, "Should we begin our trip down memory lane?" We left the deli. As we walked the old neighborhood, I took out my camera and started asking questions about who lived where, and what it was like to live here years ago. I tried to show a general interest in the neighborhood, not a pointed interest in him. I was hoping he would grow comfortable enough to say things he hadn't meant to.

As we walked, Bill handed me pieces of his family history. He said he lived at home until his late twenties. Once again, he said he was a typical "Irish guy," but this time I think he meant that he'd been a layabout and not a drinker (or was he a layabout *because* he was a drinker?). He said he knew David mainly through his own younger brother. "Michael and David were best buddies. I used to drive them places. Teach them to play sports. David was a small kid but he loved to play with us bigger guys. He was tenacious. Unstoppable."

Bill told me that he worked a lot of different jobs during his twenties and thirties. Now it was car sales, but in the early 1980s it was personal computers. I asked him if he knew a lot about computers, but he said he really didn't. "I knew just enough to sell them. I'm more of a people person. I'm good at persuading people to do things. Most people have a couple basic needs, and I'm pretty good at figuring out what these are and working from there." It was hard to hear this and not think about him and David. I was looking for signs that Bill had been the guy who

David's eighth birthday, celebrated at the Donoghues' house
(photo taken by Bill)

David said he was, and even the most offhand comments might count as evidence.

Bill pointed out his old house to me, and then he crossed the street and walked up the front walkway of a house that seemed vaguely familiar. He said, "This is your house, of course." I didn't remember living there—I was three or four when we left—but the front walk was familiar to me from photos. We knocked on the door, but no one was home. The people who'd moved in after my family left had a daughter who was my age; she sat in front of me in homeroom for four years, but I never once asked her about the house or the neighborhood or the neighbors. Now every detail seemed significant.

Bill pushed past me on his way to the backyard. "You used to have a great patio," he said. We looked up at a window on the second floor, and I asked him if this had been David's room. It was a trick question, like a lot of what I asked him as we walked along, and I thought it significant that he hesitated before answering. "No," he finally said. "I was never inside. . . . Well, maybe once or twice." I pushed a little, and he said that he might have been on the first floor but never on the second. "I'm pretty sure I wasn't in David's room. My brother, Michael, was probably in there, but not me." *Does Bill know what I'm really asking?*

We walked back into the street and Bill looked toward his old front yard. "Dorny—we called him Dorny—he was on our doorstep at eight A.M. during the summer. He would have breakfast with us. Your mom was not a cook. I remember she used to make the kids cereal for dinner. . . . Dave would eat and then he'd be raring to go. Touch football, baseball, hockey. He'd never decline a sports opportunity."

I'd heard this before. I couldn't figure out how to steer Bill into telling me what had really happened between David and him. I wanted to skip to the part where he broke down crying and said how sorry he'd been all these years. But after about two hours together, I began to lose faith that this visit was going to clarify anything.

Rob had told me that David had come back to the neighborhood and confronted Bill. I wondered if this was true, and if Bill had given David anything more than he was giving me. I decided to ask Bill straight out, and he came right across with the story. He had moved out of his parents' house that year, he said, but came back one Saturday to visit. "I was standing out in the driveway for some reason, and here comes David jogging up the street. I was amazed."

I was a little amazed as well. I didn't think David had ever made the visit. I asked Bill what he and David talked about, and he said, "Just what David was doing at college, I suppose. He went to Brown, right?" I asked Bill to say more. He thought for a few moments and said, "I usually have a good memory for things, but the details of that conversation I don't recall." I imagined that David had really geared up for the meeting, the big confrontation, and that he had tried to make Donoghue sweat and squirm and apologize. I was looking for some sign that this had happened. I came at it from ten different directions, but all I got was this: "I was just real delighted to see David." And this: "I still remember he was wearing navy blue jogging shorts. No shirt . . . He was a good-looking guy, you know?" There was nothing patently incriminating about this last statement, even if I could convince myself that he had said it a little wistfully and lustily.

Bill had to go. He said he was late for an appointment to show a car to a prospective buyer. On our walk back to his car, he looked back at the old street and said: "It's been a long time. A lot of things are flooding back." I liked the idea of memories flooding back and thought that maybe Bill wanted to tell me something at last, but he quickly closed things off: "These were good times. Just *good* times."

The moment had long passed for me to push Bill Donoghue about David. I had brought my notes from David's notebooks to show Bill his name and what David had written, but I never got close to pulling them out. Was I a coward? Had Donoghue been a good salesman, successfully selling me his version of the past? I think I lost my sense of purpose when Bill made it clear that David himself had come back to the neighborhood and found him years ago. David had pursued the matter in his own way and maybe resolved it as much as it could be resolved, so what more did I think I needed to do?

VIII

Am I writing the story of David's life? If so, I have skipped over a number of important chapters. David's boyhood, for example. It's a story that I think David tried to tell in those first years at Brown, but always as fiction, often as farce—a comic grotesque—and never fully. He walked right to the edge of what he really wanted to write about, and then stepped back. He made notes about the need to elaborate on certain episodes and themes, but he never did. Somewhere along the way he developed a creeping sense of the significance of Bill Donoghue. It started around the time he told Kathryn about Donoghue, this intense need to look back at his life, to excavate something from the depths and memorialize it in words so it wouldn't be forgotten or denied. And this fed a desire for literary stardom. If he were a famous writer, David reasoned, people would listen to his story of childhood woe—of Donoghue, of the divorce. He could write this story in code, and scholars and critics would decipher it. But then Professor Coover told David, more or less, that he didn't get it. "You have here the germ for one good story . . . *one perhaps you're not quite ready to write. . . .*"

So a new chapter began: David as washed-up at twenty, done

with fiction, disillusioned with his ability to say in words what he really needed to. David would now mentor his little brother to succeed where he had failed, give him a notebook and tell him to start writing early, give him books and tell him to read.

Meanwhile, David threw himself into acting. He played small parts in main-stage productions, larger parts in smaller student projects. He switched from prose to playwriting. A first effort: *Crazy Mother,* a monologue that began: "I used to be an Artist. I made etchings. Now I'm the 'crazy mother.' I'm a bit tired of this crazy label. I'm very creative, you know. Do you have any idea what my life is really like, David? You don't. You're writing blind." A next effort: *A Dramatic Father/Son Dialogue:*

FATHER: Why have you done this to us, David?

SON: Done what?

FATHER: Put us on stage like this, put our private lives on stage.

SON: I'm not showing anything that isn't true. . . .

MOTHER *(offstage)*:   What about me? Do you think you've told the truth about me? . . .

SON: This won't work. This is too simplistic, father as all-business, mother as maniac. You're not two people, just two explanations for me. . . . This isn't drama, it's therapy.

Next chapter: David put playwriting aside and burrowed into nonfiction, starting with a series of confessional *Brown Daily Herald* columns about "my own racism," "my own sexism," "my own homophobia," "my own suburban nature."

Next chapter: Finding God. David wanted to dig deeper into his own Jewishness. At the start of his senior year, he wrote a letter to Judaic Studies professor Jacob Neusner, proposing an independent study. "Dear Professor Neusner, What is Judaism? Jewishness? How do we investigate these matters? How do we begin to worship?"

Professor Neusner was known on campus less for his scholarship, which was prolific and world renowned (he is reputed to have published more books than anyone alive), than for his high-profile role as a critic of Brown's administration and its students, both of which he frequently denounced as "third-rate." Neusner was a gadfly and provocateur, often in the same pages of the *Herald* where David was trying to be the same. When they went to put a title to one of David's columns, the *Herald* editors dubbed David "Neusner's Lost Son." Neusner responded with a note to David through the campus mail: "Dear Lost Son, Welcome Home!—Father."

When I contacted Neusner, I asked him about the "lost son" aspect of their relationship: "I don't think I cultivated my students as 'lost sons.' I didn't want David to be an enthusiast or a convert, not to me, not to anything. I didn't want a disciple. I stood for critical learning, not for recruiting for things I believed in, or for religious conversion. I think David accepted that." Indeed, after their first meeting, David wrote: "Neusner has warned me not to go seeking after God, not to stop eating pork, not to take refuge in orthodoxy when I feel at sea. Or else, he says, our lessons are through."

David came home for Thanksgiving that year and seemed more interested in Jewish things than I'd ever known him to be. He wanted to see the talis my father had worn for his bar mitzvah, he wanted to hear about our family's roots in Poland. I remember trying to joke about it all with David, but he resisted. He told me that one day life wouldn't be so funny. I'd realize that there was more to it than just making jokes, and then I might look into my Jewishness myself. He walked around the house in my father's talis and yarmulke and said he might become a rabbi.

On the train ride back to Providence, David spied a young woman reading *The New Republic* and sat next to her. He turned immediately to his notebook: "I never get on a train or walk down a street without hoping that I will fall in love with someone or something. And tonight it was her." He showed the woman what he had written and persuaded her to add her own version of their meeting. The woman's handwriting appeared next in David's notebook. Her account began with David sitting next to her, and her fearing he'd be "a pain." But then, she wrote, they began to talk.

WOMAN ON THE TRAIN: We gossiped academically, and
    name-dropped, until we both felt a little foolish. We
    talked about the Brown U. students who wanted to
    stockpile cyanide pills in case of a nuclear attack and he
    said he was one of the originators of the idea. At some
    point, he insisted on reading me lines from a play he was
    acting in, and then he read aloud from a book of mythol-
    ogy I was carrying. He said he was going to be an actor.
    At another point, he said he wanted to be a rabbi. At
    another point, it was a novelist. . . .

David had tried this gambit with a lot of people—*I'll write something, then you write something*—but few plunged into it so sincerely.
David didn't want the train ride to end. He said nothing out loud
for fear of breaking the spell. He wrote more in his notebook and
passed it back to the woman, and they went back and forth like this
for hours before the train neared Providence and it was good-bye.
"I fear it is ending," he wrote. "Our locomotive love is derailing."

DAVID: It has been a pleasure to ride with you. For the
    record, I want to be a comedian, not a rabbi, an actor,
    activist, or ascetic. And, about my family, everything I
    told you was a lie. My father is a baker, not a doctor. He
    bakes muffins at 3 A.M., seven days a week. My mother?
    She is a saleswoman. I told you that I beat John McEnroe
    in tennis when I was twelve and he was twelve, and that I
    quit the Junior Davis Cup Team after my mother had a
    schizophrenic psychotic episode and I went home and
    cried in the waiting room of the mental hospital where
    my mother was stumbling around on Thorazine and
    Nembutal. These were lies also. I never played tennis.
    And my Maybeline eyes? The lashes are fakes. I don't
    have blue eyes (they're contacts). Also: I have never
    spoken to Phil Donahue or appeared on his show.

Just a few hours after getting off the train at Providence,
David was back in his room on campus, opening up his notebook
to the place where the woman's handwriting left off. Fun and

games were over, he wrote. Old worries returned: Would he graduate? What would he do after that? "Emily From the Train is returned to her snug life, but I will never be twenty-seven and carry a business card. The standard symbols of a coherent life, the suit, the tie, and the monogrammed briefcase, terrify me. I am nothing and want nothing but to die before I have to become something or do anything."

David lit a cigarette. He had learned to smoke for a scene in an acting class that semester and decided that he liked cigarettes. They calmed him. He started with Camels and then moved on to Newport Menthol Lights. He sat on the floor of his room with his back up against his desk and took the smoke deep into his lungs. He had a paper to write for Professor Neusner. He had a column to write for the *Brown Daily Herald*. He had lines to learn for his part in *Anna Christie*. He had a letter he'd been composing in his head to my father that he kept telling himself he needed to get down on paper and send, but hadn't. He had dozens of books he had checked out of the library—the famous diaries of famous writers, mostly—but he had cracked none of them. He closed his eyes and could see nothing for himself in the future, just a field of white light. He saw the typewriter sitting on his desk. It was late, past 2 A.M., but he sat down and thought once more about writing fiction. He fed a fresh sheet into his typewriter. By the end of the night he had sketched out a last-ditch plan to stitch his stories and notebooks together into one big, bold book.

The final chapter of Dave's College Years: the Last Stand. It was David's final semester and he'd signed up for another advanced fiction class, this time with the novelist John Hawkes. David gave himself two weeks to pull together a work that would win Hawkes's respect, redeem all of the work he'd done over his years at Brown, and maybe, not insignificantly, help earn him one of the final credits he would need to graduate.

His friend Rob was out of town for winter break, so David camped out in Rob's apartment. He laid out his writing on Rob's floor and tried to arrange it in an order that made sense. He read here and there from his notebooks and manuscripts. He tried to focus, but his mind wandered. He decided to catalog the dreams he had recorded in the last year (he counted 121). What to do with these accounts? He wrote: "I resolve to not have another dream until I know what to do with them." He went to the library. He sat at a carrel and tried to read books that would inspire him, but he felt too anxious to concentrate. "Against my wishes I am becoming dominated again by thoughts of what I will do in five months when the university bids me goodriddance." He fell asleep for a few moments and dreamed that he was being scorned by William Safire for his laziness. He decided he needed some fresh air.

> *January 5, 1985 134am*
> *Just spent an hour-and-a-half in the cold. Lost hat. Retraced path and found hat. Spent $4.34 on Ritz crackers, Chicken of the Sea tuna, and Sunkist Orange. . . . I try to write, but I am afraid I have nothing to say. Coover was right? No. I must face this now, this desolation of purpose. . . . I must fix a Dornstein-ness to the page for all time. I must make myself impossible to forget.*

David spent the next few days doing the same thing I had been doing all summer in my basement room: reading his old notebooks, coding for themes, hoping to find stretches of writing that could stand on their own, the seeds of something big. Predictably, given the high bar David had set for himself and the short amount of time, he came up short. In just a week or so, he had slipped back into a place he had not been for years.

> *January 9, 1985 230am*
> *It's still cold. I am under thick black bedding. I cannot get to that typing machine on the desk. . . . Am I afraid of dying? Maybe I will die right here in Rob's apartment. If this is all I am capable of in my life, I know it's not enough. . . . I'm no writer. I'm a thinker, a talker, on my best days, a teacher. I am energy, not articulation.*

David didn't get anything together for Hawkes that week; a month later, he dropped the class. He filled a lot of notebook pages with disappointment about this, and with the anxiety he felt about his future as a writer. But that night, when he cleared his notebooks, papers, and typewriter from Rob's apartment, then locked the door behind him, I can only imagine him feeling relief.

Graduation came down to this: David needed to write one paper for Dr. Neusner, and Neusner needed to give it a passing grade; without a credit for the course, David would have to come back to Brown for another semester. He tried to clear the decks of everything else. He turned down a role in a play. He wrote to his editor at the *Herald* and resigned. ("I regret that I shall not be writing a last column on 'How to Write a Herald Column' because I have concluded that I myself do not know how to write such a column. Once again, I have given myself an assignment which I am unable to complete.") He put away his old notebooks and returned any books to the library that didn't have to do with his assignment for Neusner.

Still, the deadline approached and David hadn't put any thoughts on paper. My father called to say that he had made plane reservations for the trip to Providence and he hoped David would take care of the dinner reservations. David panicked. He began one of his eleventh-hour notes to Neusner about how he couldn't write this paper, how his confrontation with the assigned authors, the Jewish messiah, maybe God himself, had been too profound to translate into mere words or arguments. But he abandoned the note, knowing Neusner would never buy it. David tried genuinely to pray for divine intervention, then dropped that as well.

He wandered the campus seeking out everyone he knew, for conversation. He made phone calls. In his notebook, he listed everyone he spoke with that day. I counted more than thirty people. I instinctively began to copy down the list of names—what did they remember of their conversations that day?—but then I noticed my own name in the middle. We had talked for three hours—David wrote a lengthy account of our call—but I didn't remember anything about it.

A few weeks later, my family came up to Brown for graduation weekend. David had written the paper for Neusner—ten pages of careful Old Testament exegesis, nothing terribly original, just good enough to show that he'd taken the assignment seriously—and Neusner passed him. My father and stepmother and sister stayed in rooms provided by the university, but I stayed with David in his dorm. I remember how dark his room was, and how cluttered, with every horizontal surface covered in something—books, papers, clothes, half-empty jars of peanut butter, containers of orange juice, trays and silverware pilfered from the dining hall.

I remember David and me walking around College Hill at night looking for graduation parties, circling around one house or another until David felt that things were in full swing enough for us to make an entrance. I remember sweaty rooms and loud music and David dancing with wild abandon while I nursed a beer wondering if people knew I was in tenth grade. I remember returning to David's room at 2 or 3 A.M. and trying to figure out how we'd sleep in such a wreck of a place. David's idea: Let's sleep outside. We took pillows and blankets outside and set up camp under an enormous elm tree. Drunken partygoers walked by and stared, and I was cold most of the night. David was cold, too, I think, but he liked the story of him and his little brother sleeping under the stars more than he wanted the warmth of the dorm.

My mother made the trip to Providence for graduation, and a group of us went out to dinner. I didn't recall anything particular about that night, but one of David's friends who was there still had a vivid sense of it when I contacted her for the oral history project: "You were fourteen or so, I'm guessing," the friend wrote to me. "You seemed very at ease for your age and David seemed proud of you." Then she told a story that she hoped I wouldn't find "too sad."

There was a large carafe of red wine at the table, and when that was quickly gone, another soon arrived. David made faces at me across the table, indicating his concern that your mother might be drinking too much of the wine herself. He objected openly when a third carafe arrived. Your mother left the table briefly, and he quickly turned to you and told you he was very upset. Then he picked up the third full carafe and

David and Ken (in background),
Brown University graduation (1985)

drank it entirely. You and I both tried to stop him, but he shrugged you off his arm, and just kept gulping the wine down until the bottle was empty.

David hated the idea of graduation and was critical of all of the university pomp. He lambasted the senior-class orators as suck-ups, uninspired and safe (he had encouraged people to nominate him for the job, but didn't get enough votes). This, anyway, is what he wrote in his notebook. But I remember him smiling wide the whole day at graduation, clapping people on the back and coming close to tears of joy a number of times. I remember him being handed his diploma by a distinguished-looking scholar in a robe. I sat in the audience next to my father and thought that for all of David's drama, for all of the pained phone calls home, the long, searching letters, the numberless hours of torment, David had emerged on the other end looking pretty good.

His picture appeared in that month's issue of the *Brown Alumni Monthly,* among a handful of profiles of prominent graduates. He looked fit and happy, and spoke to the interviewer with confidence and wit. He was really going places, it seemed to me from the mere fact of his being profiled, even if it wasn't entirely clear where that might be. It wasn't clear to David, either. He told the interviewer how Professor Neusner had advised him to focus on one thing and not be so scattered in his pursuits. "But I'm not sure what that one thing is going to be yet." The introduction to the magazine profile said it perfectly:

DAVID DORNSTEIN: Majored in creative writing, popular columnist for the *Brown Daily Herald,* acted in various theatrical productions. Future plans: After spending the summer in Israel studying Hebrew, no plans.

IX

David left for Israel in June, for several months of study at Hebrew University that Professor Neusner had helped to arrange for him. In an essay to get the grant, David had argued that years of reading, writing, and thinking had brought him to Judaic studies, and that he might become a rabbi. But on the eve of making the trip, he reversed his logic in order to persuade himself to go through with it: "I'm a writer, not a rabbi, and the Old Testament is the foundation of Western Literature. A writer must go first to the roots of his tradition. Yes, I will study every Western language and keep thinking and keep dreaming and keep scribbling and then I will be ready to make a proper feast of myself."

David was gone for months before he finally wrote home. The letter was short, considering how long he'd been gone, but he promised my father a "ream of tales to tell" once he returned. He mentioned "Bedouin friends"—he said he was teaching them English—and Holocaust survivors whose stories he said he had begun compiling for a book. "I even had coffee with Palestinian terrorists one lovely afternoon!" I remember my father asking me if I thought David would ever get mixed up in anything dangerous. "Do you think there's a chance he might not come home?"

David began a letter to me in Israel, but he sent it from Paris, the first stop on what he thought would be an extended trip abroad. "I hope to absorb a lot of Europe—for how long, I'm not sure. My money will eventually disappear and then either I will sell my body here or come home and sell my body in New York. I'll explain it all later. I'm rushed now. This morning on the Metro, I saw a woman hit another woman on the head with her handbag and call her a 'salope' (bitch)." David asked me to write him at an address in Paris, in care of a woman named Natalie—*a girlfriend?*—but he was back in the United States before I could reply.

I don't remember asking him much about his travels, or why he had come home sooner than planned, or what was next for him in New York, which, there was never a question, was where he'd soon be living. Maybe it had something to do with my being a younger brother, or being younger by six years, or something about these particular six years, where David was launching himself into the world, and I was still riding a yellow bus to school each morning—but our lives felt very separate. I imagined David would do whatever writers did to become Great Writers, and I didn't press for details. Where in the city would David live? How would he earn money? Did he have friends in New York? It was my father's job to worry about these things, not mine.

David found work as a proofreader for a big law firm. He went to work at an office on Wall Street, and then was transferred to a different office on the thirtieth floor of the Citicorp building in Midtown. He worked the graveyard shift, from eleven at night to seven in the morning. There seemed to be plenty of downtime for reading books and making entries in his notebook and writing letters.

November 19, 1985
Dear Ken,

If you can believe this, I'm getting nearly $300 a week to sit in an office and capitalize words, put in punctuation, and correct other minor grammatical mistakes. Nobody works here, everyone sits and waits for documents to come in. Strange hours. I read all night. More challenging work? Sure, but I'd rather stay here. . . . You must understand that Artists often work tedious, enervating jobs to support their Art.

David asked me to write back to him in care of our aunt Greta, who had moved back to New York from California after her marriage split. Greta would have let David stay forever, but he left after a few weeks. He slept on friends' couches and floors, "scribbling in his notebooks," one friend said, "and having visions."

He ultimately found a room of his own on the Upper West Side, in a building called the Bertha. He had two roommates, "Arthur the dancer" and "Darci the actress." Both were older, near thirty, and both worked restaurant jobs to pay the bills. They each had separate rooms off a common hallway and shared a kitchen. The Bertha was around the corner from the colossal, never-quite-finished Cathedral of Saint John the Divine. It was also near the Hungarian Pastry Shop, a place where David would often go to nurse a cup of coffee, to read, and to meet people. This was now home.

David seemed energized by New York. He grew a mustache. He read Frederick Exley's *A Fan's Notes* and resolved to become a drunk—a regular barfly at McSorley's and the Blarney Stone and Cannon's Pub, a few blocks away from the Bertha. He got himself cast in *Life Is a Dream,* an off-off-off-Broadway production put on mostly by people he'd known at Brown. He played bit parts in experimental films and performance pieces. He kept busy and tried not to let the proofreading work drain his energies. He penned a rhyme—"I am chronically late to the work I hate"—and found new ways to try to keep the job interesting. A favorite: He walked around the Citicorp building carrying his scarlet red *Marx-Engels Reader* out in front of him, hoping to provoke a reaction from someone in a suit and tie.

He still carried a notebook, and he wrote in it whenever and wherever he could—in coffee shops, in public parks, on the job, back in his room at the Bertha. One woman remembered seeing him writing in it on the pedestrian island at Ninety-fourth and

Broadway. "I thought he was a bum. It was cold and he wasn't dressed properly, but then he said my name and I saw the notebook and I realized it was Dornstein. I hadn't seen him since he went to Israel."

David's notebook entries were thin and more sporadic than they had been at Brown, more like notes for fuller accounts he intended to write at some later time but never did. David realized this. He wrote: "Now I stand, a candycane in the city, my notebook best for killing flies and for pretending to be an Artist. . . ."

He looked for ways to collaborate on creative projects with the creative people he knew. He sent out a wave of letters, looking to see who was interested in "frantic partnership" with him. To an actress friend, he wrote, "We could be the next Nichols and May. What do you say?" To the activist friend from Brown who actually had come up with the plan to stockpile suicide pills in case of nuclear attack, he wrote, "Maybe we could team up to save the world. Maybe you got plans I could fit into?" To a friend from the comedy magazine at Brown who had just gotten a job at Disney: "Maybe we could do some Marxist cartoons for Disney? 'Snow White and the Seven Proletarian Dwarves.' 'Grumpy' as a discontented wage laborer, etc. Let me know what you think. . . ." He wrote to my father to say that he'd like to retrieve some of his writings from the Dave Archives at home. "Editors have expressed interest in seeing them."

David talked himself into a buoyant mood in these letters. He proudly announced to my father that he was in a romance with the daughter of a billionaire businessman, and that he might be in love, but the relationship proved short-lived. And so was David's initial wave of enthusiasm for life in the Big City.

He quickly tired of his job as a proofreader. He was not quite ready to quit, but he experimented with behavior that might get him fired. He stopped shaving or showering and showed up to work in ripped clothes; he was insubordinate to his bosses; he rebelled against the WASP-iness of the firm, decorating the office Christmas tree with soy sauce packets and writing "Chappy Chanukah" with Snow Spray on a plate glass window. He photocopied his face and full body, part by part, on the office machine.

One night he wrote to my father from work: "It's now 345 A.M. and I just edited an Assumption Agreement between banks in Frankfurt and Santiago, Chile. A job well done, I'd say." The next day, he walked into his manager's office and quit. He had been imagining this for months and enjoyed the moment. But he needed money sooner than he figured and in short order found himself in an even less appealing job.

February 3, 1986

You are no longer David The Proofreader. Now you are David The Errand Boy, the messenger, the carrier of important documents from nine-to-five. "David is filling in for Marty while Marty's on vacation." My station in life? Marginal. I am falling out of the sky like the space shuttle Challenger, a puff of smoke and I'm gone. I am about to cry, really about to cry. . . .

I don't understand anything about the world. Now I'm an errand boy delivering agreements to the Joseph P. Day Realty Company. Who really is the joke on? Me. In two months, I'll be 23 years and I am inconsolable . . .

February 6, 1986

On the subway train to the US. District Court to deliver papers today I fell asleep and dreamt that Mary Tyler Moore was in the back seat of a carriage drawn by apes. In writing this paragraph about that dream, I've doubled my month's output of words. Why can't I just be a writer without all of this shuffling around? Why all this seeking after God? Why no need to make stories? . . . Goodnight David-Not-The-Actor. Goodnight David-Not-The-Writer. Goodnight David the Nonplanner of Finance, David the Spouter of Unsupported Opinions, the Grower of Beard, the Tugger of Penis. . . ."

I remember feeling ambivalent about visiting David in New York. My father had seen him when he was in the city for a Broadway show, and the report from the field didn't sound good. He said that David was in bad shape, physically wasted and dirty, mentally at loose ends, financially near broke. His room at the

Bertha was a fetid, bug-infested mess. The picture my father painted of David and his New York life scared me and made me not fight that hard to see him, even though David asked all the time when I was coming.

So I was nervous as I turned onto 111th Street that first time and started looking for David's building. But then I saw David. He started toward me, first at a fast walk and then a run. The weather was still bitter, winter cold, but he was wearing just a hooded blue sweatshirt that he had bought out of the back of a truck. He was unshaven, his hair was longer than I'd ever seen it, and his teeth were stained from smoking and not brushing much. He hugged me long and hard and took my bag and said it was truly great to see me.

His room seemed familiar to me. He had his clock radio on the floor where he slept, his typewriter on a table, along with the same chrome desk lamp he had had in his room growing up. There were books lying everywhere. He cleared a spot for me on the floor and found some crackers to offer as a snack. When he took off his sweatshirt, I immediately understood two things about his life: He probably did not shower regularly (he smelled horrible), and he did not eat very much (he was skinnier than I'd ever seen him).

He walked me around his neighborhood, showing me the important places of his new life. Then he walked me up Broadway past the Columbia campus to a strip of stores at 121st Street. There was a place that sold stationery, a bodega, and a photocopy center. This, it turned out, was where David was now working: the Broadway Copy Center. He spent four afternoons a week making photocopies, mostly course materials for classes being taught at Columbia or Barnard or the Jewish Theological Seminary, which was just down the street. He especially liked the seminary packets. He would read through them while he photocopied them and then have a number of points to argue with customers when they returned.

A lot of the visit was spent in the orbit of the Jewish Theological Seminary. I didn't know what to make of David's increasingly pronounced religiosity. I got the impression that if he had been cast in plays as regularly as he wanted, or if his writing had come

easier for him, or if he'd fallen in love, or if one of the many people he had appealed to in letters had written back to him with real
enthusiasm for the kind of headlong collaboration he prayed for,
then he would not have heard the call of the rabbinate so strongly.
But none of these things happened.

I visited David again that summer at his new apartment on Riverside Drive. He had cut down to part-time at the Broadway Copy
Center and was concentrating on writing fiction for the first time
since coming to New York. This may have had something to do
with larger forces at work in his soul, or in the universe—he was a
big fan of the "biorhythms" fortune-telling machines on the New
Jersey Turnpike—but there's also evidence in his notebooks that
this return to fiction may have had something to do with me.

At the suggestion of an English teacher, and with David's
encouragement, I had applied for a summer writing program run
by the state of Pennsylvania, submitting a story about a boy driven
mad by the insidious sniffling of one of his classmates. When
I got the acceptance letter, I called David right away. He was
pleased for me, but also for "us." Our letters had fallen off in the
previous months, but now he took up the pen with a new sense of
purpose.

May 15, 1986
Dear Ken,
    I write to congratulate you again on your Governor's
School scholarship. I write to send my love to you, my hopes
for you, my admonitions for you, my insides to you. I would
love little more than to blaze a liquid trail through the glorious trauma of life with you. You are my brother, my cohort,
my prodigy, and, now, my fellow writer. You and me, we are
scribes, chanters, describers, pleaders, paupers, poets. From
far off *Mannahatta,* I drum out hope for you. . . .

He'd stuffed into this letter a dozen passages he'd copied from different authors in his pantheon—Edna O'Brien, John Hawkes,

Doris Lessing, Melville, Faulkner. Into the mix, he'd also slipped in a bit of his own writing ("Some welsh rarebit from my own pad"). Along with these passages came a set of discussion questions that seemed lifted from a teacher's edition of a Norton anthology. "What does this selection tell you about the author's world? How does the author create a sense of place?" After the passage of his own writing, he wrote: "Do you see how vastly inferior it is to the first selections?"

David's next letter was addressed to "Ken, Reaper of Commendations," and it included "more samples of writing for your constructification." Then more letters came in steady succession. My program began in two months, and David was now intent on speeding along my maturity as a writer. He copied out more passages from Great Writers. He also continued to mix in paragraphs of his own under the heading "From the Collected Beginnings of Stories Never Finished by Somebody's Brother." He wrote, "I'm readying some of my manuscripts for publication." I didn't know what manuscripts or what kind of publication—and what he had shown me I had had trouble understanding—but I imagined a world of publishing that was filled with people who spoke the same rarefied language as David, and in that world I was still convinced that David was very soon to be very, very big.

X

DAVID'S TWO CLOSEST FRIENDS in New York were Lawrence and Billy. I met them that first time at a coffee shop near Columbia. David introduced Lawrence as a writer. Billy, he said, was going to be a rock star, but for now he was driving a taxi and working his way through a Ph.D. in European History at Columbia. "Be forewarned," David told me before we left his apartment, "Billy's an anarchist." I didn't know what this meant in practical terms. *Were there things I should not say?*

Billy and Lawrence were both whip smart. The conversation flew by fast, with all sorts of shorthand and intellectual pyrotechnics and references to people and books and ideas that I couldn't follow. Billy and Lawrence each tried to draw me into the conversation, but I had little to offer. Lawrence seemed easygoing and liked to joke. Billy's way of engaging was to play the prosecutor, wrestling my occasional comments down to the ground with a withering assault of questions.

BILLY: Do you really believe that?
ME: What?
BILLY: What you just said. Do you really believe what you

> just said? I think it's preposterous, but you seem to
> believe it. Explain yourself. . . .
>
> ME: Huh? [silence]

David watched me scramble, but didn't come to my aid. This was the major work of his life now, sitting in coffee shops and talking ideas with people, and I think he wanted me to appreciate how hard it was. It was part of my apprenticeship.

So was coming to Poets Corner, which, so far as I could tell, was a kind of salon for would-be writers, a place to read and critique new writing. David, Lawrence, and Billy seemed to be charter members. I remember being put on the spot about Poets Corner, the next session of which was just a few days off. David told Lawrence and Billy that I was headed off to the Governor's School for a writing program, and he built me up as a real talent. There was an expectation that I would come to Poets Corner. "And if you come, you've got to read," Billy made clear. "Everyone reads." All I had was a story about Sammy the Sniffler, and I didn't want to read it. I'm not sure if I was afraid of deflating my own view of myself as a writer, or David's. No matter. My father vetoed an extension of my visit to stay for Poets Corner. For David, this came as another in a long line of infuriating decisions by my father to limit his boys' time together. For me it was a burden lifted.

During the rest of my visit, David took me with him on his rounds through the city. To the Hungarian Pastry Shop ("the Hung") for coffee, to Columbia Hot Bagels, where David said it was one of his rituals with Billy to ask the guy behind the counter, "What's hot today?" (The guy would usually say, "Everything," and the joke was to press him on what was really hot, right now, right this minute. *Can we touch it?*) David urged me to take Billy's place, but I didn't want to pester the guy at Columbia Hot Bagels. This irritated David. By the time I asked, "So what's hot?" none of the fun of the original joke was left; it had become pure compulsion.

We took our bagels to Riverside Park. David selected a book

for himself—Cynthia Ozick's *The Cannibal Galaxy,* about a guy who thinks he is extraordinary but who comes to realize, by blows, that he is ordinary. For me, David reached into his blue knapsack and pulled out Donald Barthelme's *Sixty Stories.* He said, "Read for an hour and then let's discuss it." I remember being glad that Barthelme's stories were short, and not as hard to understand as I imagined they might be. I enjoyed a lot of what I read. I worked up some comments, ready for David's quizzing, but we never discussed it. Whenever I looked over at David, he seemed to be sunning himself, or asleep, or talking to someone. *Did they know each other?*

One day, David left me on my own while he put in a shift at the Broadway Copy Center. Another day, he and I walked fifty or sixty blocks south through Central Park to the Ritz-Carlton hotel, where he had taken a second job as the "night butler," handling room-service calls. It always struck me as something of a surprise when work intruded on our time together, or that David had any work responsibilities at all: His time was otherwise so thoroughly his own.

These would be the New York chapters in the Book of David: David the Room Service Guy Bringing Eggs and Vodka to Celebrities at 3 A.M. David the Subletter of Friends' Apartments. David the Lapsed Writer of Fiction. David the Occasional Actor and Student of Jewish Things. David the Avid Supporter of the Arts Who Went to All Manner of Performance, Exhibition, Reading, Happening, Concert, Retrospective, Colloquia. David the Eater of Sugar Packets in Place of Meals. David the Tugger of Penis. David the Non-Brusher of Teeth, the Non-Cutter of Hair, the Non-Changer of Clothes. David Who Pretended He Was an Israeli Who Had Fought in Lebanon and Was Writing a Book About It To Get a Woman to Buy Him a Meal. David Who Pretended He Was an Assistant Professor of Russian Literature (also for a woman). David Who Pretended He Was Playing Lucky in an Off-Broadway Production of *Waiting for Godot.*

One more important chapter that at least needs to be sketched here: David the Ardent Pursuer of Romance and Sex on the Streets of the City. I cannot properly tally the number of women he tried to make eyes at, make laugh, start conversations with, impress, wordlessly seduce, follow, fantasize about, sleep with, or otherwise pursue. I don't know how many hours of how many days he filled with these activities or how often he succeeded, but hardly a page of his notebooks goes by without mention of one woman or another. If I cut the list down to just those women who said to me at some point during our oral history interview, "You know David and I slept together one time, don't you?" or "You know I had a crush on your brother?" the list would still be unmanageable.

Was David a cad? A Women's Studies nightmare objectifier and brute? He often made this case against himself and tried to expunge all that he thought wrong in his relations with women. He spent equal time puzzling over his secret pride at being stared at and desired by gay men, with notes always to mine the story of Bill Donoghue for answers. What's inescapable here is the obvious fact of David's good looks, even when he dressed those looks down in old ripped clothes and complicated them with bad hygiene. To have been that good-looking was to have had many opportunities for sexual adventure; and yet, the more one reads the notebooks, the more beside the point sex seems to be.

When I picture David pining over a woman, prowling around her, preening for her, I don't think first of a horny guy trying to get laid. I think of the person who said that he never walked down a street or boarded a train "without hoping that I would fall in love with someone or something." David clearly thought a lot about sex—sticky intimacies with strangers—but mostly he seemed interested in love. Not conjugal love that ended in marriage and kids, and not the love of religious faith in God—though he spent a lot of time on this—but burning love that consumes. Lifeboat love in which to sail away from a capsizing ship. Love as the basic ordering principle of a new life, something to devote himself to utterly. A calling. David would write of himself in his notebook, "He was called to love," and he felt he would be able to spot in crowds others who were similarly called. He often waited for hours for the wink or the nod that would tell him he was right.

One afternoon at the Hung, David thought he found one of these women called to love. Her unusual first name ("Docious," taken from Mary Poppins's supercalifragilistic-expiali*docious*) was the only thing that made it possible for me to track her down so many years later. Docious told me about meeting David:

> I had just dropped out of college and came to New York to live with my sister. She told me the Hungarian Pastry Shop was a good place to hang out and meet people, so I went. I bought a coffee and sat at a table reading and writing in a diary. A sloppy-looking fat guy was making eyes at me and I remember writing, "Here I sit being watched by one man while another doesn't see me at all. . . ." That other man was your brother. He was reading Paul Bowles' *Sheltering Sky,* drinking coffee, and writing in a notebook. I didn't think he saw me. At one point, he got up to use the bathroom. He walked by and dropped a sheet of paper on my table, then kept on walking. He didn't stop or explain anything. I was curious what he'd written. It was the start of a story of some kind and it was clear from the way he had left it that I was supposed to continue it. I decided to play along. . . . We sat together and finished the story. It was called "How to Tell True Love from a Refrigerator." We exchanged numbers. . . .

After that first meeting, David and Docious spent a lot of time together at the Hung, talking and writing and smoking Camels. Docious still cared about David when I phoned her seventeen years later—she said she still kept at her desk a copy of a story she'd written with him. And for all I know, she may have still mattered to David. But in David's notebook, she came and went in just four brief entries:

1. August 1, 1986—Morning is sweet with Docious. . . .
2. August 10, 1986—Days spent on coffee and collaboration on stories with Docious (four to date, getting more honest). . . .
3. August 14, 1986—Emotionally suicidal terrible arguments with Docious. . . .

4. August 24, 1986—Goodbye Docious. Our disputes were becoming predictable after a month.

David met "Annette" the day after his last "emotionally suicidal" argument with Docious. The two relationships seemed similar. Annette had just quit law school in Amsterdam and had come to New York to figure out if she wanted to try to make it as a dancer. She met David in the lobby of the Jewish Museum. He was reading from *A Treasury of Yiddish Folk Sayings* and laughing in a conspicuous way to get her attention. "He introduced himself and said maybe we should have coffee sometime. He told me he had to go to work at a hotel, but he would call. That night I got a call from a manager at the hotel saying David was too nervous to make the call himself. And then David got on and we made a plan to meet. . . . I knew David basically for ten days. We had a tremendous time."

This is how I found Annette: After years of using the Lexis-Nexis newspaper and magazine database for my Harvard research job, it occurred to me to type in "David Dornstein." I found articles about the Lockerbie bombing, all of them with that same one-line obituary: "David Dornstein, 25, Melrose Park, Pennsylvania." But I also found an article in *The New York Times* from a few years earlier; it was headlined "A 'Once in a Lifetime' Stroll in the Lincoln Tunnel." A group called Friends of the Parks had organized an "insomniac's tour" of the tunnel, and to their surprise, 250 or so people showed up. The tour began at the Port Authority Bus Terminal at around 2:30 A.M. By 4:30 A.M. the crowd had reached the New York–New Jersey border in the tunnel. The Uncommon Jazz Ensemble began to play a tune. When they stopped, David apparently continued the entertainment. According to the article:

Dave Dornstein, a room service worker at the Ritz Carlton Hotel, and Annette Cocheret de la Moriniere, a visitor from Amsterdam, tested the tunnel's acoustics themselves by singing "God Bless America" and "Wilhelmus van Nassouwe," the Dutch national anthem.

In his notebook that night, David wrote only "Lincoln Tunnel. 'Cocher' (Kosher) breakfast. Goosebumps. More later. . . ." This was his only reference to Annette, a curious thing considering how serious she believed the relationship had quickly become. "I was due to leave the country not long after I met David. He seemed upset by this, really disappointed. He tried to get me to stay, and then he said to me, 'Why don't I go with you back to Holland?' He was serious. He said the change would do him good. I had known him for a week at the time. The timing just wasn't right for me, so I put him off. I moved back to Holland. I came back to New York the next year and tried to reconnect with him, but it didn't happen."

Annette didn't know that David was dead until I reached her by phone so many years later, but she wasn't that surprised. She said that she had tried to find him when she came back through New York at different times in the 1990s, but had never succeeded. This left her with a sinking feeling. "David was going to be a famous writer. If he was alive I was sure I would have heard about it. He told me that his mother was crazy, so I thought maybe he went crazy, too. I last saw him in 1987. I figured it must not have gone well for him after that."

XI

IN THE FALL OF 1986, a friend of David's named Norm wrote a cover story for *The Village Voice* called "Doomed to Succeed." It was Norm's attempt to figure out why some of the smartest people he knew had signed up with big Wall Street firms to become investment bankers. Near the end of the article, he went uptown to visit David.

> I was sitting in Cannon's on 108th and Broadway recently, trying to explain my sympathy for investment bankers to a couple of pals. One of them works as a busboy at the Ritz, writes short stories, and argues in coffee shops everywhere, and the other's been driving a cab, playing in a rock band and trying to study some European history.
>
> I was saying that some of these bankers have good hearts and lots of potential to change, but they're weak. Not only that, many are the victims of seduction, not greedy slimes by nature.
>
> The Ritz busboy was in coffee shop argument mode and told me I was wacked. "They're old enough to know what they're doing," he said. "Why do you want to make excuses for them?"

"You know what it is?" I finally said. "They're scared that if they don't work for an investment bank, they'll set a rotten pattern of life for themselves. They're scared they'll be wasting away these valuable years drinking pitchers with guys like you. Hell, you know what it is? *They're scared shitless they'll end up like you,* the Dharma Bums of the Upper West Side." My pals laughed and nodded as if I'd complimented them.

The Ritz busboy, of course, was David, and Billy was the one driving the cab, although by the time the article appeared he was no longer driving a cab and David was no longer a busboy at the Ritz. He'd quit after just a few months, citing "despair over the idiocy of my labors" on the inside flap of a book of poems he was reading on the job at the time. David had left the Upper West Side as well. Now he was living in a nice building near Gramercy Park that even Norm's young investment bankers may not have been able to afford. David couldn't afford it, either. It was the apartment of our uncle Harvey—our mother's brother—who let David live there for whatever he could pay in rent.

These big changes came at the end of a tough summer for David. A number of his closest friends had made big career moves—graduate school, law school, work overseas—and come September, when each went his own way, David was left at a loss. Even a few members of his core group were moving on. His good friend Tim, the sidekick on the Sunday Brunch tape and a close companion in New York, was starting the acting program at Juilliard, and Lawrence was leaving the city altogether—leaving Poets Corner!—for New Haven and Yale Law School. David didn't hide his displeasure at this. Lawrence remembered David "helping" him move out of his apartment: "I looked over and he was throwing my things out the window onto the sidewalk. Nothing breakable, mostly clothes and blankets and pillows. He felt deeply betrayed." David wrote in his notebook: "I said to Lawrence, 'Good luck!' but I meant 'Come upon ruin and hard times.' Law school will be disastrous for Lawrence's language, just terrible. And me? I stay here and do my frightened best. My friends a-rising, me a-falling. I tremble to see everyone off to grad school while I continue on in the fabrication trade, or pretend to. Such is my life in literature."

David's new apartment was in a building off Twenty-third Street called the Penny Lane. The first floor had an arcade of shops done up in an ersatz "olde" style, with fire-red brick facing, awnings over store windows, and a barbershop just like in the Beatles song that I presume inspired the building's name. The apartment was on the top floor, a spacious one-bedroom with a balcony as big as the apartment itself, where fake fruit trees in plastic pots were arranged around a table with an umbrella.

I know there was a bedroom in the back of the apartment, but David lived, ate, and slept mostly on the floor in the living room. This was the first thing you saw when you opened the front door: a sheet laid out on the parquet floor with some couch cushions piled up on one side (later some carpet samples on top of the sheet). Arranged around the perimeter were dozens of books in various stages of being read and not being read, a fortress of books with David walled off inside.

He borrowed my aunt Greta's typewriter (his Smith Corona with the busted *a* had finally broken for good), and he tried once more to get to work. His longest effort was a story about a man named Lake who worked a variety of odd jobs around New York. Lake spends a lot of time thinking about his mother, Yehudit, who works for a temp agency. He pictures her selling temporary workers to corporations all day, cold-calling, and it saddens him. He pictures her bicycling through the streets of the city. "Other bicyclists, mostly black kids, or longhaired white messengers risking their lives in frequently lethal traffic and noxiousness looked upon the aging woman on the rickety bicycle with ridicule, astonishment, finally admiration for her pluck. Yehudit noticed them and tried to look pretty for them, and for the male drivers, and the male pedestrians. She was still hoping to attract a man who would take her away from the city and the selling."

After a few days' work, David drew big slashes across the story of Lake and Yehudit and put it in a box. "This is terrible." It

occurs to me now that my mother lived around the corner from
the Penny Lane. David may even have been able to make out the
top of her building from the balcony of his new apartment, but
he rarely saw her.

David surprised us by not coming home to Philadelphia for turkey
dinner that Thanksgiving. He cloistered himself in his room at the
Penny Lane and wrote: "I try to re-accustom myself to the non-
work world, to solitude, to all day alone in the apartment. The
voice: Fame! Get an agent. . . . Get published. . . . The other voice:
Spy on naked women with Harvey's binoculars."

After this entry, a gap opened up in the record: no letters, no
stories, no nothing. Two months passed, and then the entries
began again.

> *January 5, 1987*
>
>   *I do not go out much, and when I do my eye is drawn to*
> *sadness and calamity. Saw a fire on 21st Street. Watched the*
> *flames destroy. A firefighter in a cherrypicker with a Durer face.*
> *Rough good men. I nearly cried. I did cry.*

> *January 6, 1987*
>
>   *A story on the radio: an Amtrak train crashed last night over*
> *the Gunpowder River in Maryland. I imagined I was on it. At*
> *least then my ruin would be dramatic. I'm bankrupt, spiritually,*
> *creatively, and money-wise. Billy is dissolving away from me.*
> *There are limits, it seems. The spell is breaking. He savages me*
> *for the way I live, accuses me of self-pitiful crumbling.*

David copied out a line from Stefan Zweig's novella *The Burning
Secret:* "He knew he needed people to act as a tinderbox of all his
talents, if the warmth and high spirits of his heart were to blaze
up. On his own, he was as cold as a match inside a matchbox."

When he ventured outside, it was often at night and mainly to
bars, although never ones where he suspected my mother might
show. He continued a course of sexual adventurism: Three differ-

David in a Times Square photo booth (fall 1986)

ent people said that David told them he had had an affair with a
rabbi's wife that involved holing up in her apartment for days
while the rabbi was out of town. Two different people told me a
story about his going to a bar to pick up the fattest woman he
could find to sleep with him. This seemed like the premise of one
of his fictions, but when I mentioned it to Lawrence his face lit up
with recognition: "David and I were once in a drugstore and he
called me to his side. 'Look! There she is. That's her. That's the fat
lady I told you about.' The woman was truly obese and a little
disheveled, like a street person. David hid behind an aisle until she
left."

David was almost out of money. He needed work. He got a
part-time job waiting tables at a restaurant across from the Port
Authority Bus Terminal. He worked random shifts, and seemed to
have been fired for some combination of antics with customers
and wanton slovenliness. Total wages earned over some two
months: $724.87, according to a W-2 form I found stuffed into his
copy of *Major Trends in Jewish Mysticism*. Even with undeclared tips,
even with my uncle as his landlord charging a token three hundred
dollars a month, David was scraping by.

Where to turn? My mother really did work at a temp agency—
several different temp agencies over the years—but David never
asked her for help. He flipped through *The Brothers Karamazov* and
copied out this sentence: "Where, then, was he to get the means?
Where was he to get the fateful money?"

David tried to write himself out of his situation, but the words
didn't come. He reread the notebooks he had kept at Brown, and
the stories, poring over the old fragments in search of some larger
order, but his thinking became only more disorganized in the
process. He slept a lot. He had frequent dreams that writers he
knew at Brown had already published novels to great acclaim. He
had one dream often enough to shorthand it: "Rick Moody Book
Dream Again." (For the record: If Rick Moody was the measuring
stick, then it's probably important to note that he was doing
arguably worse than David during the winter of 1986. A memoir
Moody later published referred to an "Unexplained Panic Event
of Christmas Day in 1986"; this was followed by bouts of crying

at work, heavy drinking, suicidal thoughts, hallucinations, and, ultimately, a stint in rehab. Somewhere in all of this, Moody did write a few chapters of a novel, but it wouldn't be published for another five or six years.)

Reading his old notebook pages made David think about Kathryn. *Where was she?* He called her parents' apartment in New York, and her mother told him that Kathryn had been living in England, trying to paint, but she would be home for the holidays in a few days. The next week, she met David for coffee.

Kathryn thought David didn't seem entirely well, but he was compelling as always when he got around to arguing for why they might give it another try as a couple. They walked back to Dave's place at the Penny Lane. Kathryn was unprepared for what she saw there. The smell, the mess—David told her that he often opened his balcony to the homeless, and it seemed to her that they'd left some of their stuff behind. In the clutter, Kathryn noticed her sleeping bag from college, and this cemented a feeling in her: The past with David had been intense and physical and sometimes sweet, but there was no going back.

David often reached out to my father in a crisis, but not this time. He didn't call or write for more than a month, and he didn't visit over New Year's. He wrote in his notebook: "I should, for certain, not run home. Nothing worse than to be lost and miserable in Father's quiet castle. When one is lost, one must be among the lost."

XII

M Y FIRST TRIP to the Penny Lane was during this time, in early 1987. I don't remember why my father allowed me to make the trip: maybe because my birthday was coming up (eighteen!), maybe because he wanted a report on how David was really doing. I remember being impressed by the Penny Lane. David knew the doorman, and the doorman knew him, and here was a lobby with shops like at a nice hotel. David's apartment had a musty odor and a dirty feel, but it was clearly a nice apartment, with a big wall of glass looking out at the lights of the city. David had tried to clean and straighten for my arrival, and I knew enough, even at the time, to find this touching.

I remember David smoking on his balcony while pointing out to me who was who in the different windows around his building (this lady likes to eat dinner with her cat sitting next to her at the table; this guy likes to masturbate at such and such a time). Sleet began to fall. I ducked inside, but David stayed out on the balcony smoking. He came inside a half hour later, his hair and woolen sweater iced over and matted. He told me to look at him, "wet and defeated," and not to forget the sight. He handed me a letter that my father had written to him a few weeks earlier. It began:

It is time to start clarifying your life, David. It's time to answer to yourself and do something with your life. It's time to stop deceiving yourself and to do a square accounting of who you really are. It's time to leave behind fantasy and to deal with the real world. Growth means to change and you are in dire need of change. Your old formula is not working. You need a new one.

He went on to tell the story of Icarus and his fall, from the father's point of view:

Remember Daedalus. He was an inventor, artist, architect who was captivated by hard problems and was driven to find solutions, but he was also realistic and prudent and he recognized limits beyond which even he dared not to venture. Daedalus tried to convey a sense of these limitations to his son Icarus, but Icarus flew too high, the wax on his wings melted, and he was lost forever in the depths of the sea. Maybe with Daedalus in mind, you might alter the scope of your writing, David. Finish one story before starting another. Or put the writing aside for now. Ease your burden. Find other work. Don't fight everyone and everything. Don't make it so difficult for people to love you. It's a self-imposed exile and it need not be.

Back at home, I reported on the visit to my father. He seemed surprised and a little dumbfounded about all David and I had done in the city—restaurants, museums, two tickets to Jackie Mason's popular one-man show on Broadway. He asked: "Did David say anything to you about work?" I said that I thought David worked occasionally at a restaurant, or at least that he used to work at a restaurant. In any event he seemed to have plenty of money. The next week, David offered up his own account to my father.

Dear Dad,
I write you because it's been too long and I miss you. No doubt you've surmised the reason for my lack of contact

with you: no job, the shame that accompanies the shameful behavior, the fear of sharing my fear with you, and all the attendant foolishness that is your son.

By the time he sent this letter, David had already begun to rally—maybe this is what had made it possible for him finally to write home. He started going out again with friends, and he had a lead on a job. His friend Billy worked at a nonprofit called the Interfaith Hunger Appeal. Down the hall was another nonprofit called the Coalition for the Advancement of Jewish Education, and CAJE (this is what everyone called it) was looking for help. Billy suggested that David check into it. A job in Judaism just down the hall from Billy? This sounded good to David, and any suggestion from Billy counted double or triple suggestions from others. My father's voice was always in David's head—Find satisfying work! Clarify your life!—but it was the way that Billy echoed this that I think ultimately made the difference. David bought a new notebook and wrote: "My friend Bill advises me to get a job. Bill finds my bellyaching about work tiresome. I HAVE TO GET A JOB, BILL SAYS. I HAVE TO KEEP A JOB."

Billy walked the walk. He was a model of industry, running the office of the Interfaith Hunger Appeal, finishing his master's at Columbia and then going for the Ph.D. He also wrote songs and played regular gigs with his band. Billy's apartment on the Upper West Side felt much more like a home than Dave's place. His sleeping area, living room, study, and kitchen were distinct from one another; he had a coffee table and cable TV. He also had a live-in girlfriend named Sarah. When David slept over, Billy and Sarah would play at being the parents, tucking David into his spot on the couch come bedtime.

Billy defies easy summary. For my purposes here, it's only important to say that David loved him, and respected him, and wanted nothing more than to spend time with him, talk with him, write stories with him. (They began one called "Reiss Ranter: Investigative Polemicist," which they actually finished, thanks to Billy's insistence that it be finished, I imagine.) David liked to play at being Billy's band manager, helping him plot out a career as a rock star, scouting other bands at Maxwell's in Hoboken and other clubs. He liked to talk ideas with Billy, joke with Billy, sit quietly in a room with Billy. Even at David's lowest point over the winter, he bought books on subjects relevant to Billy's Ph.D. program and he read them, on the chance that he could help Billy with his studies. David often wasn't sure what he was doing in New York, and sometimes this terrified him. But if he could do it with Billy, it seemed, then everything would be all right.

What became of Billy? Deep into the summer of the Dave Oral History Project, I decided it was time to find out. I found a phone number for him and left a message saying that I was coming to New York and I wondered if he had any time to meet. Billy called back that night. He seemed glad to hear from me. He wanted to meet but wasn't sure how much time he'd have. "I'm studying for the bar exam this summer. . . . You know I went to law school, don't you?"

I didn't. I still thought of Billy playing gigs and driving a cab and studying at Columbia, maybe teaching now. I still pictured him in his white T-shirt and dark jeans, with the slightly dangerous look of the young, trim Springsteen from *Darkness on the Edge of Town*. As Billy talked, I took in the full extent to which he had moved on. "I'm married, you know. Did you know that?" I didn't. There'd been a woman's voice on his answering machine message, but I'd assumed she was a girlfriend. Billy always had a girlfriend. "My wife's Iranian," Billy continued. "She's in Tehran, spending time with her family. I needed the time to prepare for the bar. She left a few weeks ago." Billy paused. "Do you need a place to stay when you're in the city? You can stay in Jacob's room. The boys are in Tehran, too." *The boys?* Note: Billy's a father.

I congratulated Billy about the wife and the kids, but I meant something more, like *How could you do this?* I felt betrayed, like David watching Lawrence and Tim and everyone else going off to graduate school. *My friends a-rising, me a-falling.*

The next week, I met Billy at his apartment. He opened the door and I walked in—no big ceremony, just a sort of stunned look initially, as if I'd shown up by surprise, and then a smile of recognition. He outstretched an arm, showing the way inside, and offered a comically formal greeting like "Welcome to my humble home" or "Enter."

Billy gave me the quick tour: The living room doubled as an office, with a desk off to one side that served as the headquarters of his wife's design business. He showed me to a bedroom in the back, where his boys slept. Sam and Jacob were two and four, respectively. Their toys were neatly arranged around their beds. Billy pointed out his favorites. "This is Banana Man," he said. "And this is Tommy the Torah." This would be my room for the weekend.

We walked into the living room. I looked at the stereo and asked Billy about one of his CDs, but he said he didn't listen to music much anymore. I asked him where he kept his guitar, but he said he hadn't played it in years. On a shelf in the front hallway I noticed a framed picture of Billy and David. It was the only photograph displayed anywhere in the apartment. *Had he put it out for my visit?* I didn't think so. Neither of us mentioned it.

Most of my oral history sessions had been entirely about David, but this one was different. This was Billy. For me, the subject was him: How had his life evolved in the years since David died? What kind of sense had he made of David's life? For Billy, it seemed, the subject was me. The tour of the apartment took about ten minutes. Once we were on the couch, Billy launched a thoroughgoing inquiry into my life. Where was I living? Did I own or rent? Did I keep in contact with any of David's friends? What about Rina, in Israel? Had I spoken with her? Billy said that he and Lawrence had had some kind of falling-out over David's death, but he didn't spell it out. "Lawrence is fiercely intelligent. He's a professor now, did you know that? Amherst." Billy stopped there. "Do you have friends? Do you have people in your life you can talk to? It's not essential, but there are dangers in isolation. Are you isolated?"

I answered Billy's questions as fully and as thoughtfully as I could. It seemed important to me to tell the story of my life and have Billy think it made sense. We talked a lot about K. I was surprised that Billy didn't know anything about our relationship. Few of the people I had contacted for the Dave Oral History Project knew about it. For years I'd been convinced that she and I were the subject of gossip and cruel judgment, and I was ready for the toughest examination on this from Billy, but he only listened and asked respectful questions and said he could see how complex it might be for us. Later he talked about his own married life; he even let me in on some tension between him and his wife over whether he should work at a law firm or teach. I felt privileged that he would talk so honestly with me. For a few moments, I felt almost like a peer, and there was no higher status. I wondered if this was the kind of talk I would have had with David.

The next day, Billy and I fell into some Dave oral history of our own. He walked me around his neighborhood and showed me David's old haunts as I took notes and photos. We wandered into Cannon's Pub on Broadway and saw some barflies drinking before noon. We walked to Columbia Hot Bagels and asked the guy behind the counter, "What's hot?" (What would David have made of the fact that the words came out of my mouth so easily with Billy?) We stopped into the Broadway Copy Center, but "Eva," the owner, wasn't around on the weekends and no one else had been there long enough to remember David. At the Bertha, I left Billy outside while I snuck my way through the front door. I knocked on apartment 4E and got the tour of the place from the current resident, a playwright roughly the same age as David when he'd lived there.

Billy and I walked the entire afternoon. We strolled in and out of stores and wisecracked; we developed running jokes just like I remembered him and David doing—a recurring line about his dentist, something about a "recession special" at a hot dog stand (we wondered if there was a council of economic advisors somewhere certifying that the recession was still on to continue the special).

Back at the apartment, Billy returned to the matter of my "career." I told him I had published a book, but he knew that a book was not a career, especially when I made no real money from it. I told him I sometimes did television documentary work, and he shot back: "But that's not a job. That's freelance. What's your job? *What are you going to do for a job?*" His questioning grew more pointed. I tried to explain the life of the "independent contractor," hoping to slow his attack, but he exploited cracks in my logic to reveal fundamental flaws. "Do you have health insurance? Have you started a retirement plan? Do you have any idea of the benefits of tax-free compounded interest over a thirty- or forty-year time horizon?"

I had never had this kind of conversation with anyone. Was this Billy's way of looking out for his dead friend's little brother? Was this why I had come: to get a dose of the same medicine he had given David once upon a time, when David was in a plummet?

The more we talked, the more irritated Billy grew. Once, when I was in the city with David, I had seen Billy throw down his guitar in the middle of a gig, and then practically assault his drummer for screwing up one of the songs; another time, I had watched as he almost got into a fistfight on the street. I found these episodes funny and surprising, but now his anger was directed at me, and I didn't know what to do about it. He fumed, "Why the fuck don't you think you need to get a job? Are you better than other people? Do you operate according to a different set of rules?" Billy's tirades sometimes had a mock quality to them, like he was channeling the words that, in this case, a really strict parent might say to a really wayward teen. But this particular rant seemed to be coming from someplace real in him. "You don't need a job? You must have gotten this from your brother. He never thought he needed to get a fucking job. It was preposterous when he said it, and it's still preposterous. Do you know that?"

He grew quiet for a moment, and then he reversed course completely. A smile came over his face. The anger seemed to have blown through, and he seemed almost apologetic for having come down so hard. I told him I appreciated his taking such an interest in my life and challenging me to explain myself. It's what David might have done, I thought, and I'd take big brothering in whatever form I could get it.

Billy began talking about himself. He said that he was about my age when he'd made the decision to drop his Ph.D. and his music and go to law school. "It seemed the right course, a solid choice. But the case could also be made that I'm just a coward." David's friend Tim later said to me: "It's hard to understand the depth of Billy's loss over David. All of the wind went out of Billy's sails on being a rock star after David died. Ask him why he gave up music. Maybe he'll tell you the story, but I doubt it. It's still too raw." I thought about Norman's *Village Voice* article, Billy as a cabdriver, Dharma Bum of the Upper West Side—it wasn't a very good depiction of Billy at the time, but who could have imagined how completely off it would prove to be ten years later? Could David's life have gone in this radically different a direction?

I told Billy that I'd thought about law school myself, but he jumped on this, too. "Do what you want about a career, Kenny. All I'm saying is that the problem of work never goes away. You need to figure out how to get paid a salary at a job you can make peace with." It seemed to physically pain him to have to lay out these hard truths for me. I felt that everything he said to me that night he might equally have said to David, and I wanted to absorb it all for both of us.

Billy left for work first thing in the morning. He was a summer associate at a big law firm. He kept a closet full of nicely tailored suits in the room where I was staying, and he came in the night before to pick out what he'd wear the next day. I was lying there in his four-year-old son's bed, using Tommy the Torah as a pillow. I felt an unmistakable sense that Billy was the adult and I was the child, and I wondered if maybe this was how David sometimes felt around him: shamed by a comparative lack of drive and direction, ultimately embarrassed into making some kind of change. In David's case, he had taken the job with CAJE. What was I prepared to do?

I went to the Hungarian Pastry Shop for breakfast. I don't drink coffee, really, but I bought a cup and sat down at a table near the back. I wanted to imagine what David had felt here, sipping coffee and writing clever things in his notebook, so I did the same. I felt that what I wrote at the Hung was more important than what

I might have written elsewhere for the knowledge that David might have sat in this very spot doing this very thing. But the feeling didn't last. I finished my coffee and read a section of a newspaper, and then I didn't know what else to do. It was 11:35 A.M. *How did David spend whole days here?* I looked around and concluded that this was a roomful of people without real jobs. *Like David,* I thought, feeling a little superior. *But I guess like me, too.*

I thought about my desk in my rented basement room in Cambridge, covered with the notebooks that David had written in at places like this, and I wondered how long I would dedicate my life to retracing his steps. I thought about K back in our old apartment in Cambridge. With Billy, I had rehearsed every one of my arguments against continuing as a couple with K, inviting him to confirm my darkest fears that me and K were a bad idea. But when the dust settled and the hours of talk with Billy were through, K and I were still standing.

Back in Cambridge, I reread the letters K'd sent me from Los Angeles, the e-mails she'd sent to me on the job at Harvard, the faxes when I was in Lockerbie. It was unmistakable: They had all been written to me, not to David's little brother. I'm not sure how I had come to see us so thoroughly in terms of David over the years, but now I was seeing us more clearly. I thought: This is how the story of me and K ends, with a bold, life-affirming act, a great leap forward and no more looks back. I would call K the next morning and propose marriage.

FICTIONS

Two books are being writ, of which the
world shall only see one, and that the
bungled one. The larger book, and
the infinitely better, is for Pierre's own
private shelf.

Herman Melville, *Pierre, or, The Ambiguities*

I

I KNEW THAT K wouldn't go in for the bended-knee routine, the engagement ring hidden in the box of Cracker Jack, the singing telegram. She didn't want this brand of romance; we'd talked about it enough for me to know this. But I'm not sure that she wanted what I had to give, either.

K and I went for a walk through the streets of Cambridge, past all of the great old houses we'd fantasized about living in for years. K told me she'd finally made a bold real estate move, putting a bid down on an apartment, and the seller had just accepted it. The place was in great shape, on a top floor, and full of light. She said it made her feel hopeful about the future again to be there. I told her that I was trying to be hopeful about the future as well. I brought her up-to-date on the Dave Oral History Project. I'd dropped the investigation into David's old neighbor Bill Donoghue, I said. I was struck now by the ways that David's closest friends had moved on with their lives. "Billy is married, you know. And he's got two kids. Tim's married, too, with a son. Norm's got two boys. So does Lawrence. Did you know Lawrence?"

The walking and talking went on for hours, and then it felt like time for the big reveal. *I guess you're wondering why I've called you here today.* . . . I began to spill out words that I hoped would add up to a convincing case for marriage. Kathryn was wary of more talk; she was listening for the bottom line, for evidence of real change, the sound of someone really committing to spend his life with her. I should have begun with something straightforward. *This is why I love you.* But I trusted that our years together had been their own argument. The commitment she wanted had actually been made long ago.

I loved K. What I needed to explain were the flare-ups of doubt, the answers I'd come to on the question of David. I led us through lengthy excursions into the nature of love, memory, grief, and the "struggle toward self-realization," a phrase I'd borrowed from the psychologist Karen Horney, whose book *Neurosis and Human Growth* I had just read and felt transformed by. The Horney book had been David's. He'd underlined passages in black pen just like I had. Not all the same passages though. I decided that David and I were different "types" on Horney's classification scheme of neurotics. But we both starred one key passage toward the end of the book. Horney asks of the neurotic who has resigned from making any of life's most important commitments:

> Does he want to keep whatever is left of the grandeur and glamour of his illusions, his claims, and his false pride, or can he accept himself as a human being with all the general limitations this implies, with his special difficulties but also with the possibility of his growth? There is, I gather, no more fundamental crossroad situation in his life than this one.

K and I had circled our Cambridge streets three times before I came to the stirring conclusion that, all things considered—all the proper qualifications laid out and caveats made, all the expert opinions weighed and the negative tax implications set aside—we should consider very seriously the notion that we would be much happier together than apart. And if being together meant getting married, then that was what we should almost definitely be prepared to take under very, *very serious advisement.* I was doing my frightened best, and K was able to make the translation. We were getting married.

The wedding was planned for just a few months later. It was a bit of a rush job after so many years of foot-dragging, but neither of us wanted a big ceremony and both of us wanted it done.

On a rainy day in early November 1997, K and I took the Cross Sound Ferry to Long Island, where the wedding would take place on the back lawn of her parents' summer house. We arrived at the East Hampton town clerk's office late in the afternoon. A woman looked up from a crossword puzzle and asked, "Can I help you?" Of all the possible responses, we offered what felt to me to be the least likely in the world: "We're here to get a marriage license."

I watched as the woman typed my name and address and place of birth under "Groom." Then she typed K's name, *her full name,* right next to mine. Those two names were linked now in a permanent way, and not through David.

The clerk handed us a copy of what she'd typed, as well as a newlyweds' gift bag filled with trial-size boxes of laundry detergent and dishwashing soap and other staples of what someone imagined to be our new life of tidy domesticity together. We were contestants on a game show, the Big Winners, and the clerks circled around to wish us well. We were Youth. We were Love. We were Hope. And we had not come for a dog license or an application for a zoning variance, like the others in line. We were getting hitched.

November is not the high season for outdoor weddings on eastern Long Island, and this, perhaps, is for a reason. It was cold and raw, and at the time of the ceremony, it had been raining for two days. I stood on the front porch and watched the wind whip through the trees. It looked like a hurricane was organizing itself just off the coast and was about to come ashore.

The tent was sturdy, set up by professionals, but the rain beat down and leaks began to appear—drips at first, but then small, flowing streams, tributaries leading to minor rivers across the dance floor. As the first guests arrived, K's father was still running around in a mackintosh and boots, trying to divert the water off the bandstand; her brother and uncle Eddie were laying out plywood on the front lawn to keep guests from slipping on the mud on their way inside.

I hadn't been looking forward to the ceremony, even the scaled-down affair it was supposed to be: the procession down the aisle, the vows, the kiss, the toasts. I told myself this was the fire I would have to walk through to get to the other side.

The rain didn't let up that evening. It seemed to reach a new pitch of intensity just as the moment for the vows arrived, but this was okay. It muted things in a nice way for me. I could hear K, and she could hear me, and I didn't really care how many others could follow along as we read the vows we had written together. We placed the rings on each other's fingers—I guessed the wrong finger at first, and K nudged me toward another. A look of impatience and judgment flashed across her face, then a smile. It was a relief to me—a sign among all the frippery and lace that this was still the K I knew and loved who I was marrying. We kissed and broke a glass, a nod to a traditional Jewish wedding that we otherwise were not having, and then we scooted back down the aisle, through the tent walkway, and back into the house.

We danced the first dance and did that awkward feeding of the cake to each other that we knew to do from movies, but these were the only forced notes in a night that was otherwise pitch-perfect, free and easy and lovely in just the way that K and I would have planned it if we had actually done the planning. When it came time for the toasts, K thanked her parents for the nicest night of her life.

Billy came to the wedding. It had been only a few months since our time together in New York. When I left his apartment, K and I were still split. I don't know what he made of the wedding coming so soon thereafter, but I hoped he'd see me as having made a decision to be a grown-up. I wanted him to certify that I was doing something that David had never lived to do. Billy and I talked, but we never mentioned David. No one mentioned David. By the end of the night I was feeling feverish. *Was I coming down with something?*

K and I flew to Florence and stayed the first few days of our honeymoon at the posh J & J Hotel, which K's parents had lined up for us. We started off strong, taking in the big museums and the Old Masters, eating bread, fruit, and wine on the banks of the Arno, finding tourist kitsch on the street to mock and beautiful sights to explore. We had someone snap a shot of us—K and me at the start of a long stone path lined with cypress trees that trailed off to forever. It would be the happy-ending shot I had imagined when I decided to go back to her at the end of the summer. This was the way I had been conceiving of marriage, I think: as the end of a long road. But, really, it was the beginning. *What had I talked myself into?*

I told myself that I was plowing new earth, going places where David had never gone. This was my story now, not his, and I would write its first few pages on stationery I took from the J & J Hotel: "A glorious sunny day in Florence today. Lunch on the Pontevecchio. More later. . . ." I began keeping a honeymooner's journal confidently, but then the writing became a little more desperate. I tried to retrace the steps of logic that had gotten me to marriage, hoping it still made sense. Question: Is this how one makes real change in one's life, by telling a story about change over and over until it stops feeling like a story? By pretending at first until the pretending feels real? Is this how you become a Husband? A Father?

Another question: What do you do if your story starts to fail? What if your story breaks down when you're far from home, locked into a week's stay in a farmhouse in Tuscany, let's say? One answer: You might try writing down your story on more of those nice sheets of white stationery you grabbed from the J & J Hotel. Start with a travelog, and see if that grounds you; if you must, catalog your feelings. If you're afraid that your new wife might come upon your sheets of paper and discover your dark thoughts and be disappointed by your slide—*another slide*—you might want to write your story as if it were someone else's. "His" story, say—some nameless "He" and not you. If anyone asks, you can try to claim, implausibly, that it's a start at a short story loosely based on your experience. This was David's game, his style of autobiographical fiction; maybe you can play it, too. You're struggling, and you don't have any better options, so you begin:

> He is in the bathroom of the rented farmhouse in Tuscany, on all fours feeling sick. His new wife is reading in bed. He pleads his problems are gastro-intestinal, but he knows they are really existential. He knows that she knows this too. She knows him very well. They have been here before—one year ago, two years ago, three years ago. He thought his troubles were behind him. He thought he could assert these troubles away, and he convinced her of this as well when he came to her over the summer. He felt solid then, but now he is dissolving. He roots around in his toiletry bag for the Xanax that his sister prescribed for him the last time he came apart at the seams. He's only got a few left, and seven more days in Italy. He must ration the pills. He looks at his new wife seated across the breakfast table and sees a woman trying to conduct a marriage by herself. He must get it together, he knows this. But how?

I tried to avoid complete collapse, or at least to postpone it until we got home. I resolved: K and I would go out into the countryside every day. We would visit the places written up in the guidebooks—the great walled cities, the abbeys, the olive groves, the vineyards, the ruins. We would buy lunch at simple shops in ancient places and eat them under the Tuscan sun just like the guidebooks told us. We would enjoy ourselves.

I'm embarrassed at how hard this was for me. My mind kept churning out dark thoughts. I was fixated on the cost of the wedding. As I went over it in my mind, the numbers grew to astronomical levels. The food, the music, the tent, the flowers—I estimated the price of everything, added New York State sales tax where relevant, and came up with ballpark figures. Then I thought about how I could start to pay it all back to K's father. I rehearsed the speech I would make to him when we got back. *When you invested in this wedding it was with the assumption that K and I would last a lifetime. Since we made it only a few weeks, you are entitled to a full refund. Here is a check for fifty thousand dollars. If it's not enough, please let me know and I will write you another check for the difference.* It was a ridiculous speech, not least of all because I didn't have fifty thousand dollars to give and couldn't imagine having it anytime soon, but I went over the argument for repayment a thousand times. I wanted to figure the size of the loss to the last dollar and pledge the rest of my life to pay it back.

In the name of balance: I know that K and I managed some moments almost worthy of a vacation, if not a proper honeymoon. Playing cards at night, taking hikes through unknown places, making a joke of the pizza place outside of Siena where we kept ending up for dinner. At times, I can remember some of what we experienced there free of all of the turmoil I felt inside, and they are sweet memories.

One afternoon we ate lunch at the home of Lamberto, the man who owned the farmhouse where we were staying. We'd put it off for most of the week, hoping I'd feel better soon, but when I didn't, we went anyway. Everything about that lunch should have been pleasant, but it pained me. Lamberto and Anna were not much older than we were, but they seemed so comfortably husband and wife. They had their land and their stemware and their young baby in a bassinet in the corner. And I had half a Xanax wrapped in a tissue in my pocket that seemed to me to be the most important thing in the world.

Lamberto asked good-naturedly, "You're married now. Are you planning to have babies?" The only answer was to say yes, or to smile dumbly as if the only possible answer were yes, or to look at K and hope she'd answer. But then she wanted to hear the answer from me as well. I tried to summon up the look of someone who might soon embark on fatherhood, and the conversation mercifully moved on to other things. I sat through the rest of the lunch hoping that no one could see how destroyed I felt inside.

When we returned from Italy, people asked about the honeymoon, and we didn't know what to say. I had made a wedding into a funeral. I couldn't look at the photos; they seemed like the history of an error. The same insidious voice inside my head kept saying, "You've made a terrible mistake, don't compound it by staying. Give K a chance to live her life. Pay back her father, every dime. Leave."

K tried to be patient and empathetic over the weeks that followed. She hoped that the storm would blow over and things would get better. But they didn't. A last straw? One night, I complained that the gold wedding band on my finger hurt. *It's too tight,* I said. *I think it's cutting off my circulation.* I asked K if she would mind if I took it off, and she started to cry. And then she got mad. And then she said she couldn't live like this anymore. She had troubles of her own. She'd decided to leave academia for clinical work in psychology, doing a postdoctoral fellowship in the adolescent wing of a big psychiatric hospital, but now her mentor was leaving and the whole program was in danger of folding. Her work had been the haven that our newlyweds' apartment should have been, but now she'd been denied that, too, and was too unsettled to keep holding up the relationship for both of us. For all of my thoughts about leaving, and my brief experiments with it, it had never occurred to me that K had the option of leaving as well.

II

I COMMANDEERED the dining room of our new apartment as my office. I filled it with David's books and papers, my crates of research about the bombing, my enormous map of Lockerbie, with colored pushpins showing the exact grid reference where each passenger from Pan Am 103 had fallen. This is where I spent my first few months of marriage: seated at the dining room table, determined to read every last word of David's, somehow to finish with it, and then put this stuff away for good. It felt like the best thing I could do for all of us.

I picked up David's notebooks where I'd left off the summer before, with David getting a job as "conference assistant" at CAJE in early 1987. David saw CAJE as another in a string of employments necessary to support his writing and maintain his sanity. He set his alarm each day and tried to make it to the office on time. He handled correspondence with the group's membership of Jewish educators, helped with the quarterly newsletter, and did the things that low-level workers do in offices. This was his first desk job. More than a desk, CAJE supplied him with a computer, which he quickly learned to love. He began staying after hours to type stories he'd written in longhand over the previous year. He revised as he went along—the computer made this so easy for him now—and he began a few new stories as well.

David also used the office computer to write letters. His first week on the job, he sent me an urgent appeal. "I propose to you that we make MANDATORY a weekly letter from me to you and you to me, to be mailed no later than TUESDAY morning, each and every Tuesday morning from now until the postal systems of the planet collapse. I propose there be *no exceptions,* ever. I have had a bitter few months in virtual isolation, bitter enough to scald me for the rest of my days, the harshest time I have yet known, Ken. I cannot, and shall not, die for two months, and bear your death for two months, ever again. I make the same proposal to Dad. No shame, no pride, no forgetfulness, no excuse of paucity should bar contact. Nor gloom of night. Nor snow. Nor freezing rain. Please agree to this."

David mailed his letters to me on Tuesday, and they arrived at our home in Philadelphia each Thursday, like clockwork.

February 16, 1987
Dear Ken,

   I am typing this letter on Monday morning in the office to make the Tuesday deadline. I am trying not to look at my keyboard to improve my efficiency as an office worker. Hence the many mistakes. . . .

February 23, 1987
Dear Ken,

   This is the report from the world of work. I phfumpher about doing whatever business they give me and mostly it's boring. Maybe it would be more exciting to fix a patella, or report news from Nicaragua. Or write a story about it all. Probably it would be more exciting to do just about anything that you aren't currently doing. Is life supposed to be exciting? Maybe it's supposed to be boring. Otherwise you get carried away. Be assured, Ken, that not all of my letters will be this narcoleptic. One hopes that thrills will be again. Remember your Tuesday deadline! . . .

March 2, 1987

Dear Ken,

My schedule crept away from me this week and I have to rush to meet the Tuesday AM deadline to you. Are you honoring your weekly deadline to me? I have not been to Aunt Greta's to check my mail, but I understand there is a letter there from you.

David sent me some of the new stories he'd been writing on the CAJE computer. There was odd science fiction with heroes named Nit and Joresh. There was a start at something about "a woman from Warsaw who was a refugee of music" and a story about a man in a park feeding a chipmunk, daydreaming, and then meeting a woman (or was this part of the daydream?). "Reiss Ranter: Investigative Polemicist," the story he wrote with Billy, was much longer and more complete than anything David had ever sent. It centered on Ranter, a tireless fighter for just causes, who takes an assignment from "a Vermont-based environmental magazine" that leads him to a polluted lake in Rhode Island. Here he meets a woman named Dahlia, who changes his life. Ranter starts out to save the world, and to take down Monsanto Corporation for polluting the water, but by the end of the story, he realizes he could be happy simply settling down with Dahlia. This last part felt like it had come from David. He was ever ready to give up everything for love.

I visited David in New York that spring. I showed up at the Penny Lane apartment around dinnertime, but he was still at CAJE, so I let myself in. He used his clock radio as a security system, playing talk programming loudly all day to deter potential thieves. As a further security measure, he kept all of his money hidden in a book on a shelf near his kitchen, a big wad of cash stuffed into his copy of *The Irrational Man*. (Why didn't David trust banks? A character in one of his newer stories says, "If you wouldn't lend money to the same people that banks lend money, then you should keep your money out of banks.")

I called David at work and he told me to take some money from *The Irrational Man* and meet him at CAJE. The office was in a gray stone building on Central Park South. I remember being surprised to see David dressed in a white shirt and dark pants handling a phone call in a very professional way. He motioned to me that he'd *be a minute,* just like busy people in offices did.

He seemed as proud as ever to introduce me to the people he worked with. "Do you think we look alike? Same blue eyes." His co-workers seemed curious to see what a brother of David's might be like. I tended to grow quiet around David in such situations; it was his show. The others in the office seemed to fall into the same role. David had not been on the job very long, but he seemed to dominate the room. People watched with nervous smiles to see what he'd say or do next.

I visited again a few months later, letting myself into the Penny Lane, taking money from *The Irrational Man,* meeting David at his office. This was the rhythm of his life now: much more steady and clear than I could remember. He had a job. He had money and the use of a fax machine. He was meeting the world halfway and he was proud of himself. He realized things were going pretty well and he wanted to underline this feeling, to crystallize it in some way before it dissolved. He decided to have a party. A Big Party at Dave's Place. A blowout, a happening, something no one would ever forget. This is why I came into the city. This party, David wrote me in his Tuesday letter, could not be missed.

I helped David with the final party preparations. We cleared the living room and the terrace, where he wanted to arrange for a band to play. He told people to come prepared to sing a song, read a story, perform a scene. He found two screen doors in the basement of the Penny Lane and persuaded a friend to paint them with the words BLAKE'S DOORS OF PERCEPTION. (Blake once wrote, "If the doors of perception were cleansed everything would appear to man as it is: Infinite.") The idea was for people to walk through the doors on their way out to the terrace performance space and then give themselves over completely to their song or poem or whatever.

What about the neighbors? David had thought of this, too. He bought a roll of industrial paper and made a banner to hang over the outside wall of the terrace. It read: I HAVE JUST GOTTEN ENGAGED. . . . PLEASE COME TO APARTMENT 817 IF YOU WANT TO CELEBRATE. He thought that people would be less likely to call the cops if they thought it was an engagement party. He expected the party to go all night.

David sent me and a friend on a beer run. He told us to fill my car with enough beer and alcohol for 150 people, and he gave me a big wad of cash to pay for it. He told me that he had spread word about the party to everyone he knew in the city, but I couldn't imagine anything like 150 people showing up.

As the hour approached for the start of the party, I felt more dread than excitement. The Big Party would never be what David had imagined. A handful of people would show up, maybe a few dozen spread out over the course of a long night. David might read a story, and people would listen uncomfortably, and no one would follow suit. He would make sarcastic, bitter, scolding remarks and throw the microphone. He would be disconsolate for weeks. He often saw himself as the last guy at the party, standing by as his friends made career moves and left the city and gave up on Art. Now, it seemed, out of some horrible, unconscious drive toward the truth, he had engineered the perfect event to cement this interpretation.

I could not watch this unfold. I went to dinner with my mother. (David stayed away, but if I was in the city I felt I needed to see her.) I stayed away from David's apartment during the crucial few hours when he'd said the party would really take off. I inched my way back to the Penny Lane at around ten thirty.

I was surprised to find the place packed. Really packed. And people had shown up in exactly the spirit David had imagined: They'd brought food and drink, and out on the terrace a band was really playing, and different people were walking through Blake's Doors of Perception to perform original works of every kind—songs, poems, monologues. It's probably safe to say that more than 150 people passed through the Penny Lane apartment that night. David was the ultimate host and loved the sight of his apartment filled with people, maybe all the more so for all of the time he'd spent there alone. He loved the sense of common purpose among the partygoers, however brief. He loved the idea that he had created something that no one who'd come would soon forget. He wanted to be remembered; it didn't matter how.

The next morning, a running joke got started that David would reference right up through the last time he and I spoke. He'd say: "It was a heckuva party, wasn't it?" And I would say, "Heckuva party. One for the ages." Then he'd say, "No, really, it was a great party, wasn't it?" He'd keep trying to step outside the lines of the joke to get a real answer, and ultimately I'd give it to him. "Yeah, really, no kidding. It was a truly great party. Truly." He loved the party and he loved the joke about it, which always ended with him laughing in disbelief at how much pleasure and satisfaction he'd actually gotten from throwing a party.

III

I LEFT FOR YELLOWSTONE NATIONAL PARK a few weeks after Dave's Big Party. I settled in for a summer of work at the Old Faithful Snack Shop, grilling hamburgers and scooping ice cream. I hoped to work for a time and then spend my last summer before college driving around the West with a friend. But when I called my father to say I was quitting Yellowstone and hitting the road, my father told me to stick it out on the job.

Something about this incensed David. Over the course of a few hours on the phone, he decided that the matter of how I spent this summer before college was of the gravest importance to him. He wasn't sure what needed to be done, but he would think on it, maybe counsel with Billy, and get back to me soon. Later that week I got a ten-page letter from him:

July 9, 1987
Dear Ken,

Here at 155 pm in the office, I realized what I have resolved to do: I am sending you $500 in a money order. You will pay me back in time.

What is most important to me is that you have the

chance to get away from the job without fear of finances. I am not being self-sacrificing. I am being self-ennobling. It is my chance at heroism. You will have the rest of your life to remit the loan. I am stuck in my job at CAJE. There is no chance I can use this money for what you can use it for: travel. And that is what I will use money for, eventually.

Here's $300 enclosed to start. If you want to hang out at your job for a couple of weeks, I'll send you the rest. Call me collect if you have a problem with any of this. I don't mean to get tough with you in that hackneyed, Do it or I'll kill ya kind of way. I just don't want you constrained by money: it makes *me* feel constrained by money. I'm current on my rent. I have money plenty to live, and the only thing I require of you are letters and secrecy concerning this transaction.

Please get away on a bus, or something. Be careful. Find campers to get wild with, anything. Maybe you can get an Ameripass on Greyhound. I did that one summer and it was a glorious, soul-expanding good time. Work out a deal with someone who is staying at Old Faithful to get your mail read to you, or sent to you, or something. Even if it's only for a few August weeks, join your friends or join the welkin west and be free. Don't get killed or butt-raped by malevolent hitchpickers, or I'll never have a moment's peace from Dad. Also, don't get hurt and hospitalized. Just get away safely, tracelessly. Be back for your flight from Montana. See things. Okay?

Look away! Look to the grasses, the hills, the geysers. Oh, Kenny, I'm raving again. Take this money. Let me know you got it, and live unfettered for a brief while.

Love,
Dave

P.S. Okay, today is July 10 and I have thought more on it. Lucky I did not have the money order when I wrote the letter yesterday. So here's what I'm thinking today. If you want to go against father's wishes, you'll have to do it to his ear or eyes. You'll have to work out a compromise with him, like a few weeks work for a few weeks travel. It's too risky for me to aid and abet you covertly. He's the U.S., and you're a South American country, allied to the U.S., but with leftist tendencies in your underdevelopment. I'm CUBA, but I can't behave like CUBA. Yet. I cannot be responsible for you. . . .

Do you understand that I despise all of this, that my original instinct to send you the money and the letter is so much better than all of this responsibility brio?

You can't sneak away from Yellowstone without telling him. It's not fair under the current paradigm. But you can plead your case. I urge you to do what you are urged to do. You have to fight your battles, you understand me? Even if you sort of made your bed, you don't have to lie in it. I will give you the financial means to do it. I'll tell Dad myself. But you, oh diplomat, hybrid of dueling stars, best of both worlds brother, you must strike the deal.

I love you. I pull for you. God curse your guilt. If you make any decisions based on my finances, I'll hate you. You won't be able to conceal it from me.

Remember, everything is significant. What kind of trees are out there? The air quality sounds so agreeable. I'd probably be etherealized in it. You want to know about New York? I'll tell you once we've unstraightened all of this out.

Love,
Dave

P.S. I decided to send the money order anyway: some serious grandstanding going on.

I took David's money order, but I didn't spend it. I stayed at Old Faithful and worked. On my days off, I traveled, hitchhiking to wherever, taking up with strangers in bars, trying to improvise adventures good enough to share with David. I wrote long letters to him filled with the details of all I was seeing. Every week I called him from the pay phone near my cabin and tried to convince him that I had not squandered my summer by staying. I'm not sure I succeeded, but he never made me feel guilty about it.

I see now in the journal David kept on the CAJE computer that he felt that he was doing some serious squandering of his own that summer, wasting away on the job. Six months at CAJE, and some of the wind had gone out of his sails on staying late and writing stories. Now he was just a guy working a job, with no secret plan for greatness in the works, just nine to five.

He clipped an article from *Esquire* about a guy giving up a serious New York publishing job to climb a mountain. (It began: "Each morning, I struggled into my suit, picked up my briefcase, went to my glamorous job, and died a little.") In one notebook entry, he complained that even his dreams had become dull. "One recently ended with me saying, 'That is a topic we can take up at another, more suitable time.'" He ended an entry about his souring mood: "I'll not write these same thoughts again until I get away from this city."

Bad news: David came home from work one day to find a flyer slipped under his door at the Penny Lane. The building was going co-op; tenants either had to buy their units or clear out. What would my uncle Harvey do? David was pretty sure this was the end of Dave's Place.

More problems: David received an outrageous long-distance phone bill fat with my collect calls from Yellowstone, which sometimes stretched to four hours and amounted to more than a hundred dollars each. Also: He needed emergency dental work: an old filling in one of his molars had cracked and fallen out, and after two years of eating raw sugar packets for "fuel," he was pretty sure he had a mouthful of cavities. How was he going to pay for this? He found himself dipping into *The Irrational Man* for more and more cash and finding less and less there. He was already a month behind in his monthly payments to Uncle Harvey, and now he needed to know if he should be looking for another place to live entirely. At the end of a long letter to Harvey, he thought out loud about "getting work as a writer or something" in order to help make ends meet. "This, by the way, would not be altogether a bad thing for me, I suppose, as it would force me to . . . ach, I don't know . . . I'm simply uncertain about whether you want to re-sublet to a wealthier person, or sell the place, or use it, or what." Harvey called to tell David he needed to find another place.

An apartment prospect? David's friend Norm called to say that he was getting married and leaving the city for upstate. He also said he was soon to become a father. David saw opportunity in Norm's news. He wrote to me that he thought Norm might sublet him his apartment on Twelfth Street. He ended his letter on a more sentimental note: "More news on the apartment as I receive it, but my eyes did moisten, as Norman is really the first of my friends to be a father and husband and all that."

It's hard to judge the cumulative effect of all of this change on David. My vantage point on him shifted that fall, and I never saw him quite so clearly again. I started at Brown that September and stopped meeting our Tuesday letter deadlines, stopped calling. I put all of my thoughts and energy into a spiral notebook, just like David; I signed up for a writing class and tried to write something great. I left home with David's old typewriter and forced myself to stay up until 3 or 4 A.M. trying to concoct scenes for a play. Now I was the one sitting tortured over my notebook and typewriter at Brown, and David was the one at home with the family in Philadelphia, at least as he described it to me in one of his letters.

September 28, 1987
Dear Ken,

Aww, Ken so tedious to explain the whole weekend with less than whole stamina tonight. Let's just say it was real fine. Dad took me shopping at Marshall's, Filene's Basement, Lord and Taylor's. He bought me some "Baxters" which are a kind of casual businessman's trouser, the very encyclopedia model of TROUSER, and some sweaters and shirts as well because I'd strongly intimated to him that I had no clothes other than ripped jeans and soiled thin shirts and sweater-rags, nor had I funds to purchase new such. I said I was desirous of looking somewhat better than I have been and Dad responded with baronial goodwill.

Please let me in on the school life, Kensington. Big buckshot goes to college and thinks he can leave his family behind? No, I must resist even this jesting guilt. My letters to you help me. It's just that with no replies, I am forced to assume things about your experience that by definition arc untrue, as they are assumptions. So write when you will.

At the end of another month of not hearing much from me, David made a surprise visit to Brown. I woke up one morning, and there he was at my door, with Billy and a friend of mine who lived in New York City. David dragged us all to a football game and made a show of mock school spirit. *Sis boom bah, Brown U., Brown U. rah rah rah. . . .* I introduced David to my friends, and he grilled them about their interests, ambitions, political leanings, favorite foods, favorite form of birth control. He came on strong, but people seemed to like him. I don't remember his doing the "Don't we look alike?" routine. I was the Dornstein at Brown now, and he was Dornstein's brother, and no one really had a strong enough feeling about me to wonder too much what Dornstein's brother might be like.

David was amazed and dismayed at how quickly his star had dimmed on campus. He took me to an archive of old newspapers in the *Brown Daily Herald* building to find some sure sign that he'd been there at all. With me and my friends, he often lapsed into the character of a man who had given his best at something and failed, and now had only to pass along what he knew to the next generation.

I couldn't find an account of the visit to Brown in David's notebooks. In the place where I might have found it, I didn't see many words at all. Just numbers. Dozens of little problems of addition and subtraction, multiplication and long division. The number 240 cropped up a lot. *Wasn't this the amount David had told my uncle Harvey he made each week at CAJE after taxes?* The word

"Jerusalem" was mixed in with the numbers as well: The next year's CAJE conference would be held in Jerusalem.

During my Yellowstone summer, David had calculated the price of freedom for me at around three hundred dollars for a few weeks. Now he was running the numbers for himself.

IV

"F OR ONCE, I'VE GOT A LONG RANGE PLAN," David wrote
to me in February 1988. "As you know, I am in Israel with
CAJE this summer. May not come back for a while. Where to go
from there? Africa? Must get inoculated against a hundred diseases." David then offered a version of this new plan to my father:

February 16, 1988
Dear Dad,
    My life will come apart a bit soon before hopefully
coming back together—when? I'm not sure. Without long
explanations, it seems I'm out of my present apartment
when the lease is over on February 29. I'm looking for a new
place at this writing.
    Last week, I notified CAJE I'll be leaving them after the
Jerusalem Conference. Thus the future yawns, asking: What
next? Perhaps travel, then back to New York. Perhaps not
back to New York. Perhaps many things. I'll have money
(four or five thousand dollars, I calculate), and a better sense
of my basic capabilities for having done this job. In other
words, a blank slate. . . .

David moved out of the Penny Lane in March, months after my uncle Harvey hoped he would. It took a while before he ran into a woman he knew from Brown who had just rented a two-bedroom apartment uptown, at the edge of Spanish Harlem. She mentioned to David in passing that she was looking for a room-mate and was surprised when David called a few days later to take her up on it.

The woman's name was Amy. She had come to New York to be a dancer, and had found a place in an established dance company. But fifteen years later, I found her living in Minnesota, just starting maternity leave from General Mills Corporation. She said:

> As you probably know, there was some tension between Dave and me at 1646 Madison Ave. I remember him squatting in the corner of the living room, always chain-smoking, musing on what it might be like if we slept together. He kept wanting to know if I thought it would change our living arrangement. . . . We didn't get off on the right foot.

David ceded most of the homemaking to Amy. He took the less-nice bedroom, a ten-foot box off a central hallway with a window onto a dank interior courtyard, and he spent most of his time inside with the door closed. It's hard to imagine him paring down any further from his already Spartan digs at the Penny Lane, but he did. He made a mattress of some periwinkle carpet samples. He used a roll of paper towels as a pillow. His room now contained mainly books.

David's lone contribution to the communal life of the apartment was his minding of the outgoing message on the answering machine. "He was obsessed with it," Amy said. "I remember he asked me once if I cared about the message. When I said no, he turned it into this huge thing. He would come home from work and spend hours recording a new outbound message. He hauled his boom box out into the living room, along with tons of tapes, and then he'd get to work."

I remember those messages. He'd play music in the background and start riffing in funny voices. My favorite? His impression of Daniel Inouye, the senator from Hawaii, making extemporaneous remarks at the Iran-Contra hearings before saying, "I yield the balance of my time to Senator Metzenbaum. . . . Please leave a message at the beep." Who knew Inouye had such a deep voice and that it would be such a perfect fit for David's baritone?

I used to call David's machine first thing in the morning just to see what he'd come up with the night before. And then I started making messages of my own. I spent hours racing around my dorm room trying to coordinate music cues with doors slamming and other sound effects. It was my roommate's machine, though. He got most of the calls, and he didn't really appreciate my messages. His parents spoke English as a second language (Chinese being the first), and they were deeply confused by what I was doing. (A man talking in a thick Jewish accent with *Fiddler on the Roof* playing in the background: *Was this the right room?*) My roommate said he didn't understand the messages, either. This wounded my pride a little, but then, I realized, my roommate and his parents weren't my intended audience. I made my messages for David, and ultimately I think he made his messages for me. Those messages were little subversions of our respective households, creative outlets for people who weren't quite sure about their medium, notes in a bottle sent toward each other's distant shore.

It was spring break before I visited David at the new apartment on Madison. I came with a friend from Brown named Adam, whom David took an instant liking to. Adam was an extraordinary character, tall and misanthropic and very smart, and more widely read than anyone I'd ever met, except maybe David. Adam and David traded literary references and felt each other out about what they knew. Who remembered that passage from Henry Miller's *Plexus*? (Or was it *Sexus*?) Who could recite more lines from Pound's *Cantos*?

It was good-natured literary sparring between two heavyweights. I maneuvered them into the ring, picking up *Naked Lunch* from David's shelf and saying something about how I thought Adam had memorized a big chunk of it. (David: "Really? Let's hear it.") And then I sat back and watched as the two slugged it out. I couldn't always follow the shorthand; I hadn't read any of the books they were talking about. I was listening for the signs that one of them had scored points. I was watching for the big gap exposed in the other's knowledge of books, the knockout blow. And I was rooting for Adam.

Did David sense a change in my allegiance? I don't know. But it's in this context that one other incident from that visit comes to mind.

David's favorite song of the moment was "The Evil That Men Do," written and sung by Ira Kaplan of Yo La Tengo. David cued it up on his tape player many times during the visit. It's long, maybe seven or eight minutes, but we sat and listened to it straight through. No talking. The song begins with pulsing drums followed by two or three minutes of wild, driving distortion guitar. Then it settles into something more melodic. A man's voice—Kaplan's presumably—starts intoning, "It's a lot of time . . . It's a lot of time for a man who walks on me. . . ." This last line is repeated over and over. "When a man walks on me." The words are sung at first, and then screamed over and over: WHEN A MAN WALKS ON ME! Then the guitar goes wild again. David gave himself over to the song entirely.

One night, when we were getting ready to leave the apartment to meet Billy and Tim for dinner, David wanted to listen one more time to "The Evil That Men Do." He said he wanted to start a new ritual. He'd say, "When a man . . ." and it would be my job to finish the line: ". . . walks on me." *Got it?*

David wanted to try it. He said, "When a man . . ." and then he looked over at me and Adam. I tried to laugh it off at first, but David persisted. "I said, 'When a man . . .' " It would have been simple enough to have responded ". . . walks on me," but I didn't want to, and the more David pushed, the more deeply I resisted. I don't know exactly what was at stake for David here, or for me, but after several minutes, he grew belligerent. He screamed the lyric with more furious abandon than Ira. "I SAID, 'WHEN A MAN . . .' "

Now it was impossible for me to say, ". . . walks on me." Adam looked at me for a while then looked down, at a loss as to how to act. I don't know if the whole scene would have played out differently if Adam hadn't been there, or if it would have happened at all if it had been just the two of us. But it wasn't just the two of us. And maybe this was part of why it seemed so important to David that I make it clear whose team I was on. "I SAID, 'WHEN A MAN . . .'" Now David was in my face, pushing my shoulder, trying to provoke me into saying my line, but I clammed up. All I had to say was ". . . walks on me," and then it was off to dinner. But I couldn't. I didn't.

Two years later, when David was dead and I was back at Brown, Yo La Tengo was playing in a downtown Providence club. I got there early and talked my way into the band's dressing room before the show. Ira Kaplan was a thin Jewish-looking guy with bushy, unkempt hair; he wore a hooded blue sweatshirt and jeans like David might have worn. (Had David styled himself after Ira?) Kaplan's girlfriend, Georgia, was a full partner in the band. She played the drums, and if you were lucky she would sing outrageously beautiful harmonies with Ira. The two of them sat and listened as I tried to explain myself.

My brother, David, was a big fan, I said. He and his friend Billy used to come to the shows at Maxwell's in Hoboken and shout things at the stage. "You're a Jewish rock star, Ira!" *Do you remember this?* I assumed that David had really done the things he'd said he'd done, and that Kaplan had found them clever or endearing or at least memorable. In any event, I assumed that he and Georgia would feel sorry for me when I told them that David had been killed in the Lockerbie bombing and that this would give me license to tell them David's story. They didn't know what to say when I was done, and I wasn't really sure what I wanted from them, except to make the connection. I told them about "The Evil That Men Do"—how much David liked the song, how he and I made a ritual of "When a man . . . walks on me," even though we decidedly had not.

I stood in the crowd as the club filled and Yo La Tengo took the stage. About halfway through the show, the drums began to play the long intro to "The Evil That Men Do," and I paid special attention. Ira mumbled something about David. It went by quickly. Did he say, "This one's for David"? I lost myself in the song. This was the way it worked that night: Ira would say, "When a man . . . ," and I would say out loud, ". . . walks on me." David wouldn't have believed how easy it now was for me to do it.

V

DAVID'S PASSPORT ARRIVED IN EARLY MAY. Plans for Jerusalem were going forward, and he felt good about it. He was ready for a change. He was tired of going to bars and coffee shops, tired of listening to people's stories and making up ones of his own, tired of sex with strangers. His love affair with New York was over; now they were just living together out of convenience. "New York is getting predictabler and predictabler," he wrote to his friend Jena, who had just left New York for graduate school.

> We all just want to be in love, Jena. This is all there is, I am more and more convinced. No new sentences, no better machines, no more mordant insights into Nature's mind. No solutions, and no new problems. No new characters, no better references. Just love to befall us, to make everything bearable and maybe sweet. That's all I want, anyway.
>
> I'm headed away soon. I am uncertain still about my plans, although I have generated a certain take it or leave it attitude toward nearly everything and everyone here, except of course Billy. I am more sure each day that I will try to live elsewhere

for a while, until my money runs low. I suppose the departure of others here from the city into graduate school or couple-dom makes it easier to leave city and country. *That, as well as the divergence I currently experience from my brother's nature . . .*

Italics mine. *What divergence?*

Over the years, David had stored boxes of books and papers with different friends, but now was the time to gather everything in. He asked me to drive my father's Buick Regal into the city to help him get it home, but for some reason I was slow to do it. As the day grew closer for him to clear out of his sublet, he wrote home.

> June 13, 1988
> Dear Family,
>   My heart is heavy in upheaval this week—women, work, the whys. It probably has been the hardest week for me for a year at least. It's getting ridiculously morbid everywhere I look in this city and real emotion terrifies everyone. I don't think I'm just projecting my inner state. On the upside, Billy's rock band is playing in more clubs, and I'm getting plenty of Vitamin C. I see the end of this job and that solaces me. . . .
>   Ken, when are you coming to New York to fetch me and my stuff. It's got to be this weekend or next, or else let me know so I can make other plans.

I drove into New York the next weekend. There was a lot to do, David told me. We made a number of stops, filling up the big trunk of the Buick with boxes and loose items, causing the back end of the car to ride low under the weight.

Late in the afternoon, we picked up amplifiers and guitars from someone's apartment, worked them into the backseat of the Regal, and drove them to a club in the Village where Billy's band was playing. At the start of his set, Billy announced that this would be the last gig in the "Dave Farewell Tour." He made a

number of cracks about the farewell tour, how it had been dragging on for months now, how everyone would be glad to see it
done. David, sitting at the bar about ten yards away, chimed in
with some comments of his own. I remember him fielding questions from the crowd about what was next for him. He said, *Who
knows?* He said, *Wherever the wind takes me.* He said, *Won't miss much,
but I'll miss nights like this.*

The next day, we packed up David's room at the Madison
Avenue apartment. I remember David being not quite ready to get
on the road. He turned briefly grave. He propped himself on his
carpet samples in his otherwise empty room and told me that he
really didn't have any plans beyond the trip to Israel. *Really.* He was
working without a net, he said. *No joke.* He was trying to tell me
something, but I had trouble hearing him. It was late, and I just
wanted to get on the road.

These were the last few days I'd spend with David. I remember us
driving into downtown Philadelphia to buy him a Walkman cassette player at one of those cheap electronics stores that promised
big bargains. The place was run by Israeli men who shouted things
across the store at one another: "Moshe, do we have the Pana-
sonic AVX-900, dual cassette?" They shouted things at you as
well: "You pay cash? You buy today?" David told them he was
headed to Israel, and they insisted on buying him a coffee. I was
afraid that he and the sales guys were getting too chummy. I had
come here to bargain, to haggle, to beat the prices advertised in
the newspaper by the big chain stores. I still had the three hundred
dollars that David had sent me at Yellowstone the summer before,
and I planned to blow it all on a big send-off gift, but I still wanted
a good value. We picked out a fancy Walkman made by AIWA.
("Better than Sony," the Israeli guy said, "but same price.") When
I went to pay, David balked at first, but then I explained where the
money had come from, and he loved how it had come full circle.

David spent a lot of that last week at home upstairs in the
Dave Archives, organizing his notebooks and papers. One afternoon, he came away agitated. He told me that if I ever looked

through his box of stories and came across one I liked, I should feel free to finish it for him. I don't think he was willing his literary estate to me so much as proposing a collaboration on terms I might actually accept: I'll leave the stories behind, and you can do with them what you will. The net result was the same, however. In six months, the Dave Archives would be mine.

I last saw David at Philadelphia's Thirtieth Street Station. He in his too-tight khaki shorts and thinning T-shirt; he with his dark, curly locks and the worn canvas sneakers with no socks. I was leaving town first, headed on a summer drive to Alaska by car. It was the adventure I'd missed out on the summer before when my father insisted I stay at Yellowstone; it was the road trip that David and I would never take.

David was not leaving Philadelphia for another few days, and he wasn't leaving for Israel until the next month, but I needed to get on the road. Now, of course, I wish I had stayed the rest of that week with him. He said a dozen times that he was not going to come home for a long while, but maybe I didn't believe him. Maybe it just wasn't that important for me to spend time with him. Things were not as easy between us as they'd once been. We had had a standoff one day about whether I would drive him to the Reconstructionist Rabbinical College to say hello to some CAJE members he'd corresponded with, and these standoffs were becoming more frequent. I was getting tired of being David's little brother. I wanted to get away with my own friends, with my own money, on my own adventure. So that's what I did. David and my father drove me to the train station after dinner one night, and off I went. This was David: waving, returning to the blue Buick Regal with my Dad, receding, gone.

When I returned home from Alaska, I found a letter from him. He said that CAJE was going as expected, with plenty of hassles and complaining Jewish educators whom he suffered with extraordinary equanimity. "Off a duck's back," he wrote. "My mind is already traveling." He asked about my travels: Had I made it to the Arctic Circle, where I had told him I was headed? He related one bit of bad news: The AIWA stereo-cassette player had broken, gone mono. (He said he suspected that Moshe from the electronics store had screwed us with a cheap knockoff model.) He also had one very good piece of news to report, and this was his top story from the Holy Land: He had just met a woman he liked very much. "Her name is Rina."

VI

IN VLADIMIR NABOKOV'S *The Real Life of Sebastian Knight,* the narrator, identified only as "V." (read "Vladimir"), goes looking into the life of his older brother, Sebastian Knight, a novelist who died young while living abroad. Knight left a bundle of letters marked "To Be Destroyed," but V. can't help but look at one that escaped the fire. It is from a Russian woman whom Knight had met at a hotel in the south of France. The two spent a week together, and Sebastian wrote that it was the finest time of his life. The romance ended suddenly, and badly, and Knight was devastated, wrecked, never again to be the writer he might have been. He died not long after that, of an inexplicable illness.

V. feels a lot of regret over his brother's death. Sebastian had tried to persuade him to visit and to write, but V. didn't make any efforts in his brother's direction until it was too late. Now V. wants to do something for his brother. He wants to correct the misimpressions of the biographers and to solve for himself the mystery of who this Russian woman had been for his brother. He enlists the help of a private detective he meets on a train, explaining, "It's really quite simple. My dead brother loved her and I want to hear her talk about him. . . . I want to write a book about him and every detail of his life interests me." The detective is worried that V.'s efforts are well-intentioned but misguided. He warns V. in his thick Russian accent: "Please donnt search de woman. What is past is past. She donnt remember your brodder." V. won't hear anything of giving up, however. "[This Russian woman] is the missing link in Sebastian's evolution and I must obtain her," V. says. "It's a scientific necessity."

It had been more than ten years since David left Rina in Israel; and just a few years less since I'd seen her in Boston. Where was she now? Her last letter to me listed a return address in Tel Aviv, but it seemed unlikely that she would still be in the same apartment. She may even have left Israel. I kicked myself for letting the trail grow so cold.

Then I remembered her cousins in the United States. I'd stayed with Ralf in Boston. *Was he still in that place on what's that street?* I got lucky and found his number on the back of an old scrap of paper. And then I got luckier when I reached a voice on an answering machine that sounded very much like his.

Ralf called back to say that Rina had moved several times over the years, but she had never left Tel Aviv. He gave me her phone number, but I didn't dial it right away. I had budgeted a lot more time for the chase—camel rides into the desert, fishing trawlers in the Aegean—so when the chase proved so short, maybe I had too much time to think about what I really wanted to say. And how could I begin to apologize for the shabby way I'd treated her that last time in Boston?

A year or so later, when I finally dialed her number, I reached an answering machine with a man's voice speaking Hebrew on the outgoing message. I hung up. I called back and reached the same man speaking Hebrew. *Who is this guy?* I stammered through a message. When we finally spoke a few days later, Rina told me that my voice on her machine hadn't sounded like me. I joked that the voice on her machine hadn't sounded like her, either, and she said what I suspected: that the man on the machine was her husband. "I got married a few years ago." She had much bigger news as well: She had just become a mother. She said her baby girl, Neta, was feeding as we spoke. We talked for a few minutes or so before the baby started to cry and Rina had to go.

I called a few weeks later, and we spoke again. I told Rina that I had begun to write a book about David. She listened and offered to help in any way she could. "I still have some of David's stuff, you know. Books. Quite a few books he left on my shelf. And a few of David's notebooks, too." She couldn't say exactly what was in the notebooks—it had been a while since she'd seen them— but there were three of them, and they were filled with David's writing.

I pressed her about the notebooks—had David written more in Israel than I knew?—but by the end of the conversation, she said she wasn't sure if she still had them. She said that she'd carried a box of David's stuff with her as she moved from one apartment to another in the years after he died. She hadn't looked through the box much, but she couldn't get rid of it, either. She kept it in a closet, and that's where it had remained until just last year, when she got pregnant and she and her husband realized they needed to move to a bigger apartment.

She remembered packing her things and carting them out. That old box of David's was one of the last things left in the closet, and she felt ambivalent about taking it with her. Now that she was telling the story, she said she felt clearer: She hadn't thrown out that box of David's things; she could never have done that. But she hadn't taken the box with her, either. She said she remembered just leaving the box in the empty apartment as she and her husband and her not-yet-born baby girl closed the door behind them. "I just couldn't take David's stuff off the shelf one more time. Maybe the next person would find it and do something with it."

I tried to show compassion for Rina's choice—I was deeply ambivalent about my own boxes of David's stuff—but it was difficult. I felt completely stricken by the loss of the notebooks.

I hung up with Rina and pounded my desk. I raged around my

apartment and then I cried and I raged again. I felt like David had when he left his notebook out in the rain in front of our house in Philadelphia. Now three notebooks were lost—perhaps David's last words, maybe the only completed work of his brief life—and the suffering was all mine.

Rina and I lost touch for six months or so, and then I called again. Her baby girl, Neta, was now in day care, and Rina was back at work, doing art therapy out of a spare room in her house and also teaching at a university in Tel Aviv. "These were good days in my life," she said. I asked her if I could come to Israel and visit, and Rina said, "It's time."

Rina met me at Ben Gurion Airport. Her new apartment was not far away, in a rural area of farms and pine forests midway between Tel Aviv and Jerusalem. Her husband wasn't home—Rina said he was still at work—but a friend of hers was there. She was the first of the guests to arrive for a big Israeli Independence Day barbeque that night. There was a party atmosphere in the air, with stacks of paper plates and cups and bulk bags of potato chips on the kitchen table. Rina and her friend took a seat at a plastic table and chairs in the backyard and slipped deep into conversation. I felt that I was interrupting something.

I passed my first few hours in the house hardly saying a word to Rina. All of this seemed understandable at the time—she had a lot to take care of—but later I started to worry. Had Rina wanted another adult around when I first arrived in case things were awkward? Was she going to find a polite way to keep her distance the whole time? Why no hug or kiss at the airport?

Rina's husband, Tano, returned home in the early evening. His hair was gray and he wore a button-down work shirt and slacks. He carried a briefcase. He seemed like the dad who was returning home to a houseful of kids, me among them. We shook hands, and then he and Rina disappeared into the kitchen to talk. *Had he known I was coming? How had Rina explained my visit to him?* On the phone, Rina had assured me that she and Tano had discussed my trip, but now I was feeling that I should have stayed at a hotel.

(Nabokov's V. knocks on the door of one of his brother's old loves and finds the husband at home: "My wife is not keen to recall past friendships, and you will forgive me if I say quite frankly I do not think you should have come.")

As the sun set, Rina's house filled with guests. Several of Tano's friends set up a giant "Argentinian barbeque" outside on the driveway—they were all originally from Argentina, descendants of Jewish émigrés from Europe. I stood at the fire trying to bond with Tano and the others, but I was starting to fade. My day had started more than twenty-four hours earlier.

I didn't see Rina for several hours, and even when we finally sat down to eat, she seemed always to be just beyond my reach. I watched as she laughed and joked and ate. I thought: So this is how Rina's life has turned out. I felt like the Ghost of David Past hovering over the night.

The next day we took a drive, Rina, Tano, Neta, and I. We ended up at the waterfront in Old City Jaffa, walking along a path of rocks that jutted out into the Mediterranean. Tano pushed Neta in a stroller, and Rina walked alongside them. I kept dashing ahead to videotape them. It was all wrong to be filming them so soon after arriving, and without asking, but I couldn't help myself. I hadn't recorded anything of my first visit with Rina, and it felt important for me to capture this scene of her and the family she had made.

A strange moment: On the drive home, we passed through Tel Aviv, and Rina asked Tano to slow the car so she could point out a sign for the Super Charter travel agency. This is where David had purchased his airline ticket home. I knew this because I had looked through my Lockerbie relics before I left for Israel, but I was amazed that Rina had remembered and that she still cared enough about it to have noticed that the Super Charter office had just closed for business a few weeks before I arrived. This was the first real thing Rina had said about David on this trip. What did Tano think of his wife still caring so much about her old boyfriend? I didn't know. Tano kept driving. Every so often I caught his eye in the rearview. I imagined he was suffering this tour through his wife's tragic romantic past through gritted teeth.

That night before bed, Rina had a pleasant surprise for me. She handed me David's three "lost" notebooks. She hadn't left them behind after all; she had recently found them in her closet. I stayed up half the night reading.

The first notebook began promisingly, like a novel, with a character named Shneirson, who "was something of a student, though no one seemed to know exactly of what." But Shneirson's story ran out after just a few pages. This was not the "lost novel"—it had not even been written in 1988, I soon realized. These notebooks were from David's first trip to Israel in 1985, right after he had graduated from Brown. He must have grabbed them from the Dave Archives to bring along on his return trip for comparison.

It didn't matter. I'd felt alone in Israel, and now David was there with me. I got swept up in his accounts of his travels. His motto that summer came from Sterne's *A Sentimental Journey:* "What a large volume of adventures may be grasped within this little span of life by him who interests his heart in everything." One particular adventure from those notebooks stretched over thirty or forty pages. David had just arrived in Israel. His program at Hebrew University was not starting for another week, so he decided to leave Jerusalem on a bus and then hitchhike north. He made his way to Tzfat, where he walked the labyrinthine streets of the old city and wandered in and out of shops and synagogues and art galleries. He attracted two women, Danish tourists, and somehow persuaded them to listen while he read them the entire Song of Songs.

Tzfat is built on the highest elevation of any city in Israel, and, late in the day, David set off alone to its very peak. As he looked down on a valley of ancient Jewish graves, an old man approached from behind. "You want to see something?" the man asked. "Come, I show you something interesting. Don't worry. I don't want to take your money. You are a mensch. You know how I know? You are alone. You go your own way. Let me look at your forehead." The man cradled David's head in his arms and studied his forehead. "Yes. Hmm. You are a mensch. You are a little stubborn, but you know what you want. You are a Hassid. I know. One hundred percent. You are a Hassid. Your great-grandfather was a Hassid, a very holy man. You don't know, but I know. Your family is from Poland."

This probably was not that hard to guess, a Jew with ancestry from Poland, but David was swept up by the man's spiel. His name was Mordechai Jakower, a "fiery, soothsaying Kabbalist" with "bright blue eyes, an aging, blazing, orange beard and braided *peyut* down to his waist." David and Mordechai left Tzfat in Mordechai's van. Mordechai whipped through the winding roads of the old city, talking a blue streak. "You will stay with me. I will show you things. Stay with me a year. Give me one year. You will not pay a penny."

Mordechai explained to David that he was an electrical engineer by training, but worked in Tzfat as a refrigerator repairman. It paid the bills, he explained, and supported him in a lifestyle of learning and spiritual devotion. He talked a lot about "honest labor"; he contrasted this with the "faking" work of professors and rabbis. "I'm not a faking professor, making money for my faking speeches about my faking belief in higher things. . . . I'm not a faking rabbi standing in front of my congregation spouting faking words for money."

David spent the night and the better part of the following day as Mordechai Jakower's disciple, living the life of spiritual questioning and devotion that he'd often imagined for himself. But just before sunset, he began to worry over his situation.

July 2, 1985
All day with Mordechai. My soul is jarred. I ache. He speaks wisdom to me and I think about the suntan I could be getting. He can prove, clearly, the existence of God—Dear God I know that you exist, that you have set it all in motion—but I am young and must be free again. I am a tourist, truly I am a dabbler a dilettante, a puff on the wind, a pretty whisper.
You are a man of great beauty, Mordechai. Doubtless you

*could teach me the world. Doubtless you could fix up my life,
but it shall not be. It hurts me to run away like a grandmother,
to cause pain rather than back away nicely. I must follow my
heart, my instinct, my mind. My soul says, "David, you are a
liar and a sneak and a cheat and you are not yet ready for a
righteous life of Torah."*

*The honest thing to do is to run away like the scared
animal I am. I am that weak, vacillating, confused boy on the
telephone whom you said did nothing but waste your time with
his faking interest in higher things. Like him, I will not be one
of your boys, Mordechai. I pray for you not to stay awake for
me. Maybe you knew when you went to pray that you would
never see me again. I will become one of your stories and you
will become one of mine.*

*You fed me, as much as I wanted, food made to order, and I
ate. Why should I continue to steal from you? Go to sleep
Mordechai. I pray you know what I have done and that you
have already said to God, I have fulfilled my obligation to a
fellow Jew—now let him act like an idiot. Let him burn, stupid
animal, let him quiver in the world of hypnotized idiots. He
does not want to see truth when I offer it to him. He does not
want to be a Jew. He does not want to know even a thimbleful
of Jewish wisdom. Let him freeze to death in the idiot
winter. . . .*

*I am headed back to the center of town. If I'm lucky those
Danish nymphs will still be there. I could stay in Tzfat for
these women. I would stay forever in the green pasture of sex,
but not the pasture of wisdom or comfort. For this I would not
stay.*

VII

I WAS AFRAID TO OVERSTAY my welcome at Rina and Tano's, so I took a bus to Jerusalem for the weekend. I made a plan to meet Beth, a friend and colleague of David's from CAJE who still lived and worked in Jerusalem. She drove me up Mount Scopus to Hebrew University, where we walked the campus and talked about David. Beth said she remembered David and Rina talking the night of the CAJE conference opening ceremony. They were off to the side of the stage looking at each other in a way that gave Beth the idea that they might soon be a couple. "I asked David about it the next day, and he just smiled."

After the CAJE conference, David stayed with Beth at her apartment in a faux-Tudor building in the "German Colony" section of the city. Photographs that Beth took of him in that apartment show him shaving, reading, looking at maps, and clowning with some of the other people staying there that week. He is not wearing a shirt in any of the pictures. This is because he was proud of his body—his square shoulders and his trim stomach, his thick chest hair. It's also because he'd spent a day at a beach in Tel Aviv, falling asleep in the sun reading *Tristram Shandy,* and had come back with a burn that nearly required hospitalization. He

David in Jerusalem (August 1988)

couldn't wear a shirt for days; Beth remembered her and others spreading aloe and whatever other creams they could find on David's blistered back. A few months later, these would be the photos that everyone wanted. David's bronzed body and flowing curls seemed to tell the whole story: Beautiful boy cut down in his youth.

David shut down the CAJE computer for the last time in mid-August. He sent a floppy disk with all of his writings on it to Billy, who kept the disk for years before handing it over to me when I visited him that summer in New York. One of the last documents modified on the disk was a letter in which David seemed to be apologizing to Billy for not having written any stories yet, or done much traveling. "Perhaps next letter I'll have gotten down to some serious touring with all sorts of saturnalia and facts and observations to relate, things you can't get in a guide book, the marrow, the raw data of human experience." By the next letter, David stopped promising foreign adventures entirely.

> I've moved to Tel Aviv. I haven't been away a month even Billy, but I think I'm happier here with Rina in her apartment doing normal things than touring around right now. Happy with the little normalcies. "Piece of cake?" "Let's go to rest." Wash clothes, clip them to the line. Boil water for tea. Phone ringing. It's Rina's mom for the third time. That's daily life, with plenty of time for siesta.

Rina and I had our first big talk the night I returned from Jerusalem. I told her about my visit with Beth, and I asked her about those early days and weeks with David, after the CAJE conference. This conversation opened up things between us. I seized the moment to express regret again for the way I'd let our relationship drop so abruptly. Rina said there was no need to apologize. She said that it was a long time ago, that we were all doing the best we could under the circumstances, that I was young, that she now understands some of the complication I felt at the time with K. . . . But then there was that night in Boston all those years ago;

Rina didn't want to let it go completely unremarked. "We only saw each other for a few minutes before you ran off. It was strange, don't you think? I felt silly sitting in that restaurant after you left. Really silly." I think this was her way of saying she'd felt humiliated and hurt. She was not one for indirection, but the time for harsher words had already passed, and silly and strange seemed to be all that remained of those old feelings. The past was the past. She wanted us to turn the page.

Before bed, Rina said, "I still have the letters you sent me all those years ago. Do you want them? I put them in your room." The archivist in me should have been pleased to recover such an important source, but I wished I could have made them go away. There was no more intimate record of my reaction to David's death than this, but I didn't want to read it. I thought: Just more to apologize for on those pages. Then, before sleep, a different thought came to mind: Maybe one day I'll feel less derision for the person who wrote those letters to Rina, and more sympathy. Maybe that is how I'll know when this project is finished.

One morning, Rina and I drove into Tel Aviv. We went looking for the apartment where she had lived when she knew David. She had trouble finding it. The buildings all looked the same—a cluster of nondescript apartment houses near the Hayarkon River. She walked up to the front entrance of one building and cupped her hand on the glass to look inside. "This is it. We lived on the second floor." A few minutes later: "No, I think it was this building. Number twenty-three. We had a large kitchen."

I brought with me a copy of a letter Rina had written to me after David died, in which she explained, "There was a bench in the park nearby, this one particular bench, and it was like David's office. He would sit there and complete his 'mission impossibles' of so many pages a day, reading and writing. He knew the dogs that walked by, and the birds that flew around, and the gay men on roller skates. He knew where he could urinate without being seen. I would sometimes drop by and surprise him and I'd always get a big hug. I'd sit with him for hours and he'd tell me the latest news about the dogs and squirrels and the different couples and the old men. If you came here someday, I'd show you this."

The park was just a few blocks away. Rina and I walked there together. I watched as she moved from one bench to another looking for something, staring out at the water. She said, "I haven't been back to this park since the last time I was here with David. I ran away from here after he died." For the first time, I felt that she was experiencing something for herself on this trip, not just acting as my tour guide.

Rina and I continued along the waterfront, past the old men fishing and the lovers and the guys in speedboats, until the bike path spilled out onto the street. At the corner of Yirmeyahu and Yeshayahu was a café with outside seating and a place that sold newspapers and cigarettes next door. "David used to get coffee here and read and write letters." (He had once written my father from here: "What's my day like, Dad? I write stories, crazy little ones really, read the papers at a little café near me and Rina, practice Hebrew, read novels. It probably sounds to you like early retirement, but in fact it's not so different from the life of any as-yet-unpublished writer.")

Rina and I stopped at a lunch place for hummus and falafel sandwiches. The woman behind the counter looked us up and down and then said: "You two young people look so nice together. So beautiful. You will get married. I know these things. You will marry her." Rina and I laughed at how much the woman didn't know.

Rina looked at her watch and realized she was running late. She wanted to know if it was okay if we cut short our tour of the old neighborhood; she had errands to do before picking up Neta at day care. She thought I might be disappointed, but I was emphatic that she do what needed to be done. Socks for Neta and bread for Tano were real, it seemed to me, while I was just chasing after things I would never properly get hold of.

One night I showed Rina photocopies I had made of David's letters to me from Israel, including the random artifacts that he liked to enclose: the top from a bowl of Israeli Cup-a-Soup he'd just eaten; a package of Lebanese-made Chiclets gum, which were called "Chicfulls"; a thin square of tissue ("This is what passes for toilet paper in this struggling nation"). I wanted to see if any of this stuff shook loose any memories for Rina. She stopped on one page in particular, a brochure from the *Disco Piper* cruise ship that they'd traveled on through the Greek Islands early in their relationship.

Rina examined the brochure, back and front: "Have I ever told you the story of that trip? David's the one who first suggested it. He said he wanted to travel. He'd looked through guidebooks and had the money to spend: lots of traveler's checks. But then weeks passed, and he stopped talking about it. I pestered him. 'I thought we were going to cruise the Mediterranean.' But David said he didn't want to go now." Rina said that David chastised himself about how little reading and writing he'd done since leaving CAJE. "He said, 'I don't deserve such a nice trip.' "

Rina wouldn't let the trip drop, though, and David finally relented. He wore a scopolamine patch to avoid seasickness and it made him drowsy; he sulked on deck and resisted the lure of the sea. He said he wanted to get off the *Disco Piper* at Zorba the Greek's island (Crete), but Crete was too heavily touristed for him, at least the main port city was, so he and Rina crossed over a mountain to a quiet seaside town outside of Heraklion. Rina said that she and David spent just one night in this town, but it was among the most memorable nights of her life with him. She told me, "After that night, I knew he would stay with me. I knew he wouldn't go off and travel." I asked what had happened to make her so sure, but she seemed reluctant to discuss it.

A few days later, the night in Heraklion came up again. Rina said, "David fell apart in the hotel. He got very manic, and talking seemed to make it worse. I didn't know what to do. He lay on the bed crying and rolling around. I couldn't help him. He was not reachable, inconsolable. He looked so vulnerable on the floor. I started singing Turkish children's songs to him, like he was a little boy. I now sing these songs for Neta. I didn't know I remembered them until the words just came out. I held him and sang, and it calmed him. And then he fell asleep."

Rina stopped for a moment and asked, "Why was David in so much pain? He was in tremendous pain. Do you know this?" I don't know what I said at first, but after a few minutes, I found myself telling Rina about Bill Donoghue. How I'd heard about him from one of David's friends from Brown, how the abuse had happened around the time my parents split up, maybe magnifying its impact. Rina seemed to know what I was talking about. I got the impression that David had told her the story on that trip to Greece, maybe during that night in Heraklion, and she was holding these details close. I don't think she trusted the way I was talking about Donoghue. My detachment, maybe. The way I seemed so pleased at having put the puzzle pieces together, but not curious enough about this pain of David's that she was talking about.

We dropped it. Later, I found a few loose sheets of paper among the things of David's that Rina had saved. What was written on them seemed like thoughts of the sort that David would have recorded in his notebook if he'd still been keeping one. He begins with several accounts of dreams of himself going to school as a young boy: "It was always dusk and the yellow buses were always leaving and the walk home was cruel and humiliating if you missed yours." There are references to "busy parents, latchkey children, neighbors on the prowl." David writes: "I should have outgrown all of this by now. But here I am still dreaming of school while my body lies next to someone I am trying to love, but now believe I will leave instead." At the bottom of the page was a strange sort of aside to me: "Dear Ken, These are the themes of my life—sexual abnormalady, family division, Herzogovinian revolt in my soul. They make telemovies on scantier, right?" What was the purpose of this note? A final word to the curator of the Dave Archives? "Don't forget the divorce. . . . Don't forget Donoghue. . . . Don't forget *me*"?

It wasn't clear where I should slot these pages into the chronology of David's Last Days that I had brought with me to Israel. From what I could figure, they fit just before this letter:

October 27, 1988
Dear Ken,
        I just left the Super Charter office where I reserved a pair

of tickets. One on the 18th of December to London, one on the 26th (or thereabouts) to New York. My heart is in my throat, my stomach in my heart, my head in my hands and my hands raised up in supplication: "What am I doing?" I haven't been panicky but for the times I've thought what to do?

I realize I could make a life out of devotion to Rina. She's fine to belove, it's just so damned contingent on me, my internal affairs. Am I simply biding clockticks until such time as my brother or my friend Bill join me in some palimonial enterprise? I'm afraid that nobody's fist is raised for such adventures. Castles remain handsome in the mist, and my needs, Ken, those terrible driftwood spears, remain jagged and monitored. . . . Am I being clear?

I know you're busy with your life as are others, and it pains me to be so groping with you, yet there is instability. . . . I'll be back just after Christmas and we'll hang around for some of January? I've still got pretty much money and maybe after skiing we'll go somewhere? Why don't I come back soon and we'll make some full scale farces and sell them, get some money, travel, eh? Do you still want to write funny things for the television? Maybe I'd like that too.

Are we still pals, Ken? Please tell me how you are. Is your hair long? Mine just got cut short by Rina. I wanted it so. Are you smiling? I hope with every petal on my flower that you write soon.

David's letter crossed in the mail with one I'd sent him from Providence. I'd put a lot of time into it, taking the better part of a week away from classes. It was an elaborate, late-in-the-day attempt to make up for not having written to David all those months. I used his old Canon camera to take photographs around Brown and Providence, which I taped into a small spiral notebook. Then I laid down a running commentary on a cassette that David was supposed to sync up with the photos like a filmstrip in school, turning the pages at the beeps. I thought he could play it on his AIWA, which he said he was getting fixed. I threw some fall foliage into the envelope, grabbing what was near at hand, as he used to do, and I added a brief note: "You're far away. We haven't seen each other for months. Can you hear me across the Sea of Reeds?" Rina said that David listened to the tape a lot, trying to explain the different jokes to her. She said that he laid the leaves out on the floor of her apartment and walked around in them barefoot until they were reduced to almost nothing.

I asked Rina many times and in many ways if she understood why David left her that December, and if she believed she would ever see him again. She replied many times the same way: "I had no unfinished business with David." Toward the end of our visit, she said more about this: "The ski trip was David's way out. He was so happy to be included in your father's plans, he didn't need any other plans than this. He talked about duty, his family duty. He said, 'My father's asked me to go, so I need to go.' Like it was out of his hands. I was frustrated with him. I wanted to shake him, but there was something he wanted from going home that he could never get by staying."

Among the papers David left behind with Rina, I found a handwritten manuscript running around twenty pages. It was a little piece of fiction about a young man living abroad. His name, Paul Criss, seems to have messianic overtones. His place in society is sketchy. *He's some kinda drifter. . . . Not the typical American abroad, sorta different. . . .* It's not clear where Paul lives, but it's near a border, a kind of nowhere-place, where identities—geographical, personal—are unclear and open to influence from all sides. Paul has lived in this borderland for a long time, but now he knows he's got to leave. *He had to get away from this place, he knew its border atmosphere was driving him nuts, he threw rocks at the fence.* Paul has exhausted all of his own myths, ridden every daydream out to the end of the line. Leaving this borderland, the reader comes to understand, has become for Paul a matter of his own survival.

This is when he falls in love with a beautiful border guard named Rita. The two notice each other, make eyes, and wonder what might be. And then they start talking. The more they say, the more they feel there is to say, even if most of the time actually saying these things isn't necessary. "Their connection was beyond words."

Paul isn't sure what to do. He needs to leave the border, for reasons he can't quite articulate, but now there's Rita. Can he take her with him? Will she leave her post? Will their relationship work somewhere else, or will he find that it looks beautiful only in the haze of the border? Paul walks the border looking for a sign, some clue to action. One afternoon, he's approached by some men who want to smuggle illegals over the border. They know Paul's got a relationship with Rita and they want him to exploit it, to distract Rita with conversation while they slip past. It's a ruinous idea to jeopardize the one thing that feels hopeful in his life—Rita—but Paul considers it.

> Paul Criss was anxious to hasten his growth. He needed to take action. He wondered how could he get over that fence with the smuggler and his men? He needed to do a kind of pole vault out of one life and into another. He had hit that spot on a long approach where the vaulter says JUMP! JUMP! But could he actually take the leap? Would he help the smugglers? Would he declare himself to Rita and stay here with her at the border? He needed to do something and it didn't really matter what. Just this once, might he act to save himself?

That's it. The story of "Paul Criss at the Border" ends unresolved, with everything up in the air.

A last story from Rina: The weekend before David left Israel, he and Rina traveled to the north of the country, near the border with Syria. Rina told me that the mood of the trip might well have been downbeat—David was leaving, and their future was unclear—but they decided to suspend that knowledge and have a good time.

They went to Tel Dan, a large nature reserve near the base of Israel's tallest mountain. At the front gate they took a tourist pamphlet. For the next hour, David made a big point of finding a spot that the pamphlet referred to as "the Garden of Eden." This would make a great story, he said—he and Rina in the Garden of Eden. They set off on trails that snaked through streams and trees, following signs for the Garden of Eden until the signs ran out in a little wooded spot of rocks and gently rolling water. They walked around the area trying to take it all in. Nearby stood a majestic old tree on a small hill that could have doubled for the Tree of Knowledge. David made Old Testament jokes; Rina played along.

It was funny for a while, but Rina was tired. She wanted to leave, but David insisted on staying. She said that he wouldn't leave until he had written something in this special spot. He took out a pad of paper and started a letter home. The letter was dated December 12, 1988, and it arrived at our house in Philadelphia about two weeks later, after we had already held a memorial service for David.

I remember being home alone in the afternoon when the letter arrived. I stared at the envelope as if it were a message from the hereafter. The letter began: "Dear Family, I have walked through the Gates of Heaven and have entered Paradise. . . ." David went on to describe the trees and the flowers and the birds in the Garden of Eden. He made up fantastical animals and wondrous sites that he said he was seeing all around him. It was nice to think of David there. To the extent that Jews have a conception of the afterlife, the Garden of Eden is the place where the good and the righteous ascend, freed now from the cares and burdens and disappointments of this world. Who wouldn't want to receive a letter from a dead relative reporting a safe-and-sound arrival in Heaven?

Rina told me that David walked off from the rock where he'd written the letter feeling pleased that he'd finished what he'd set out to write there. His letter closed: "It's pretty here in the Garden of Eden. I couldn't resist writing to you. See you all very soon."

VIII

IN THE MONTHS AFTER I got home from Israel, I began, again, to write a book about David's life. I had done my gathering and reading and tracking down of people. I had gone to the end of the road with David in Israel, and now it was time to make something of it all. I needed this to be over. For me; for me and K. David had become the crazy uncle in the attic, the relative who had stayed too long, and now he needed to go.

So this is what I was doing at my desk in the dining room: trying to find the most decent way possible to usher David out the door. Week after week, month after month, I worked on this book about David. David was no longer my brother. He was my subject. He was my occupation, the thing I did from just after breakfast to just before dinner. He was my job, the thing that paid the bills. (I'd sold a proposal for the book and was living off the first advance payment.) I thought it was ironic that the story of David's underemployment, and his casting about for what to do with his life, had become a livelihood for me. I thought for a time that this might even be a blessing, David's way of taking care of his little brother from the grave. But then it began to seem like a curse: I had gotten sucked into the world of David's notebooks, but what if I couldn't find my way out? Who said I wanted to write books anyway?

A turning point: One afternoon, I got up from my desk to have lunch—the usual turkey sandwich eaten at the usual time—and I turned on the television. I was watching *Columbo*? *Hogan's Heroes*? And an ad came on for a technical college course to learn to become a truck driver or a nurse's assistant. Another ad told me to call a 1-800 number to fix my bad credit. Another asked if I felt depressed or anxious or had trouble leaving my house—if so, I might need to ask my doctor about a breakthrough new drug. I thought: These ads are cynically targeted toward the unemployed. Here was this vulnerable population home in the middle of the afternoon, maybe a little down on their luck, looking to television for a little escape from their situation, and these vultures, these sharks, were trying to capitalize. *Disgraceful.*

And then it occurred to me that I was a member of this vulnerable population myself. *I* needed a trade. *I* needed to pay off big credit card debts. I was the target audience, the sad-sack demographic so prized by afternoon programmers. I tried to sit at my desk and get back to work after this, but everything felt off. I was no longer a writer doing what writers did during the day, just as lawyers or accountants did what they did. I was more like an unemployed person in his apartment pretending he wasn't really unemployed by busying himself with papers.

I can't say that I acted immediately on this bit of self-knowledge. Another month passed before I bottomed out. K was unusually stern with me once I gave her an opening. She said I needed to put the writing aside and find a job that would take me outside of the house during the day.

I bought a local Sunday newspaper and looked through the employment listings, circling different ads. A small southern New Hampshire newspaper needed someone to cover the police beat. There were a number of jobs in advertising. Here's one that looked good: The *Oil and Gas Pipeline Reporter* needed someone to cover offshore drilling news, oil spills, "and more." The ad mentioned an office not far away, in Cambridge, and that was all it took to hook me. I wanted so badly to sit at a desk anywhere but in my dining room. I had been living on the daydream model of career advancement for years, thinking, like David, that good things would just happen for me, or that someone—maybe even David, somehow—would step into my life from offstage and save me from my worst self. But now the daydreaming was over.

I wrote letters expressing my interest in various jobs, and went on an interview. I got offered a job at the best of the places I approached—public television, working on a show I actually watched. I started right away. I told myself I'd keep working on the book about David on the side, at night, on weekends—but I didn't. I got up from my desk in the dining room, shut off the light, and walked away. A week or two passed without my touching David's notebooks and papers, and I felt bad about it, like I was letting David down. But as the months passed, it got easier to stay away. K and I even talked about reclaiming the dining room for dining.

This is how the story of me and K finally trying to have a baby begins: with me putting aside David's papers and getting a job in television. A job, I found, came with certain perks—a salary, for one thing, health insurance, an office. It was a kind of one-person economic revitalization plan, giving the unemployed not just a paycheck, but also a sense of pride and belonging, just like the politicians say. Regular showers were forced on me, as well as the purchase of new shirts and pants and twice-a-month trips to the dry cleaner's—good for me, good for the local economy. If I'd had some kind of caseworker, I would have reported that I was very happy with my job placement. I would have said that this job had really turned things around for me and that I would do everything I could to keep it. Apologies to David if I'd given up on the hard road in life—the Artist's tortured and lonely way—but I couldn't continue in his footsteps. Maybe if David had lived to the ripe old age of thirty he would have concluded the same.

Another job benefit: Not spending all day reading about David (and about David and Kathryn) helped me to see a little more clearly the relationship that K and I had made together—its strengths and potential, and not just its peculiar history. Once upon a time, K and I had gone to a couple's therapist, a tart-tongued Indian woman who listened to us talk about our situation for half an hour or so before rendering swift judgment: "This relationship is *incestuous*. Can't you see how *incestuous* this is? It cannot work. You must separate right away." But now we'd found a different therapist, who seemed utterly uninterested in the history that connected us through David. The more we talked with her, the less David seemed to stand in the central position where I'd placed him between us.

So did all of this add up to a decision to have a child with K? This much is clear: One afternoon, K and I had unprotected sex after years of protected sex. I was thinking about having a baby just moments before, but in the abstract—a baby as the emblem of the kind of change I might one day want in my life, a baby as a happy ending to a story about loss. I am almost positive that I was not thinking of the real flesh-and-blood kind of baby, the crying-in-the-middle-of-the-night kind who comes into your life and really does change everything.

I am not disavowing any willfulness on my part here. On the contrary, I know that I initiated the unprotected sex that day. Because I *wanted* a baby?

Here's what I can say about my state of mind: On that particular afternoon, in that stopped time with K on the floor of our apartment, I let something go. I was lifting a latch on a door that had been locked for years. I was not being careful after a lifetime of carefulness. I was making K mine and not David's—making her *Kathryn*—and if there were consequences for doing this, then I resolved not to be afraid of them.

Kathryn. I said her name and told her I loved her, things I usually found a way around. She started to cry and hid her face, but I glimpsed what I think she didn't want me to see: how hungry she had been to feel something this strong from me, how starved, and yet how ashamed she'd grown always asking for more.

Kathryn. To say the name once was to want to say it over and over. I wanted to articulate things usually left unsaid during sex. I wanted everything that had been murky to be clear, every middle position pushed to a decisive end. I wanted to say yes to Kathryn in some grand way. I wanted to make Kathryn pregnant that afternoon. I wanted nothing else.

A few weeks later, I was back at my desk in the dining room rooting through David's papers and thinking I should get back to work on that book about him. Then K walked in. She was K again; the moment had passed. She said she needed to talk. She wasn't feeling well and said she had classic signs of pregnancy: frequent urination, nausea, tenderness in her breasts. She had been saying this for days, but not wanting to hear something is a powerful disincentive to actually hearing it.

The next morning, K came to me with a home pregnancy test. The blue indicator line was faint, she explained, but that it was there at all meant almost certainly that she was pregnant. I tried to fend off her conclusion, seizing on the faintness of the blue line. *Was it really there at all?* Maybe it was some kind of trick of the light in our apartment. And what about false positives? I questioned whether the generic brand of home pregnancy kit that K was using might be inferior to name-brand kits. *Where are these things manufactured?* I was off in any direction but the one in which the test clearly pointed. We needed to repeat the test, I said. This time K used the most expensive kit on the shelf. Now the blue line was unmistakable.

I was terrified. I made K pledge not to tell people, not even her family. "Until when?" I didn't know. I wanted time to decide how I really felt about her being pregnant before other people's reactions got mixed up in it. I replayed events in my mind. I remembered how K had done some funny exercises after sex that she said would increase the chances of conception. I briefly pursued the theory that she had tricked me into impregnating her, but then I remembered how much I had insisted on doing the impregnating, how ecstatic I'd been about it, in fact. I remembered that afternoon, those few moments of transcendent connection there on the floor of the apartment. It was impossible to measure the distance from that place to the spot where we stood now.

We said little about the pregnancy for a few days. There were blood tests, ultrasounds to do. Anything could happen, right? We were into the realm of "wait and see." We slipped back to our separate ends of the apartment.

Weeks passed. Then one afternoon, I found K at her computer. I hadn't planned to say anything particular, but a flood of words came out. I had with me a little red car that I'd bought at a toy store that was going out of business. I had gone there looking for a gift for our little niece Ella, but came away with the car for no child in particular. It was cheap, and I liked its big rubber wheels *and who knows who might want to play with it some day*? The red car found a place on top of our mantelpiece, a symbol of a future that K and I might have together as parents. But now that future was closer than ever, and the red car only made me sad. I asked K: How could I invest my stingy heart in new life knowing, so intimately, how investments like this could blow up? I wondered aloud: Was this what my father meant when he suggested that David's life had been a waste—that to love a child was to open oneself to the possibility of colossal loss? Could I be this open? And what did a baby mean for my own relationship with David? That thin blue line would separate David and me forever, sending me off into a whole new family of my own in which he would just be a story I told.

I said all of this to K, and she listened. I went to my bookshelf looking for passages in books that confirmed my gloomy view of fatherhood. I found this from Mikal Gilmore's book about his brother, Gary, the murderer: "Though I may have spent years telling everybody that I wanted a family, in part so I could redeem some of the destruction I'd seen in my own home, the simple truth is I never had that family. I never made the right choices that could have made that dream real, and now I had to wonder if I'd ever really wanted it in the first place."

These words seemed wise because they did not discount completely the possibility of growth or change or transformation through marriage and children. Gilmore had striven in this direction, but had come up short for whatever reason, and now he had the courage to tally his loss. The best I believed I could hope for was similar courage, and that's what I thought I was summoning up with K. And yet once I had said all I had to say that afternoon, the arguments didn't feel as potent. In having made my case—or, more important, in K's having listened to it without getting too upset—a little bit of space opened up for me to imagine things actually working out much better than I feared. The baby would be born in August, K calculated. We were back to wait and see.

What did I feel when I saw the outlines of a little child on that first ultrasound? How did I react a few weeks later when K told me in tears that blood tests showed too much of some critical hormone (or was it too little?), and miscarriage was almost certain?

I know I went with K to the hospital for the medical procedure that would remove this seed of new possibility from our lives, but I wrote down nothing about it in the journal I tried to keep while working on the book about David. Was it too painful to write about? Or was my relief in this case so shameful that I dared not record it? In any event, where had the whole episode left K and me? Would we try again to have a baby? We were both buckling under the weight of statistics that promised complication and tragedy to the woman who conceived a child beyond the age of thirty-five, but K was more likely to be crushed by these statistics. Was it my intention to crush her?

It was another shaky time for K and me. She needed to know that we were going to try again to have a baby, but I couldn't assure her. She pushed, and I resisted; the old dynamic kicked in again. The loss of that little life was terrible for her, even if it had barely registered on the scale of losses in my life. She had her own ambivalence about trying to conceive again. She and I were really very similar in our fears about parenthood, but she was six years older—David's age, lest I forget—and it felt like now or never. She needed to plan for another baby, to get the nest ready. She fixated on our apartment and how less than ideal it would be for child rearing. "How would you get a baby, a stroller, and sacks of groceries four flights up with no place outside to park and unload?"

K decided we needed a house. She worked through the real estate listings, and I agreed to go along with her to open houses on Sunday afternoons. So many couples with babies in strollers and backpacks and slings and papooses—I felt the pressure to procreate just standing among them. And then there were the real estate agents, who set themselves up near the front door. They'd hand you a sheet listing the lot size, the type of heating system, the annual taxes, etc., and then ask you to sign your name in their book. This seemed to me an especially useless gesture. Couldn't they tell I had no intention of buying? Was the ritual designed just to shame the unserious into leaving?

K took the information sheets and did the signing for both of us. And then she was off, going room to room, trying each place on for size. I spent my time gathering evidence for the case against each house in the event K really liked it—signs of terrible water damage, an old boiler that looked like it was about to blow, nightmare defects of any type that would prove the point that home ownership was a Pandora's box of problems, not for people like us, not now. Rejecting a house on these trumped-up terms seemed smarter than saying what I really felt as I stood in those houses: There was no chance K and I would be making a bid. I was not willing even to consider it.

A few months later, K and I bought a house.

We sold our apartment in Cambridge and moved a mile or so away in a cheaper direction. We had a driveway now where we could unload groceries and a stroller, and no more four flights of stairs to climb with it all. On the second floor was a room for a baby. The third floor was going to be my office. This was where I would finally write the book about David's life and then get on with living my own. I carted David's corpus up those three flights of stairs, but I couldn't imagine unpacking it and settling back in to work. I couldn't imagine a baby asleep in the room below. I had worked up some hope about the house at the time of the purchase—another brief moment of desire as I thought about the life that K and I might make here—but now that feeling was gone. A new feeling had taken its place: There would be no Holly-wood ending to the story of K and me. The house was too much, marriage was too much, and kids would be too much. Maybe David knew this about himself when he left Rina, and now I felt I knew this about myself as well. I couldn't stay.

THE END

———

I thought I could describe a state; make a
map of sorrow. Sorrow, however, turns
out to be not a state, but a process. It
needs not a map, but a history, and if I
don't stop writing that history at some
quite arbitrary point, there's no reason
why I should ever stop.

C. S. Lewis, *A Grief Observed*

I

APRIL 2000: I came home from work one afternoon to find a phone message from the producer of a radio show. She said she was doing a program about the trial of the two Libyans accused of the Lockerbie bombing and wanted me to be part of it. The trial had been in the news since early 1999, when the Libyans were turned over to a special Scottish Court in the Netherlands, but now the trial was due to start, and there was a new wave of interest in it. "Will you be going to the Netherlands?" the producer asked. "What do you think about the prospects for justice?"

I knew what the producer was looking for—the victim's perspective—but I had trouble giving it to her. She had seen a magazine article I'd written about my trip to Lockerbie and assumed I would have something to say about the Libyans, but I didn't. I should have just said no—it was an uncertain time for K and me—but maybe for that very reason immersing myself in the facts of the bombing once again seemed attractive to me. I took out my old files with the clippings about the bombing and spent the weekend trying to drum up thoughts for the Monday program. I searched newspaper databases for answers to questions I thought the host might ask, things about the investigation I thought I should know. I tried to grasp the whole history of U.S.-Libyan relations during the Qaddafi era so I could put the bombing into proper context. I researched what other relatives had been saying about the trial: Most spoke in one way or another about "justice"—how long they'd waited for it, how they owed it to their lost loved ones to see that it was finally done, how this trial, despite its flaws, might be the last best chance to get it.

I looked at the newspaper photos of the two Libyans charged with the deaths of 270 people, one of them my brother, and I tried to see evil in their eyes, to hate them. Abdelbaset Ali Mohmed al-Megrahi was the older of the two suspects. He was in his early thirties at the time of the bombing, and reportedly worked as head of security for Libyan Arab Airlines. Al-Amin Khalifa Fhimah was a few years younger and much more junior in rank, the manager of a Libyan Arab Airlines office on the island of Malta, a few hundred miles off the Libyan coast. Both men were accused of being Libyan intelligence agents—Libyan Arab Airlines was reportedly a well-known cover—but both denied it.

I remember seeing news footage of Megrahi and Fhimah standing on an airport tarmac before being put on a plane for the Netherlands. I remember being surprised that the handover was actually taking place, that the plans for a trial were moving forward. For so long it seemed that the story of Pan Am Flight 103 had a clear beginning—a bomb exploding in the cargo hold of a plane and all of the people inside being killed—but no ending. I got used to the annual calls for justice from the relatives and the U.S. president, the statements of defiance from the Libyans, the alternative theories of the bombing that surfaced from time to time. The file on Lockerbie would always remain open, it seemed, the evidence always secret, the questions forever unanswered. I had grown to accept this, maybe even to like it. So long as the bombing was officially unresolved, I felt better about not wrapping things up with David. But now Colonel Qaddafi was going off script. Newspaper articles said that the Great Libyan Leader wanted to put the past behind him, to retake a place on the world stage again, to move on.

What to say about this? The trial was set to begin in two days, and I was on the radio, broadcasting to a national audience my indifference about it. I don't remember exactly what I said, but it was enough to trigger an angry call from a woman whose daughter had been killed on Flight 103. She disagreed with me point by point about the two Libyans not being worth pursuing because they were low-level operatives, as I'd argued, or because Libya itself might be only one part of a larger puzzle of state sponsorship that may well have included Iran and Syria. The woman said she was glad that there was finally going to be a trial after so many years and she was grateful to the people who had worked so hard to make it happen. She said she had already made a reservation to fly to the Netherlands to see the trial firsthand. She said that she imagined staring "Mr. Megrahi" and "Mr. Fhimah" straight in the eye and trying to discern guilt or innocence for herself. This, she said, would be a very meaningful thing for her. Earlier in the show, I had discounted the power of such a moment. But when the show was over, I thought the woman was right: I should probably go to the Netherlands and see Megrahi and Fhimah for myself.

The Justice Department set up a special site in downtown Manhattan for Lockerbie relatives who wanted to see the trial of the Libyans but couldn't make it to the Netherlands. This was a good solution for me. The trial could be unpredictable; it was never clear when court might be in session or which witnesses might testify when, and I couldn't manage weeks out of the country anyway, now that I had a day job. But on short notice I could drive from Boston to Manhattan and watch a closed-circuit television feed from the Netherlands. A room was set up for the Lockerbie families on the twenty-first floor of the Javits Federal Building. Two large-screen televisions sat on big carts at the front of the room, and chairs were lined up in neat rows behind them. There was space for about sixty or seventy people, but on the first morning I went, there were just three of us.

The sound from the courtroom in the Netherlands was difficult to understand, distorted as if it were coming in over short-wave radio. It took me a while to orient myself to the pictures.

There were several different cameras filming the proceedings, with someone choosing which angle to show when. One shot was clearly the judges: four men in white robes and white wigs sitting on a raised platform with the large seal of Scotland hung behind them. Several more shots alternated with the judges: more men in robes and wigs. One side was the prosecution, I presumed (the Scottish lawyers were referred to as "the Crown"), and the other was the defense; but which was which? And who was that guy sitting alone across from the judges? A witness? Another mystery: In the background of one of the shots were two men in some kind of traditional dress—white robes and round, black head coverings. One of the men wore glasses that made him look like a professor. *Were these the Libyan lawyers?* At the morning break, one of the other relatives set me straight: "Those are the defendants," the woman said. "That's Fhimah, and the one with the glasses is Megrahi."

I tried to focus on the testimony—to chart the connections, note the inconsistencies—but I was distracted. Each time another relative arrived, a series of chimes sounded—*ding, ding, dong*—and a big steel security door opened. Relatives trickled in like this throughout the morning. *Ding, ding, dong*—who's there? The noise wasn't distracting so much as my fear that the steel door would open and my mother would walk in. At the time the trial began, I hadn't had any contact with her for six years.

It sounds like a dramatic estrangement, but it wasn't that hard to split from Mom. If I saw her at all over the previous years, it was because I had made the trip to her apartment in New York. (She mostly didn't leave.) When my mother and I talked on the phone, it was almost always because I had called. Either way, the conversation was usually about things that she was watching on television (the set was never shut off), or who she might be dating. ("You were a private investigator. Could you do a background check on a guy? I think he's married.") My mother talked a lot about her physical ailments (usually something requiring pain-killers), and about her dental work (extensive, and also frequently requiring painkillers). She talked of the professionals she dealt with most often as if they were her personal staff—"her dentist," Stanley; "her pharmacist," Alan; "her acupuncturist," Hirugipol.

Increasingly, she talked about the elective cosmetic procedures she was contemplating with "her plastic surgeon," who she simply called "God."

In fact, I think this is the last thing my mother and I talked about before the line went dead between us: an expensive series of cosmetic procedures that she was planning with the money that was coming to her from Pan Am's insurers. David's life was valued at the low end of the compensation scale—about half a million dollars—because he wasn't making any money at the time he died. In the cold numbers of the actuarial tables, being a promising writer was worth about as much as not being any kind of writer at all, and about twenty times less than being a lawyer for PepsiCo, like the lead plaintiff in the case, who got millions. My father didn't say much about what he planned to do with his half of the money, but my mother talked about it for months before the money was awarded. Something about the way she worked David and the Pan Am money and a face-lift all into one sentence turned off a switch inside me. I hung up the phone with her and thought: What if I just stopped calling? What if I just didn't make those trips into New York any longer? When I thought about how this might play out over weeks or months, I could only imagine my mother, happy to be let alone to do what she wanted with her life and the Pan Am money. I'd leave her in "God's" more than capable hands.

This is as good a place as any to say that I have no idea what goes on in my mother's mind or what truly beats in her heart, and I have no insight into what kind of pain she experienced at David's death. She was his mother, after all. She would often say this to me on the phone. "I was David's *mother*. . . . I gave birth to David at Long Island Jewish Hospital." It was an assertion of something, the simple fact of birthing him, if nothing else, but it also felt like a reminder—to me? to herself?—of who she was *before*. I think she also meant a kind of denial of something—of any importance in David's life claimed by my stepmother or by my aunt Greta, who, after Lockerbie, became very active in one of the Victims of Flight 103 groups. "Your aunt Greta thinks she's David's mother, but she's not. *I'm* David's mother."

Once upon a time, the Lockerbie bombing was the biggest story in the world, and television talk shows wanted to hear from relatives of the victims. A number of grief celebrities were born in this moment, and my mother wanted to be one of them. She talked all the time about "her story"—how producers at this or that television show might be interested in it; how she would tell her story one day, and it would be broadcast to the world. My mother was quick to understand a basic axiom of the confessional age: It's more important to tell the world your story, to be recognized universally for your suffering, than to be understood by people in a position to really hear you.

As I write this, I think: There is little danger that my mother will ever read this book. Even though I'm the author. Even though David is the subject. If she knows anything of this at all, it will be through television. That's where she lives now. That's what she knows. Oprah and Joan Rivers and those ladies on the home shopping channels selling skin revitalizing cream, and those call-in psychologists (she had a long, phone-only relationship with one named "Roger"), and whoever's currently being featured in the twenty-four-hour news cycle—these have become the principal members of my mother's family. I don't know how much of her descent into herself to attribute to David's dying, but my guess is that his death only made her feel more entitled to her solipsism. It didn't cause it.

The last time I heard my mother's voice, it was out of the blue, a message left one evening on my answering machine at home. At first I didn't realize it was my mother. She sounded like Joan Rivers, and I wasn't expecting a call from Joan Rivers. *Why was she calling?* I couldn't figure out what my mother was saying the first few times through, but ultimately I got it. She was talking about the trial of the Libyans at Kamp van Zeist in The Netherlands. She said, "I'm the one who made it happen, all very hush-hush, behind the scenes." She explained that she had attended a meeting in Washington, D.C., with Madeleine Albright and suggested to the secretary of state that she should enlist Nelson Mandela to help persuade Qaddafi to hand over the bombing suspects. "It worked like a charm. You didn't realize your little mother was responsible for the trial, did you? Now you know the inside story. It's an exclusive. I haven't told it yet to any of the networks."

Why mention all of this here? Why mention my mother at all? I've tried not to, and for the most part, it hasn't been that hard to keep her out of this account. She was much more of a crazy presence for David during his first ten or eleven years before the divorce; even in David's last few months in Israel, talking to my mother on the phone could reduce him to tears, Rina told me. For me, my mother was more of an absence, a voice on the phone, a name and face to put in the space where a real mother might properly have stood. Since she and I stopped talking, I had gone to New York many times without ever really thinking of visiting her. But my visits to the Javits building were different: Her phone message had put me on notice that she was following the trial of the Libyans, and her apartment was just a fifteen-minute taxi ride away.

Did my mother have an official ID badge from the "Scottish Court in the Netherlands" to get her into the room with the closed-circuit feed? During a lunch break, I found the guard desk unmanned, and decided to find out. About midway through the guard's binder, I found a color photocopy of my mother's ID badge. I didn't recognize her at first. Her hair was wispy and blond when it had always been jet black and unnaturally straight; her face was a different shape than I remembered, and she was wearing some kind of black vinyl or leather coat that I had never seen her wear. I could imagine her telling me about all of these changes on the phone: the hair dye she bought from a cable TV shopping channel, the jacket that a salesman had insisted she take for next to nothing because it fit her figure so perfectly, the work that "God" had done on her face.

What did I feel as I looked at my mother's picture? Not much. I was focused mainly on the fact that she had an official ID card, and lived in New York, and could walk into the room at any minute. Every *ding ding dong* of the security chimes made me feel like I was part of an episode of *This Is Your Life. And now, please, welcome the woman who gave birth to you, a woman whose "story" we all know and love, the one and only mother of David Dornstein. . . .*

I tried to keep centered on the trial. I listened to the testimony as many days as I was able to make it to Manhattan. I took notes and attempted to understand the evidence. I talked to some of the other relatives and tried to feel, for once, that I was part of the group.

After months of following the trial, I was no longer indifferent to what went on in the Scottish Court at Kamp van Zeist. I had begun to invest myself in the possibility that those men in wigs and robes might actually establish the facts of who had placed the bomb on Flight 103. They might even go a long way to proving that Lockerbie was a Libyan plot from beginning to end, with none of the other long-rumored players or countries being involved in any significant way. With each witness heard from, every document entered into the record, every dot connected to another, I was coming around to the idea that this trial might truly end the story of the bombing of Flight 103, and that an ending might actually be a good thing.

II

The Crown's case against the Libyans was circumstantial, they often reminded the court. There was no smoking gun. Megrahi and Fhimah were linked to the bombing by just a few pieces of documentary evidence (passport stamps, hotel records, diary entries, airline tickets) and by the testimony of three main witnesses: a Swiss engineer whose company had designed the timing device that set off the bomb; a Maltese shop owner who had sold the clothes that were wrapped around the bomb; and a defector from Libyan intelligence who had worked as Fhimah's assistant in the Libyan Arab Airlines office in Malta.

This was the core of the Crown's case as I later came to understand it:

- Libyan intelligence had planned for years to bomb a passenger plane. Edwin Bollier, the Swiss engineer who supplied the timers, testified that he'd attended tests in the Libyan desert in which planes were blown up.

- Megrahi was a member of Libyan intelligence who was well aware of these plans to bomb a passenger plane. Abdul Majid Giaka, the defector from Libyan intelligence, testified about a conversation he had with Megrahi in the fall of 1986, just a few months after the U.S. had bombed Libya in response to years of Libyan-sponsored anti-American terror. Giaka told Megrahi that it would be possible to get a bomb in an unaccompanied suitcase onto a passenger jet at Malta's Luqa Airport, and he claimed that Megrahi told him, "Don't rush things."

- By the middle of 1987, Megrahi had been issued a "coded" passport by Libyan intelligence allowing him to travel under a fake name, "Ahmed Khalifa Abdusamad."

- Megrahi used this coded passport for various trips to Malta, checking into the Holiday Inn there as Abdusamad during the summer and fall of 1987.

- Early in 1988, Megrahi and another Libyan intelligence officer rented office space in Zurich in the same building where Edwin Bollier's electronics company was based, and Megrahi made several lengthy trips to Zurich in the fall of 1988.

- In late November of 1988, Libyan intelligence requested more MST-13 timers from Bollier, and Megrahi's partner in Zurich personally approached Bollier about them.

- Around the same time in Malta, Lamen Fhimah, the second accused in the Lockerbie trial, made notations in his desk diary about taking Air Malta luggage tags from Malta's Luqa Airport, where he used to work. Fhimah referred to Megrahi as "Abdelbaset" at times, but also by Megrahi's fake name on the coded passport, Abdusamad.

- On December 7, 1988—two weeks before the bombing—a man walked into a clothing shop in Malta just before closing and began pulling items from the store's shelves without much care: a pin-striped shirt, a pair of pajamas, a BabyGro jumpsuit for a two-year-old, a T-shirt. The store's owner, Tony Gauci, recalled: "[The man] was looking at things and he started saying, 'I'll take this, and I'll take that,' and then when I asked him to try on the trousers, he told me, 'These are not for me.'" It was the same story with the tweed sport coat. "He did not want to try on the sport coat. Absolutely not." For a tailor, a man buying a sport coat and trousers without trying them on was deeply concerning. It stuck in Gauci's mind some ten months later when Scottish police officials first visited his shop to tell him that clothes from his shop had been wrapped around the bomb that blew up Flight 103. Initially, when asked to identify the man who bought the clothes that night, Gauci was sure of only one thing: "He was Libyan."

The Crown's case rested heavily on its ability to prove that this Libyan man was Megrahi, and that Gauci had sold him the clothes on December 7, 1988, the date the Crown could prove Megrahi was in Malta. In the absence of any clear recollection from Gauci, or solid independent proof, they went about establishing the date with testimony about: if it was raining on the night of the purchase (Gauci said it was drizzling, but the weather report cast doubt on that); if the Christmas lights on Gauci's street had already been hung on the street lamps (he seemed to remember that they had been); which soccer match Gauci's brother watched earlier that afternoon. If it was Juventus against Liege, then December 7 might well have been the date of the clothes purchase. But if it was Roma against Dresden, then there would be major problems for the Crown's case.

The Crown enhanced its case for the seventh by tracking Megrahi's movements in the two weeks that followed. They showed that:

- Megrahi left Malta on December 8 and landed in Zurich, where he spent a week, presumably visiting his office in Edwin Bollier's building and making further contact with Bollier about the MST-13 timers.
- Near the end of that week in Zurich, Bollier was asked to carry a Samsonite suitcase full of clothes to Tripoli and deliver it to one of the higher-ups in Libyan intelligence.
- In Malta, during the week before the bombing, Megrahi was on the mind of Lamen Fhimah, who made more

notes in his desk diary: "Abdelbasset arriving from
Zurich." "Take taggs [sic] from Air Malta. OK."

On December 18, Fhimah and Megrahi each flew back to
Tripoli—the Crown could clearly prove this—but the evidence
about what the two Libyans did over the next few days ran thin.
The Crown looked to its defector from Libyan intelligence, Majid
Giaka, to help fill out its case.

Giaka testified that Megrahi had once brought plastic explosives to the Libyan Arab Airlines office in Malta and that Fhimah
had stored them in his desk drawer; Giaka also said that he saw
Megrahi and Fhimah on the night of December 20, arriving in
Malta on a flight from Tripoli with a brown Samsonite suitcase of
the type that was later shown to have contained the bomb.
According to Giaka, Fhimah's role in the plot was to use his status
at Luqa Airport to get the Samsonite bag with the bomb in it
through customs and security without its being searched. This testimony seemed to seal the case against both Fhimah and Megrahi,
but Giaka's credibility was seriously undermined by the defense,
who won unprecedented access to previously withheld CIA
cables detailing his early days as a Libyan defector. The cables
painted Giaka as a liar and a fraud. Most damningly, in the few
years following Lockerbie he had told his CIA handler several different times that he knew nothing about the plot to bomb Flight
103. In a withering cross-examination, the defense lawyers made a
convincing case that all of Giaka's most incriminating testimony
seemed to have been invented by the former Libyan intelligence
agent to persuade the Justice Department to take him and his
family out of Libya and into the U.S. Witness Protection Program
(where they now live, all expenses paid, for life).

Without Giaka, the Crown was left with little to establish
Megrahi and Fhimah's movements in Malta during that crucial last
day before the bombing. On the evening of December 20, the
Crown showed, Megrahi and Fhimah did indeed fly from Tripoli
to Malta. Vincent Vassallo, a Maltese man who had agreed to start
a travel agency with Fhimah, testified that Fhimah and Megrahi
showed up at his house right after they landed. "I was watching

television upstairs and my wife called me to say Lamen [Fhimah] was here," Vassallo said. "As I was coming downstairs, I called out to Lamen, and I said, 'Come in, Lamen.' And he said 'No, because I have a person in the car with me, the person I told you who might help us with the travel business, the person who has a relative who works for an oil company.'"

This is who Vassallo believed Megrahi was: someone who would help bring in big blocks of foreign oil workers as customers for his fledgling travel agency. Vassallo insisted that Megrahi come inside for coffee. The Scottish Police hoped Vassallo might give them a few more details: Did he remember what kind of car Megrahi and Fhimah were driving? Were they carrying any luggage—a brown Samsonite bag, maybe? But Vassallo's signed statement read: "I have been asked if I can remember either Lamen or Baset to have a brown Samsonite suitcase but I can't say that I ever did. On the evening that Baset arrived at my house with Lamen, they had coffee, then left."

That night, Megrahi checked into a Holiday Inn in Malta using his coded "Abdusamad" passport. Early the next morning, Megrahi made a call from his room to what turned out to be an apartment not far from the airport where Fhimah had been living since the summer. The call was brief, less than thirty seconds, according to the Holiday Inn's billing logs, but the Crown suggested that this was just long enough for Megrahi to tell Fhimah to set the MST-13 timer on the bomb and come get him at the hotel. The bomb went off some thirteen hours later—over Scotland, instead of over the Atlantic Ocean, where the remnants would have been unrecoverable. One Scottish investigator later said this was because Fhimah likely failed to account for the one-hour time difference between Malta and London. *Is this what happened?*

The Crown lawyers prepared to cross-examine Megrahi and Fhimah, but there was little likelihood that the suspects would ever take the stand. This is when I arrived at Kamp van Zeist myself: In November 2000, when the Libyan government finally agreed to let one Libyan intelligence agent testify. His name was

Mansour al-Saber. He walked into the Zeist courtroom with the demeanor of a man who completely disdained the proceedings. From start to finish, his body language in the witness-box was pure Fuck You. He didn't look at the Crown lawyer who questioned him. He twirled a set of prayer beads and waved them around in front of his face while the lawyer talked. He slung one arm over the back of his chair and leaned back as far as the chair allowed. The Chief Judge told him to sit up, closer to the microphone so his answers could be heard by the court, but a few minutes later Saber was swaying way back again. Even Megrahi and Fhimah exchanged looks of exasperation over him. *What did this guy think he was doing?*

Just ten months before Lockerbie, Saber had been arrested in Dakar, Senegal, in connection with a briefcase full of bomb-making supplies, including an MST-13 timer and Semtex explosive of the same sort that blew up Flight 103. Saber was jailed in Senegal for several months, but then let go, reportedly because of a bribe. A photograph of the contents of his briefcase was turned over to the CIA at some point, and this, along with another MST-13 timer seized from Libyans in Togo a few years earlier, is what led the CIA to identify the fragment of timer found in the woods outside of Lockerbie.

So the Crown called Saber in order to cement this bit of the investigation. They also seem to have called him for reasons of dramaturgy: He would play a kind of understudy role for Megrahi and Fhimah, who would never take center stage. This, anyway, was why I was so interested in him. He would likely be the closest I'd come to seeing a Libyan intelligence agent directly respond to questions about timers and bombs and planes.

Saber tried to be as unhelpful to the prosecution as possible, denying the obvious and the already proven. He said he couldn't recall whether he'd been jailed in Senegal for months. He said he didn't know anything about a briefcase with a timer and plastic explosives in it. When asked why he had traveled to Dakar in the first place, he said he was visiting there on holiday, even though the Crown produced a transcript of him telling a judge in Senegal that he was a bank employee traveling on official bank business.

Saber admitted to being a Libyan intelligence agent, and he was forced to concede that he'd traveled to Dakar using a fake name written on a coded passport of the sort Megrahi used on his trips to Malta before Lockerbie. Asked repeatedly why he might travel using a coded passport, Saber finally allowed: If I used a coded passport, it would only have been for the purpose of carrying out a "military mission" for the state. *Would this have been Megrahi's answer as well? Was this the Libyan view of Lockerbie—a military mission?*

On Saber's last day on the stand, I sat on the Libyan side of the public gallery to be nearer to Megrahi and Fhimah. My idea was to study their faces for signs that they knew Saber personally. It was guilt by association: Megrahi, Fhimah, and Saber were roughly the same age, and they all had been employees of Libyan Arab Airlines, which Saber all but admitted was a cover for Libyan intelligence. Had they all been colleagues? At different times, had they each traveled with briefcases full of bomb parts? How would Megrahi and Fhimah react as the Crown confronted Saber with evidence about MST-13 timers and Semtex? Any signs of recognition about the coded passports? Any worried looks? I was not talking about the sort of evidence that the judges might consider. This was for my own private file.

So this is what happened: During the morning break, I stayed in my seat in the public gallery while everyone else cleared out. The courtroom was divided from the public gallery by a wall of soundproof glass (we listened to the trial on headphones). I watched Megrahi's defense team huddle on the other side. After a while, I realized that one of the lawyers was talking to another and pointing in my direction, and then the two of them pointed me out to a third. I had been staring at the defense lawyers without realizing I was staring—and doing it from the Libyan side of the courtroom—and now they were staring back at me. Megrahi's lawyer, Bill Taylor, seemed slow to pick up on what was going on, but I watched as he was briefed on the situation. Taylor walked toward the glass, his eyes fixed on me.

I felt exposed, but I refused to look down or walk away. Taylor was an imposingly large man, and a bully in the courtroom. I was trying to stand my ground. I felt that I had come to this courtroom to see something for myself, and that morning, I finally had. Now, with my staring, I was telling Bill Taylor that I had seen it as well, this thing that he had been working every day for years to obscure. That is: The Crown was right. I felt this now in a way I hadn't before. I had seen Megrahi and Fhimah riveted by Saber's presence in the court, looking at him and then trying not to look too hard, and then looking hard once again, fiddling anxiously with their prayer beads and headsets. At several points during the week, I'd watched as both Fhimah and Megrahi dozed during testimony (at one point Fhimah fell stone-cold asleep on the shoulder of the Scottish policeman at his side). But the two defendants did not nod off during Saber's testimony. They *knew* him. I was sure of it. And if this was true, I felt, then much of the rest of it was likely true as well. Megrahi's purchase of the clothes in Malta, Fhimah's diary entries about luggage tags, the coded passports, the connections with Edwin Bollier in Zurich and the MST-13 timers—all of it likely meant just what the original indictment said it did: Megrahi and Fhimah, both Libyan intelligence officers, *had formed a criminal purpose to destroy a civil passenger aircraft and to murder the occupants therein.* . . .

I knew this now, and I wanted Bill Taylor to know it as well. This was my moment to say what I only then realized I had come to say: You tried to destroy my brother, whoever you were, hiding behind big, bewigged Bill Taylor. You tried to destroy him and then to conceal that fact forever, and you did not succeed. I knew this now and I resolved to stand in that courtroom, silent and behind a wall of soundproof glass, as long as it might take for someone—*David?*—to hear me.

III

THE JUDGES AT KAMP VAN ZEIST gave family members one day's notice to get to the Netherlands for the verdict. I got word in the morning and was at the airport later that afternoon. Most other relatives were flying from New York City, and I was told that with one quick connecting flight from Boston, I would meet up with them. That was the plan, but the ticketing agent at the airport couldn't find my reservation. Then the flight was delayed—initially for an hour, then indefinitely. Someone said something about lightning having hit the incoming flight. I waited in lines. I talked to customer service agents, managers, supervisors. I brandished my laminated photo ID from "The Scottish Court in the Netherlands," but this didn't get me anywhere. I kicked many chairs. I hoped and lost hope a hundred different times, and then, at around 11 P.M., an announcement was made that the flight for Amsterdam would soon board.

We arrived at just after 11 A.M. local time. A Scottish police constable met me at the gate and rushed me through customs. Outside, several Dutch policemen sat on motorcycles ready to escort me to Kamp van Zeist, lights flashing and sirens screaming. All of this confirmed my fantasy that I was on a special mission to save David—the bombing was just about to happen, and I was rushing to stop it. But then the Scottish constable told me that the verdict had already been delivered. The judges had read it right around the time my flight had landed. Megrahi had been found guilty, he said, and Fhimah had been acquitted.

The trial at Kamp van Zeist was largely a story with no pictures (no photographs could be taken inside the courtroom), and there were no daily comments from the lawyers (that's not the Scottish way). In a situation like this, the other family members and I were a big part of the daily story. "The Victims Arrive." "The Victims Have Come for Justice."

I walked past a rope line of photographers and television cameramen and ducked into the courthouse. A Scottish court official led me down a hallway and into a room she called the "Families' Lounge." It was a nice space, with comfortable leather chairs and a kitchenette. I recognized a few of the other relatives from the Javits building in New York; some of the more outspoken relatives were familiar from years of television and newspaper stories. Maybe there were fifteen of us there that day, none of them my mother, I was relieved to see.

I asked about Megrahi and Fhimah—*how had the Libyans reacted to the verdict?*—but got conflicting accounts: Fhimah leapt up from his seat in exultation at his acquittal. Fhimah let out a cry. . . . Megrahi bowed his head. Megrahi mouthed some words to his wife in the public gallery. Everyone had his or her own version of the story, and I felt sorry that I had been denied my own. Then someone reminded me about the videotape that had been made for the closed-circuit feed to the United States. By Scottish Court rules, the tape would be destroyed at the end of each day, but had it been erased yet?

I was told that a senior Scottish official would come find me to discuss it. It turned out to be Brian Sutton, the Scottish policeman I'd met on my trip to Lockerbie five years earlier. I was kind of a stray dog then, poking my nose around the town for scraps about the bombing, and I didn't look that much better now: no sleep, no shave, asking for a favor.

Brian took a kind view of me once again. He wanted to talk. He surprised me by remembering Kathryn's name. "Are you two still together?" I was proud to tell him that we were married now. He put his hand on my shoulder. "Any wee ones?" I told him that Kathryn had been pregnant once, around a year earlier, but that she'd miscarried. He told me to hang in there and it would happen for me. In those moments, I wanted nothing more than to have pictures of two wee ones in my wallet to show Brian Sutton. The way he talked about having a child seemed so wholly positive that I didn't dare tell him what a protracted mess I had made of it. The best I could report wasn't anything of the sort that he would want to hear about: Kathryn and I felt solid again as a couple, the ups and downs smoothed out with the help of a kooky-but-effective couple's therapist, and we were starting to talk about babies once more.

Brian bent the rules and ushered me through back rooms of the courthouse to the control room, where he said the video team was set to replay the verdict for me. The Zeist courtroom was equipped with six cameras, all remote-controlled. The woman who directed the filming told me that there was not an inch of the courtroom she could not see, but she had had strict instructions not to be too editorial with angles, close-ups, or cutaways. "Nothing too dramatic," she said as she pushed a VHS cassette into a machine and let the verdict play.

The reading of the two judgments was done in less than a minute. I tried to watch the faces of the suspects as the verdicts were read, but I had a hard time making out expressions. Fhimah smiled, but Megrahi seemed generally impassive. When I said this to the camera operators, they disagreed. They had one angle on Megrahi that they could not show, but which they said showed a tear forming in his eye as the Scottish Lord Advocate took the stand to recommend a sentence of life in prison.

I was in the courtroom myself when the actual sentence was handed down later that afternoon. "Abdelbaset Ali Mohmed Al Megrahi, the mandatory sentence for the crime of murder is imprisonment for life, and that is the sentence that we impose." It was a powerful moment; it felt as if I had heard the word *murder* in connection to this case for the first time. Arranging for a bomb to be placed on a plane was such an abstract way to kill, but the verdict brought home the raw fact of it. It all played out quickly in the courtroom. The sketch artists in the front row had hardly finished a first outline of the scene before it was over. Megrahi walked off for the last time. And then, so did we.

The prosecution had not been wholly satisfying. Fhimah left the courtroom a free man, despite what seemed to me to be his clear involvement in the crime; and there were at least a half-dozen other Libyans whose names came up during the trial who would never be held accountable for their roles in the bombing. And then there was the matter of Megrahi's sentence: The judges said life, but it turned out that he'd be eligible for parole in twenty years, and the sentence would be served in a specially built cell that photos in a British tabloid would later reveal to be more than comfortable, complete with a living room, television, private bath, and guest room. Still, I don't remember feeling anything but grateful for that last moment at Kamp van Zeist. A lot of bombs have gone off over the years, killing a lot of people, and it's the rare case that ends with anything like a trial, much less a conviction.

In the Families' Lounge, people cried and hugged. The Crown lawyers stood in front of the room and accepted a standing ovation. The Scottish Lord Advocate made some remarks about the long road to justice, the admirable perseverance of the relatives, the appeal options still open to Megrahi. And then he stood awkwardly, not sure what to do next. He said, "Well, I guess that brings proceedings to an end." One of the relatives asked the Lord Advocate if it was all right to give him a hug. She didn't wait for a response before locking him in a full embrace. The look on his face was equal parts embarrassed civil servant and assault victim. It was over.

I took a short flight from Amsterdam to London the next day, and then an hour's train ride south to a town called Farnborough. I was met at the rail station by a man named Mick Charles, the lead member of the British team whose job it had been to reconstruct the fuselage of the Pan Am 747 destroyed over Lockerbie. The remnants of the *Maid of the Seas* had been stored in a hangar at the Farnborough air base for more than ten years, but now that the trial was done, no one knew what would happen with them. Any relatives with an interest in seeing them were encouraged to make the trip after the verdict, so I did.

Mick Charles began with an elaborate slide presentation about the bombing—before and after photos of the plane and the disaster site—but I was impatient to get out to the airline hangar. I had come to Farnborough for one thing, and I suspect the few other relatives who'd come were there for the same reason: to see the *Maid of the Seas* up close and personal, to stand there next to the wrecked 747, maybe to touch it. I wanted to feel whatever it was I might be able to feel from those pieces of aluminum and plastic before they were moved to an aviation museum or sold for scrap.

We walked outside in a line behind Mick Charles, past lesser wrecks being investigated, until we reached a high-security door. Charles told us to wait outside while he turned off the alarms, and then he asked us to step in. "Here she is," Charles said, walking right up to the plane and touching the side as if he were visiting a horse in a stall. He reached up to a panel of aluminum that had been blown out from a center point like the petals of a flower. "The bomb exploded right here, on frame seven hundred. This frame right here."

The *Maid of the Seas* was both much more and much less than I had imagined. That is, she was enormous, twenty times larger than anything else in the hangar, and yet the amount of the original plane that was actually represented on that scaffolding was a small fraction. I had pictured an almost completely rebuilt 747 sitting in this hangar, with a cockpit, a tail, wings, engines, and seats—all I'd need to do was somehow put David back in his seat, and the situation would be fixed. But Charles explained that his team had reconstructed only those parts of the plane relevant to pinpointing where the bomb had detonated. It was strange: Even standing right next to the plane didn't relieve me of the need to imagine it.

Charles carried with him a seating chart for Flight 103. He said to a mother and son who were with me: "You want to know his seat position, don't you?" I watched as he read out the seat number of the woman's husband and walked with her to the spot on the scaffolding where row 15 would have been. A few pieces of the plane's aluminum skin hung there, along with a small belt of windows. The son moved in for a photograph.

Charles looked down at his clipboard and turned to me. "Your brother, David, right? . . . That would be seat 40K." He looked toward the far end of the hangar and said that 40K would have been "way, way down there," well past where the scaffolding for the reconstruction ended. "We could pace it off, if you like." I walked with him down to where he felt seat 40K might have been. It was hard to believe how long a 747 was.

Charles was respectful of the relatives' relationship to the reconstructed fuselage. He offered to step outside if we wanted to be alone with it. I wasn't sure what I'd do with a few minutes alone with the *Maid of the Seas,* but I said yes without hesitation. The others left as I moved in close to the skin of the plane and touched it. Some dirt from the ground in and around Lockerbie was still on the underside of the plane. Some loose wiring and thin bits of insulation hung off the scaffolding. I lingered. I had a sense that this was a last chance at something and I didn't want to leave anything undone. *What did this old wreck really matter to me?* There was no real connection between the way David had died and the way he had lived his life, even if some poetic interpretations suggested themselves; there was no meaning to a fall six miles down to the ground, just pain. It was terribly unfortunate that David chose to fly Pan Am Flight 103 on the twenty-first, but it wasn't a tragic choice to find the cheapest flight home. It wasn't a suicide. If anything, the tragic part had happened weeks earlier, when David decided to give up on the love he had found with Rina for a ski trip.

I was done with the *Maid of the Seas.* I walked outside, and Charles shut off the lights in the hangar behind me.

I rode the train back to London, reading my chronology of David's last days along the way. A passport stamp told me that he had landed at London's Gatwick Airport early in the morning on

December 19. A receipt from the Travelers Exchange Corp. found in his pockets by the Scottish police told me that he had taken a train into London's Euston Station and exchanged a one-hundred-dollar traveler's check. There were museums near the train station—did David stop in? Did he grow tired of lugging his bags around over the course of the day? Was he distraught about leaving Rina? I know only that he phoned Billy and told him that he was feeling tired and lonely and not interested in being a tourist in London. He had planned to spend a week there, he told Billy, but he now thought he would come home much sooner. He didn't call home to pass the word along. It would be another of his surprise arrivals.

On a scrap of paper returned with David's things from Lockerbie, I found handwritten notes about several youth hostels in and around London. I was pretty certain that David had stayed at one of the places on the list—his International Youth Hostel Association Guest Card was stamped twice, once for the night of the nineteenth and another time for the night of the twentieth. But which hostel was it? David wrote detailed directions to only one of the three places on his list, the Holland House in Kensington, so I decided I would spend my last night in London at the place where he likely had spent his.

The Holland House was set back from the street, deep inside a gated park; it was big, made of stone, and had the look of an asylum. A plaque inside read: IN THE FIRST PART OF THE 19TH CENTURY LADY HOLLAND HAD A SALON HERE, ATTENDED BY SUCH FAMOUS NAMES AS SHERIDAN, SIR WALTER SCOTT, LORD BYRON, WORDSWORTH, AND DICKENS. (I remembered someone telling me that David had flipped out when he wasn't cast in a production of Romulus Linney's *Childe Byron*. He said: "THIS IS RIDICULOUS. I *AM* BYRON!") Now I was sure that the Holland House had been his choice that last night.

The Holland House had the feel of a college campus, with buildings arranged around a common grassy area, cheap institutional food available at a cafeteria, and signs posted on bulletin boards advertising roommates and cheap train tickets for sale, last-minute. At twenty-five, David had been closer to the median age of the guests here than I was now at thirty. This was a place for young people, it seemed clear, and I felt distinctly not-young there. I wonder if David had felt a little old for the student's life as well.

I left the Holland House and walked the Kensington high street from one end to the other, trying to imagine what David saw that last night, what he felt. I found a café that felt like the local version of the Hungarian Pastry Shop. Maybe David sat at a back table nursing a cup of black coffee, thinking about New York and what he might do when he returned. I found a seat near the back and nursed my own cup of coffee. I took out a notebook and began to write down everything I could about the trip to see the *Maid of the Seas* earlier that day.

After a time, I felt someone watching me. I looked up to find a young guy at a nearby table trying to get my attention. He was a couple of months into a beard that wasn't growing in very well. With him was a woman with long dark hair and piercings who was writing in a notebook of her own. "Are you a writer?" the guy asked. Before I could answer, he pointed to the woman's note-book. "We're writers, too." They moved their chairs closer. The guy said that the two of them wrote poetry, plays, short stories— "nothing published yet, but so much of publishing is bullshit, isn't it?" They wanted to know what kind of things I wrote, *if you don't mind saying.* . . . I didn't mind. I said: I don't really write anything. I'm not a writer.

I was trying to discourage conversation, but the guy with the beard wasn't discouraged. He started talking about how he saw himself as a latter-day beatnik. He said he was carrying on in the grand tradition of Americans who traveled abroad to make great art. The girl with the piercings seemed to have been antagonized by my line about not being a writer. She showed me pages from her notebook, some writing mixed in with a kind of scrapbook of her travels, and then she asked me about the spiral notebook I was carrying. "If you're not a writer, what have you been writing for the last hour?" The guy with the patchy beard wanted to know as well. It was late. I decided to tell them a story.

I'm not a writer, I said, but my brother was. He was going to be

one of the great writers of his generation—*everyone knew this.* He
lived in New York for a few years, but then he decided that he
needed to see the world. He traveled for a while and then met a
wonderful woman and moved in with her. He was an Artist, a
writer who was finally going to write his first novel, and she was
an Artist, too. She painted silk scarves at home and sold them to
tourists. Some of the scarves were framed like paintings and sold
to galleries. It was a partnership like neither of them had ever
known. They pushed each other to make better art and to be better people than they might ever have been on their own. They
were in love, and this love transformed both of them. With her in
his life, his novel came to him faster than he had ever imagined;
after just a few months, he completed a full draft. He surprised me
with this on the phone the week before he was set to fly home. I
wasn't sure he was even trying to write a novel, I said. I thought
that maybe my brother had actually tired of his ambition to be a
great writer and was trying to find a way to stand down from years
of raised expectations. I thought he was just hiding out overseas,
but I guess ambition doesn't die so easily, does it?

The guy with the beard and his girlfriend seemed caught up in
what I was saying. Most of it wasn't true—it was the story I
wished had been true for David—but now I had to finish what I'd
started. *Do you remember the Lockerbie bombing? Pan Am Flight 103?*
My brother was on the flight, I said. And that great first novel of
his was lost. The guy and the girl seemed stunned and saddened—
not for my loss, I imagine, but for the loss of that book they
believed David had written, like the loss of their own notebooks,
the very flower of someone's youth, scattered through the woods
and streams somewhere in Scotland.

I agreed that it was sad, but I offered them this consolation: I
had found my brother's notebooks, and I had tracked down a lot
of the people he had talked with over the period of years when
this novel was percolating inside of him. I had retraced all of his
steps and tried to experience everything that he had, so I could
recreate this novel and get it published. This was why I had come
to London and, more specifically, to this café on the Kensington
high street. I was pretty sure that this was where David had sat and

drunk coffee late into the night making a last set of revisions to his manuscript. I showed them the page I had written in my notebook describing the café. I have to get down all the details I can, I said. You never know what might have influenced him.

"What was your brother's novel about?" the guy asked me. "What was it called?" I said something about it being semiautobiographical, *like so many first novels are*. "David had planned to call it *The Memoirs of an Unknown Author*." The guy with the patchy beard and the woman with the piercings agreed that it was a great title and said they wanted to read it when it came out. I bought us another round of coffees. For a few moments, it felt as if we were all writers, brothers and sisters in arms fighting the good fight against a world that didn't care about what we were scribbling in our notebooks, a world that we would one day surprise and delight with the words we had troubled to set down that night. It was nice to feel this with someone again.

I returned to the Holland House. Something about the bunk beds in my room at the Holland House, and the colors of the blankets, made it feel like a child's room. Before bed, I looked around at all of the men and boys tucked in for sleep. I wondered who knew that they were there. Who was missing them tonight? If one of them died tomorrow, I thought, how mysterious this night might come to seem in the eyes of those who loved them, how hard to picture the sight of their warm breath in the cold air escaping up toward the windows. I tried to imagine David tucking himself into his bed that last night, a little boy under his blankets with no one to come to kiss him good-night.

The next morning I left the Holland House and rode the Underground to the airport, just as I imagined David had. I pictured David's last few hours on a split screen, with David's actions on one side and the progress of the Samsonite suitcase with the bomb in it on the other. At the time that the bomb entered the baggage system in Malta—at about 8 A.M. London time—David might still have been sleeping. At the time the bomb reached Frankfurt in the midafternoon, David was likely on his way to the airport. And when the bomb was finally loaded onto Flight 103, just after 5 P.M., I imagined that David was at Heathrow. He had probably already eaten the meal later described in the coroner's report. Maybe he bought a magazine or a book or candy, trying to spend those last few British pounds from the original fifty he'd gotten at the ATM outside Euston Station three days earlier. He sat in the lounge in Terminal 3. Did he talk to anyone? Was he reading his paperback copy of *The Flowers of Evil,* thinking about going with Billy to France to help work on his dissertation? Did he wonder if his letter from the "Garden of Eden" had already made it home, thrilling everyone with a sense of the great things he'd seen during his time abroad?

Flight 103 began boarding at 5:30, and David, with his seat toward the back of the plane, likely was among the first on. The gate agent for the flight was called as a witness early in the trial at Kamp van Zeist. I wondered if David had said anything to her. Did he seem happy? There was a time when I might have dedicated my life to finding this woman, hoping for that one last detail about David from that one last person still living who'd had contact with him, a detail that would somehow end David's story in a way I could live with. But as I boarded my own flight out of Heathrow, I decided that that time in my life now had to be over. I had to get back for work on Monday. I was looking forward to seeing Kathryn and telling her everything.

IV

I VISITED KAMP VAN ZEIST one last time in March 2002. I saw a Scottish judge tell Abdelbaset Ali Mohmed al-Megrahi that none of the grounds for his appeal was well founded, and then watched Megrahi being led away by Scottish policemen, who would fly him to prison by helicopter later that night. Once more, I ran into Brian Sutton, my favorite Lockerbie policeman. I had good news for him this time. Kathryn was pregnant, and this time nature was cooperating. An ultrasound told us that it would be a boy and he would be born in September.

The clock had been ticking for years for Kathryn on the question of having a child. Now, when I returned from the Netherlands that last time, it was ticking for me. I worried: If I don't write this book about David right now, it will only seem less important once the baby is born. I was afraid that life would sweep me along in another direction, that I would disappear into a family of my own and forget the one I'd come from. I thought: I will soon be someone's father, and this will give me a lot less time to be someone's brother. I didn't like the way this sounded, the way it felt that I was leaving David behind, but Kathryn and I were three or four months into a nine-month process and I needed to be realistic. I set a deadline for myself to finish the book before the baby was born. I strived after a perfect neatness to the affairs of my life, wanting the old cleared away completely to make room for the new.

I signed up for five weeks at an "artist's colony," thinking that this would be the perfect place to write about David. I was assigned a fine room in a grand mansion, with an overstuffed chaise longue, a settee, and a writing desk that looked out over a broad green lawn and a marble fountain. Bats flew around at night. It was a stage set from a drawing room comedy about an artist who had only so many days to write his masterpiece. I was Method-acting the role of the Great Writer, hoping for a performance worthy of David.

There were strict quiet hours in the mansion and a lot of time by myself to work, but it was the meals I spent with the other artists that I found the most challenging. I struggled to find a simple way to summarize just what it was I was doing there. I started off by saying that I was writing a book about the Lockerbie bombing. If the person seemed interested, I'd reveal that my brother was on the flight—this obliged respectful nods and questions about how old David was and *were you close?* If we got that far, I'd often go all the way and say that my brother had been a writer—*he was the real artist in the family*—and then start talking about the "lost" manuscript and the notebooks and David's desire to be famously published.

Artists are probably more inclined than the general public to be curious about the lives of other artists, and the story of a promising artist cut down before his time was irresistible. People asked all sorts of questions about David, and I found myself responding with stories I hadn't planned to tell, things about David's relationships with my parents, about my relationship with his old girlfriend, about this odd neighbor who'd played an important part in David's early life. But then I'd make clear that this wouldn't be in the book. My plan, I said, was to stick strictly to David's words, to try to arrange them artfully enough so that they would add up to more than what they had while David was alive. *This was David's book, not mine. . . .* I imagined building a great wall of David's words that people would admire without ever really peering behind. But the wall didn't really hold with the artists. And I found at the end of my stay, as I read through a draft of what I had written, that it didn't hold for me, either. I needed to start again—once more with feeling.

Kathryn gave birth a few months later. The delivery was cesarean, so I held the baby in my arms during those first forty minutes of his life while Kathryn was being stitched up. I remember the nurse handing him to me as if I knew what to do with him. I watched as his eyes flickered to consciousness. *What could he see?* There is nothing profound about this whole experience unless it's happening to you and you're sitting in the recovery room watching your wife and your son curled around each other in a bed, their chests rising and falling together, all signs pointing unmistakably to a life and a future that you had so much trouble trying to imagine. Kathryn and I never considered naming the baby David. Eight pounds at birth, he didn't need to start carrying that kind of load. We settled on Sam.

Next month Sam will be two years old. I've spent his entire life writing this book—creeping up to my attic office for stretches at my desk while he slept—and I feel as if I've spent my entire life working on this book as well. For Sam, David will be a name in a book, a historical figure as dead and gone as George Washington. David becomes a little more historical for me each day as well. Initially, I thought this was terrible, this forgetting, and I set myself against it—dedicated myself, that is, to remembering everything. But now I think the forgetting is a gift, the thing that makes life possible, and being the curator of the Dave Archives is a job I've become okay with quitting.

I'd like to be able to say that there was a particular moment when things changed for me, but so far as I can tell, it was a series of moments, a few of which I have tried to set down in this book. And the change, insofar as I can be sure it really happened, will,

I'm certain, never be complete. The plot of one of David's fictions comes to mind: A man has written the story of his life, but someone breaks into his office and cuts the book apart, sentence by sentence, scattering the pieces across the city. Some sentences are stuffed inside fortune cookies, some are rewritten as graffiti on walls, some have been tucked into books on library shelves. And the man spends the rest of his life searching for the missing pieces. If I were to try to finish this story for David, I'd look for a way to make the man realize that whatever he has lost isn't worth spending the rest of his life trying to recover, for that wouldn't be much of a life at all.

Sixteen years after David's letter arrived from the Garden of Eden, I never imagined I'd still feel the urge to write back to him, but here goes.

July 29, 2004
Dear David,

I've stopped looking for you in bus stations and restaurants. I've stopped rummaging through your old room and calling your old friends. Soon I will pack away your notebooks and your manuscripts as well. Someday, maybe, I will take them out again and read them, but not for a while. I know that you know that this is anything but sad.

I'm enclosing a recent picture of my boy, Sam. Kathryn and I took him to the beach this past winter. It was just a few days, and it rained a lot of the time, but it was a vacation, time spent being a family, and we hope to do this more now that I'm no longer spending all of my time with you.

I've got another photograph here. It's a picture of you from your ninth birthday. There's a cake with some slices out of it at the center of the table, and a man and a woman sitting on either side of you, but it's not Mom and Dad. It's the Donoghues from down the street. Bill Donoghue took the picture; his ex-wife sent it to me recently. She said Bill took it from his mother's house after she died. Looking at this, it occurs to me that you and I each had a bomb go off in our boyhoods, and we soldiered on for years in the aftermath, trying to make something beautiful of the wreckage. There was a moment when you were young and the family was coming apart. You looked up to someone for help and, disastrously, found Bill Donoghue. But I remember looking up at key moments in my own life and finding you. You were doing your best to be there for me in a way that no one had ever really been there for you, and that—I'd love for you to know now—made all the difference.

I've got to wrap this up now. Sam and Kathryn have been away at her parents' house this week while I try to finish this. I've told them I'm close to being done, almost there, just about at the end, coming down the home stretch so many times over the last year, they probably don't believe I'll really finish. Each time I've meant it, but things come up all the time to keep me from my desk. I get frustrated and think about the whole of life as a big interference. But Kathryn and Sam spent the week on a beach somewhere, and I'm sitting here in my attic with your old notebooks, so maybe I need to change my idea of what's interfering with what.

I have to go. Kathryn and Sam will be home any minute. In some ways this whole project has been a struggle to get back to the present from wherever it was that I blasted off to after you died—a fall to earth just like yours, but with hope and possibility opening up as I near the ground, not closing off for good. I feel like I've been scratching and clawing my way back for years and I'm almost there.

I hear the car in the driveway. I hear the *ding ding ding* of the door opening. I hear Kathryn saying, "We're home!" I hear Sam in the front hallway saying, "Choo choo." And then: "Daddy?"

I've got to go. I'll write more when I can.

Still your brother,
Ken

Ken and Sam in Florida
(photo by Kathryn)

ACKNOWLEDGMENTS

Thanks to Philip Gourevitch and Jeffrey Frank at *The New Yorker* for helping me get this story off my desk, and to Sarah Chalfant and Jin Auh at the Wylie Agency for believing this could be a book and seeing it through with such determination and grace.

Jon Karp, Daniel Menaker, Jonathan Jao, and Evan Camfield at Random House made this book better at every turn.

Much appreciation to David Fanning, Louis Wiley, Jr., Mike Sullivan, and Marrie Campbell at *Frontline* for letting me wear two hats.

I am deeply indebted to everyone who participated in the Dave Oral History Project—only a small fraction of which is represented here—and to the Corporation of Yaddo for the time and space to start, and nearly finish, this book.

For reading a not-quite-final draft and offering such valuable comment and encouragement, sincere appreciation to: Norman Atkins, Mark Bradford, Lawrence Douglas, Rebecca Godfrey, A. M. Homes, Tim Blake Nelson, Jena Osman, Dana Reinhardt, William Savitt, and Joan Snyder.

To Kathryn, who lived this book with me and knows its meaning far beyond the words on the page: Here's to all the chapters not yet written.

NOTES

The title of this book comes from a line in a W. H. Auden poem, "Musée des Beaux Arts," which was inspired by Pieter Bruegel the Elder's painting *Landscape of the Fall of Icarus*. Icarus is hardly noticeable in the lower corner of Bruegel's frame; his two legs dangle above the surface of the sea before going under. Auden writes in part:

> *About suffering they were never wrong,*
> *The Old Masters: how well they understood*
> *Its human position; how it takes place*
> *While someone else is eating or opening a window or just walking dully along;*
> . . . . . .
> *In Brueghel's Icarus, for instance:*
> *How everything turns away*
> *Quite leisurely from the disaster; the ploughman may*
> *Have heard the splash, the forsaken cry,*
> *But for him it was not an important failure; the sun shone*
> *As it had to on the white legs disappearing into the green*
> *Water; and the expensive delicate ship that must have seen*
> *Something amazing, a boy falling out of the sky,*
> *Had somewhere to get to and sailed calmly on.*

A general note on sources: This book relies on memory, which is famously fallible, but it's also heavily dependent on various sources outside of my own head. I've tried to make this book as transparent as possible, citing sources as I found them—telling the story of how I've come to know what I know as I go along—and, where this was awkward or didn't fit the needs of the narrative, I've added some notes below.

In the case of my main source—David's writing—a further word is in order. In many places, I've collapsed several of David's notebook entries into one. I've taken sentences from David's letters and mixed them into notebook entries from around the same time; I've done the reverse as well, and changed the dates accordingly. A lesser sin: I corrected a lot of David's more idiosyncratic spelling and punctuation. David left behind a ton of words and I worked through them all, but how to make a book out of it? I was stuck with a very practical problem: Accounts of everyday life are messy with mundane details, and sometimes repetitive, and often not that illuminating. But several entries over the span of a week or a month, distilled, cut and pasted, and reassembled in the right context, can add up to something more, and this, in the end, was what I was trying to do: to make David's life add up to more than some old notebooks and papers on a shelf in my closet.

This said, there were some rules to my witchcraft. I did not mix and match words from significantly different times or contexts. I never made David say things that he didn't actually say in one form or another, even if he didn't always say them in the form it seems. I was highly selective in what I quoted from David's writing, picking and choosing words that cohered with the very particular story I was trying to tell, but nothing was invented out of whole cloth. The subtitle of this book—"A True Story"—is more a question than an assertion. In the end, the book is only as true as I could manage. Another reader of David's writing (if there ever should be one) might find a different David than the one I've created here. In the course of my writing this book, David became my Frankenstein's monster, stitched together from stray parts, and he might well resemble his creator more than he should.

Two more things: (1) In a few places not indicated in the text I have changed people's names and some details about their lives to protect their identities. (2) A number of other people needed no protection, but they nonetheless remain obscure figures in this book. I am thinking mainly of my sister, Susan, who has her own Dave story to tell, and who helped me in many immeasurable ways to tell my own. I am also thinking of other members of the family and certified Friends and Lovers of Dave. I don't know how to account for all that is not in this book except to say that, in the beginning, I gathered everything I thought I'd need for an epic biography of an unknown writer: a portrait of his family, rich descriptions of place, essays into the cultural moment in which he was writing, every disparate line of artistic influence traced to the fullest. In the end, I narrowed my ambitions to the much smaller, more urgent story I felt I needed to tell about David and myself—who he had been for me growing up, the way our lives had become dangerously entangled after he died, and how both of us, in our way, conceived of a book that could repair the damage of the past and make us whole again. The gaps in this story may seem less confounding in light of my frame for the larger project—less biography or memoir than an act of survival.

I. LAST THINGS

I found Thomas Wolfe's words about his difficulties writing an early novel ("I had been sustained by the delightful illusion of success . . .") in David's copy of *The Writer's Craft*, edited by John Hersey (New York: Alfred A. Knopf, 1981), p. 405. This was one of David's favorite books. The most underlined essay in the collection was W. H. Auden's. One passage begins: "The work of a young writer is sometimes a therapeutic act. He finds himself obsessed by certain ways of feeling and thinking of which his instinct tells him he must be rid before he discovers his authentic interests and sympathies, and the only way by which he can be rid of them forever is by surrendering to them." Next to this David wrote, "Yes! Yes!" A few paragraphs later, Auden observes:

> Some writers confuse authenticity, which they ought always to aim at, with origi-nality, which they should never bother about. There is a certain kind of person who is so dominated by the desire to be loved for himself alone that he has con-stantly to test those around him by tiresome behavior; what he says and does must be admired, not because it is intrinsically admirable, but because it is his remark, his act.

In the margin next to this, David wrote: "Ouch."

For the story of Juan Trippe's original vision for the 747 and the subsequent design meet-ings with Boeing engineers, I've relied generally on Clive Irving's *Wide Body: The Triumph of the 747* (New York: William Morrow, 1993). For details on the construction of a 747, I read Douglas J. Ingells's booster history *747: Story of the Boeing Super Jet* (Fallbrook, Calif.: Aero Publishers, 1970), as well as some Pan Am publicity materials found in the Pan Am Archive at the University of Miami's Richter Library. This is also where I found the December 1988 issue of *Clipper* magazine.

On the role of the Lockerbie bombing in finally bankrupting a struggling Pan Am, see Robert Gandt's *Skygods: The Fall of Pan Am* (New York: William Morrow, 1995) and Thomas Petzinger, Jr.'s *Hard Landing: The Epic Contest for Power and Profits That Plunged the Airlines into Chaos* (New York: Random House, 1995). Gandt writes about the "ghosts of Flight 103 stalking the Pan Am ticket counters" the summer after the bombing (p. 282). After three years of restructurings and other plans to save the airline, Pan Am declared bankruptcy in December 1991. The Pan Am building on Park Avenue in Manhattan had been owned by MetLife insurance since the 1980s, but Pan Am wasn't forced to take its name from the top of the building until 1992. The giant *P* from the sign is being preserved in a warehouse in New Jersey by the Pan Am Historical Foundation, which hopes one day to create a Pan Am museum. I once talked to a member of the foundation at a store in Florida that sold Pan Am memorabilia (three dollars for an old cup and saucer from "Clip-per Class"; seven dollars for an economy class blanket). The woman was happy to talk to me about the glory days of Old Pan Am, but she turned grave when I brought up Locker-bie. "Lockerbie is a bad word," she said. "A real bad word."

The sequence of the *Maid of the Seas* destruction comes from the British Air Accidents Investigation Branch's *Report on the Accident to Boeing 747-121, N739PA at Lockerbie, Dum-friesshire, Scotland, on 21 December 1988.*

The account of the well-preserved body on the Lockerbie Golf Course comes from Nick Cohen of the British *Independent,* as quoted in Joan Deppa's *The Media and Disasters: Pan Am 103* (London: David Fulton Publishers, 1993), p. 75.

On the details of the early Lockerbie investigation and the different theories of how the bomb made it onto Flight 103, a number of books have been written over the years. I've read them all, as well as more newspaper, magazine, and journal articles than I could ever properly cite. Here's a field guide to the works I found most helpful:

David Johnston's *Lockerbie: The Tragedy of Flight 103* (New York: St. Martin's Press, 1989) was the first book published, and it is very strong on the immediate aftermath of the bombing. Matthew Cox and Tom Foster's *Their Darkest Day: The Tragedy of Pan Am 103 and Its Legacy of Hope* (New York: Grove Weidenfeld, 1992) adds more detail to the story of the plane coming apart and the aftermath among the victims' families.

On the early years of the Lockerbie investigation, two books initially were the most authoritative: Steven Emerson and Brian Duffy's *The Fall of Pan Am 103: Inside the Lockerbie Investigation* (New York: G.P. Putnam's Sons, 1990) and David Leppard's *On the Trail of Terror: The Inside Story of the Lockerbie Investigation* (London: Jonathan Cape, 1991). Both books start strong with the details of the investigation, then settle on a theory of the bombing that has never been proven: namely, that it was carried out by a cell of a Palestinian group, the PFLP-GC, based in West Germany, which was hired by Iranian clerics to avenge the destruction of an Iran Air passenger plane accidentally shot down by the U.S. warship *Vincennes* in July 1988. Leppard's book, published after Libyan involvement in the crime had been established, endorses a compromise notion that the PFLP-GC initiated the plot and the Libyans finished it. This still retains some plausibility—it's hard to imagine that two different groups were building near-identical bombs for the same purpose without some knowledge of each other, if not coordination—but the trial at Kamp van Zeist made a strong case for Libya's sole authorship of the plot that brought down Flight 103.

The best of the more recent Lockerbie books is Allan Gerson and Jerry Adler's *The Price of Terror: The History-Making Struggle for Justice After Pan Am 103* (HarperCollins, 2001). It's essentially an account of the effort by a handful of lawyers and relatives to successfully sue Libya in civil court for damages, but it offers a solid, general treatment of most aspects of the bombing. Gerson and Adler also seem to endorse a version of the theory that the plot to down Flight 103 was initiated by Iran in retaliation for the accidental downing of Iran Air Flight 655 in the summer of 1988. There's every reason to think that Iran initiated some kind of retaliation, but no one has ever been able to connect this to the Libyans who actually put the bomb on the plane.

A good review of the official reports on the bombing, as well as the findings from the civil case against Pan Am, is found in Rodney Wallis's *Lockerbie: The Story and the Lessons* (Westport, Conn.: Praeger, 2001).

The line about Dachau being a "perfect place to bring up a family" comes from Timothy W. Ryback's *The Last Survivor: In Search of Martin Zaidensadt* (New York: Pantheon, 1999), p. 78.

The Scottish Fatal Accident Inquiry Relating to the Lockerbie Air Disaster took place in Dumfries from October 1, 1990, through February 13, 1991. The minitrial on "pre-death pain and suffering" took place in the United States District Court in Brooklyn, New York, August 24–26, 1992. The Lockerbie coroner, Anthony Busuttil, spoke about his study of fat emboli before London's Royal Society of Medicine on June 11, 1998, and I read a transcript of it in "Lockerbie and Dunblane: Disasters and Dilemmas," *Medico-Legal Journal* 66, part 4, pp. 126–40.

To be clear: Of the many thousands of people who have fallen from passenger jet aircraft after sudden break-ups at altitude, an infinitesimally small number have ever been found alive. I know of only two cases, both the result of bombings. One, a twenty-two-year-old flight attendant named Vesna Vulovic, survived a rapid decompression and a thirty-three-thousand-foot drop after her Yugoslav Airlines DC-9 was bombed by Croat terrorists in 1972. A thick blanket of snow may have helped cushion Vulovic's fall, although she was still paralyzed for life from the waist down. She holds the Guinness world record for Highest Fall Survived Without a Parachute.

The other case is much less well-known. In May 1962, Continental Airlines Flight 11, a Boeing 707 flying from Chicago's O'Hare Airport to Kansas City, Missouri, broke apart at 39,000 feet over Unionville, Missouri. A dynamite charge had been placed in a towel bin of the bathroom by a husband looking to collect on a life insurance policy he took out on his pregnant wife a few weeks before. The wreck of Flight 11, one of the largest of the early jet age, provided Federal Aviation Agency investigators with a chance to make a unique study of what happens to passengers who are subjected to traumas at heights previously known only to military test pilots wearing pressure suits and carrying supplemental oxygen. The FAA doctors described what happened to the passengers as the plane came apart:

> Most passengers sustained one or more injuries of the crushing, amputative, and eviscerative type as the cabin came apart. . . . Also noted on inspection of the bodies was the fact that the trouser belts were broken on approximately one-half of the male occupants. This is a frequent finding in accidents with vertical decelerations. [Others have already] documented the abrupt expansion of the abdomen that occurs in such impacts.

FAA investigators were shocked to find that one of the passengers from Flight 11 had been found alive on the ground some seven and a half hours after falling 39,000 feet. Takehiko Nakano, a Japanese-born engineer living in Evanston, Illinois, had been napping across a row of seats with no seat belt on when the rapid decompression began. The seat frames apparently absorbed a lot of the shock of the impact with the ground. The FAA medical team found that "upon admission to a local hospital, [Nakano] was in shock, but he told the nurses his name, address, destination, religion, and next of kin. He also stated repeatedly that he was thirsty. He did not relate, nor was he asked, any of the details of his ordeal." The team described Nakano's injuries as "relatively minor," except for a laceration of one of the veins leading back to the heart. They said Nakano might have lived had he received care sooner, but he died instead, just a few hours after being found—nine and a half hours after the explosion that brought down Flight 11. See J. Robert Dille and Howard Hasbrook's "Injuries Due to Explosion, Decompression and Impact of a Jet Transport" in *Aerospace Medicine* (January 1966), pp. 5–11. The article refers only to a "survivor"; I found the name Takehiko Nakano in the *Unionville Republican*'s coverage of the bombing, photocopies of which were sent to me by a kindly librarian at the Putnam County Public Library.

Of all of the Flight 103 passengers, David seemed to be one of the better candidates for at least some period of consciousness: He was seated far from the bomb and the wings; he was protected from a lot of flying objects by the bulkhead wall right behind his seat; he was surrounded by a lot of empty seats, lessening the likelihood of knocking into someone; and his injuries were not in Anthony Busuttil's first, worst category of severity. The fact that David was found separate from the rest of the economy-class passengers at Ella

Ramsden's place might suggest some unique position within the plane that may have altered his fate in some way. Maybe David was asleep across the empty seats next to him like Takehiko Nakano, and this helped protect him in some way; then again, maybe he wasn't sitting in his assigned seat at the time of the explosion. For all of my efforts, it's impossible to know what happened.

Elie Wiesel is quoted from *The Town Beyond the Wall* by way of Karl A. Plank's "The Survivor's Return: Reflections on Memory and Place" in *Judaism* (Summer 1989, p. 274).

II. PRIVATE INVESTIGATIONS

My understanding of levirate marriage comes largely from two articles by Dvora E. Weisberg in *The Annual of Rabbinic Judaism:* "Levirate Marriage in Halitzah in The Mishnah" (1998) and "The Babylonian Talmud's Treatment of Levirate Marriage" (2000). Interestingly, Weisberg isn't certain that levirate marriage ever was widely practiced, even in Ancient Israel; the only stories in the Old Testament that deal with it involve cases where it didn't work out. Levirate marriage is just one of many topics discussed in Frederick E. Greenspahn's interesting study *When Brothers Dwell Together: The Preeminence of Younger Siblings in the Hebrew Bible* (New York: Oxford University Press, 1994).

Just how much is an original Red Skelton oil painting worth? A quick search shows a number of different dealers with widely discrepant appraisals. The official Red Skelton Gallery website endorsed by one of Skelton's children offers an original Skelton for sale for $85,000. Another dealer, a Persian rug salesman who claims that his father learned English by listening to Red Skelton on radio and television, says Red Skelton originals sell for $50,000 and up. All of this is supposed to demonstrate the value of the Skelton Gallery's "limited edition" canvas-transfer prints.

A taste of David's work as a *Brown Daily Herald* columnist: Early on, "Tortured Ravings" (and then "My Reality") was often a harangue against apathetic fellow students and "anemic" professors: "you neutrals, you noninvolved people, you people too busy to concern yourself. . . ." David railed against a wide variety of people: "insipid" springtime lovers kissing on the green; an Indian man named Vishnu Devananda who flew a glider over the Berlin Wall to spread purple chrysanthemums; Walter Feldman, a beloved older professor in the art department whose pen-and-ink prints adorned the cover of the University's course announcement booklet each year ("His complicated drawings confuse the already confusing matter of choosing courses—I say, 'Down with covers by Feldman!' "). David used two or three different columns to celebrate and then to lambaste "Larry the Punk," a campus figure known for his leather, chains, and spiky, mustard-colored Mohawk. David's last Larry column concluded: "My love affair with Larry is over. Proletarian Larry is stuffing tiny Ziploc bags with locks of his old lox-colored hair and selling them. . . . Vermin, lice, locusts, cattle disease, Larry. Rot, you changeling."

Several times, David used his columns to comment obliquely on his relationship with Kathryn. After their last big break-up, David made this modest proposal to the university administration:

I believe that one exhausting love affair (two for the bachelor of arts) should be made a graduation requirement. For candidates in the creative arts, this would be two or more excruciating and tumultuous love affairs that bring one to the pinnacles of ecstacy, then plummet one to the depths of despair, and cause one to repine of a paucity of creative fervor.

A note about the *Philtrum Press,* Brown's fledgling humor magazine: David didn't start the magazine—some friends did—but he pushed himself to write short humor pieces for it, even when things didn't feel that funny to him. David's *Philtrum* stories were not the funniest pieces in the magazine by my lights. They walked the line between being funny and trying to be more-than-funny. It worked in the case of "Old Men Urinating," a long buildup of things old men are terrible at (playing hockey, ballroom dancing, etc.), until David's narrator discovers one day in a men's room that old men are great at urinating. It didn't work in the case of "Babysitting in North Central Florida," a twisted story of a child being left to a serial-killing babysitter, which David had tried to adapt from a story he'd written for one of his fiction writing classes. David's stories strived after an ideal of literature that most of the other pieces didn't seem to bother with, and it was these other, simply funny pieces that I tended to like best—sketches filled with television references, absurdist bits, bodily humor jokes, cartoons. A number of articles were written by a recent grad named David Yazbek, who had become a staff writer for *Late Night with David Letterman,* according to an author's note. To the extent I could imagine being a writer of any kind, I think I was shooting more for David Yazbek than for David Dornstein.

A word about David and falling. Throughout David's notebooks there are images and references to falls. Almost always, David is reaching for a graphic way to describe a loss, a falling-short of some grand goal, but in several places he writes about actual falls, usually from a plane, and these seem worth mentioning. On a Greyhound bus climbing into the high desert around the Grand Canyon at the end of the summer of 1983, David began to imagine himself in a plane that was going down:

> Seven thousand feet above the level of the sea . . . Swallow to reduce the pressure. . . . Above your seat there is an oxygen mask if you'll watch the flight attendant. . . . Please use your seat as a flotation device. . . . Will he die in a plane? Because of a plane?

David's *Fall Journal* contains several pages of writing about a TV weatherman named Jim O'Brien, who was beloved in Philadelphia for his wacky, cornpone forecasts. In the autumn of 1983, O'Brien died in a skydiving accident, falling 8,500 feet to his death when his parachute got tangled up with someone else's and wouldn't open. David was hit unusually hard by the story. He wrote in his notebook: "The weatherman died. Fell from the sky. They photographed his parachute, puffed by the gales, caught in the branches. His body on the ground. I can't stop crying, can't stop. . . ." According to one of the news articles my father sent him, a close colleague of O'Brien's—Jim Gardner, the rocksolid anchor of *Action News*—broke down crying while relating the story on that night's news broadcast. David wondered why anchormen didn't cry more often when delivering the news. He wrote a column for the *Brown Daily Herald,* "On a Weatherman's Death," in which he expanded on how "frighteningly well" we've been trained to receive news of death "without tears or drama or a flicker of recognition that someone has suffered, often tragically, pointlessly. . . . Jim O'Brien's death was sadder'n a lame calf lowin' for its momma, as Jim might have said. And yet I think it is no sadder than the death of any of the countless so-and-so's out there who died that same day." Maybe O'Brien's death influenced the premise of the *Fall Journal* ("DIES IN AIR CRASH"). David didn't want the unknown, young writer "Dorrance-Dean" to be just another so-and-so.

Finally, in a note written in lieu of a final paper for Philosophy 8: Existentialism, David evoked Kierkegaard, Sartre, and the rest as he stared into the abyss of actually failing the class. By the end of his note to the professor, he offered a full-blown description of falling to his own death that he could have had no idea would become so poignant.

> I am seized now with a vertigo as I peer over and gaze down into the valley of the "No Credit." I fear falling into that valley, but will not fall. I will throw myself instead. . . . I shall plunge. While I am in the air falling, I shall hear the voices of all who care about me, and I shall look up to see them hovering above me, reaching out a collective hand to aid me. But I will not accept their aid. I shall scream. That it is my right, it is my duty, it is my responsibility to myself to do this, to become, to fall, and this is what I am doing. . . . Soon I will splotch the soft ground and it won't make a difference. There is only a one-letter difference between Falling and Failing, but in that one letter is the whole of the world. . . .

On David's mental state: Some readers may conclude that David was troubled in ways that neither he nor I have fully reckoned with. Many have offered their favorite diagnoses: manic depression, bipolar disease, generalized anxiety, a personality disorder (somehow related to my mother's troubles, whatever they may be), logorrhea, hypergraphia, some kind of clinical inability to finish anything. I can't reject any of these suggestions out of hand, but none feels like a true fit, with either the David I remember or the one whose life I've attempted to reconstruct over the years. If an answer ever existed on these questions, it is now lost: David was evaluated by a psychiatrist at Brown, but the university destroyed David's Health Service file (part of a regular seven-year purge) long before I requested to see it. I wrote to a psychiatrist who prescribed David medication at Brown, and later tried this psychiatrist by phone, but I received no response. David may well have had reasons for avoiding a diagnosis or treatment—his equation of art and suffering, perhaps, led him to go untreated for whatever it was that he suffered from—but I have no interest in soft-pedaling the hard facts of his mental health. I just don't know them, and my suspicion is that organic mental illness does not explain David in the total way that some readers may come to believe.

III. DREAMS

On my becoming older than David: In the clinical literature on bereavement, there is a phenomenon known as "age correspondence." Most documented cases involve the adult children of parents who died young. One case: Laura H. was five at the time her father was murdered, but just after she turned thirty—the age her father was killed—Laura H. suffered a nervous breakdown and had to be hospitalized. In another case, a twenty-nine-year-old army officer fatally shot himself in the head, leaving behind a young son who grew up, joined the army, and shot himself in the head shortly after his own twenty-ninth birthday. A few cases of age correspondence in the literature involve siblings: A young girl became mute and refused to eat after turning eleven, the same age at which her older sister died suddenly. A man whose older brother died the day after turning twelve committed suicide the day after his own son's twelfth birthday. (See John Birtchnell, "In Search of Correspondence Between Age at Psychiatric Breakdown and Parental Age at Death—'Anniversary Reactions,' " in *British Journal of Medical Psychology* 54 (1981), pp. 111–20.)

Age correspondence reactions are rarely so extreme, and yet the phenomenon in more mild form is widespread, especially in cases involving sudden or violent death. Birtchnell writes: "What emerges from most [clinical accounts of age correspondence] is a morbid identification with the dead . . . and a conflict over the extent to which the subject feels able to differentiate between him/herself and the deceased." He continues:

> Linked with this is the concept of *nemesis.* This is the conviction held by some patients that they are destined to repeat in their lives the pattern of some other person's life, usually to a tragic end. . . . There are always certain similarities, of at least a superficial nature, in the life patterns of the two individuals which tend to confirm for the patient the reality of his nemesis fears. The things that are happening to him he believes to have been previously determined by the events in the life of the person whose pattern he is following.

For a good general overview of the clinical literature on grief, I found one work most useful: John Archer's *The Nature of Grief: The Evolution and Psychology of Reactions to Loss* (London: Routledge, 1999).

In my account of Seder '84, I left out mention of Norman Mailer, who may have been part of the reason David didn't come home that year. In April 1984, around Passover, Mailer came to Brown to lecture and visit his daughter Kate. David arrived at Mailer's lecture prepared with a lot of questions. He pictured himself going a few rounds with the old pugilist in public; the crowd had come out to see the champ but David imagined them coming away mightily impressed with the young challenger.

This didn't go as planned, but David had a backup plan to get Mailer's attention. He prevailed on Kathryn to ask Kate Mailer to invite him along for dinner after the lecture.

April 16, 1984

  Lecture, reception, beer with NORMAN MAILER. Thrilling night. Mailer's got stories. "I once called Donald Barthelme an asshole. . . ." And: "Jesse Jackson? He's a jive-ass."

  Mailer and I agreed on things. . . . He dropped the top of the ketchup bottle and I picked it up. . . . Wanted to ask him about the quick deaths in his writing, sudden and abrupt deaths. The abruptness scares the shit out of me, because it's so realistic. It disorients me the same way deaths and other violences in the newspaper disorient me. . . . Maybe I'll write to him about it.

  Want to apologize to Kate for perhaps abusing her good will by inviting myself along for

drinks and then monopolizing the conversation. And must apologize to Kathryn too. She
warned me not to take over. . . . But what a night! I will write a letter to Mr. Mailer thanking
him for his time and for picking up the check. It will not be the last he hears from me. . . .

The next week, David set about writing to Mailer. He spent a lot of time on it and went through a dozen drafts. In the pocket of his notebook from that month, I found a lengthy typescript titled "Aborted Letters to Norman Mailer." It was more than ten pages long.

Dear Mr. Mailer,

Is the need for attention a driving force in your life? It is in mine. I'm not sure how I feel about it. . . .

Dear Mr. Mailer,

Torture to write to you, sir. Feel helpless conveying to you how well I think we would get on. Realize this is no audition for no play, yet I feel the pressure of a one-shot deal. . . .

Dear Mr. Mailer,

Don't worry, I'll never burden you with a manuscript. I fear nothing like I fear the possibility of being burdensome to anyone. Aim to be, if nothing else, interesting. . . .

Dear Mr. Mailer,

Not looking for a wet nurse. Don't want you to give me a break (sure I do). Don't want you to give me a chance (sure I do). Don't want you to give me a leg up (sure I do). Want you to talk to me. . . .

David didn't send Mailer any of these letters. A month after their meeting, when David got wind that Mailer was going to be back on campus for Kate's graduation, he sent Mailer a note about how much he enjoyed their night of beer and conversation and how much he would like to talk with him again. But David didn't see Mailer at all during graduation. I know this not from David's notebooks—for some reason David didn't mention it—but from Mailer himself, in this note I found in a pocket of David's notebook.

June 10, 1984
Dear David,

Sorry I missed you at graduation. At any rate, it was fun to talk to you that night, and that's saying something considering how much I had been exercising my jaw earlier, so let this be good luck to you.

Cheers,
Norman Mailer

In response, David sent Mailer an account of a dream he had of the two of them at a special hotel for writers. "Dear Mr. Mailer, I just awoke from a late afternoon rest. The sun was in my face and I had a dream in which you were a principal. I want briefly to tell you of the dream, then once again to relieve you of my burden eternally." David never heard back from Mailer and that was the end of it.

For "A 'Once in a Lifetime' Stroll in the Lincoln Tunnel," see *The New York Times,* August 18, 1986, B3.

More on Bill Donoghue: I realize that it's the nature of stories of childhood sexual abuse, and a heightened danger of David's story, pieced together as it is from stray sentences in his notebooks, his own fictionalized stories, and the accounts of others, that clarity remains elusive. This said, I have come to believe that Donoghue abused David in the way that David described, and that, over the years, David came to see this as one of the central, vexing facts of his life—still on his mind some fifteen years later, during the last months of his life. The references to Donoghue in David's notebooks are much more concrete than I have indicated, and the statements I gathered from others were consistent on the basic facts of the abuse. Also: I know of at least two other men who claim to have been abused by Donoghue around the same time, when they were roughly the same age as David. Their recollections remain vivid, and the impact of the abuse on their lives, at least for one man who has written to me at length about his forty years of struggle to come to terms with what happened, remains profound.

For Norman Atkins's "Doomed To Succeed: Cautionary Tales of Four Young Bankers," see *The Village Voice,* October 7, 1986 (cover story). Norm told me that he talked to some *Voice* editors about David in the fall of 1986, suggesting David as a possible columnist or contributor. Norm told David to follow up with a phone call, but this was during David's "plummet" of late 1986, and he never did.

For Rick Moody's "Unexplained Panic Event of Christmas Day in 1986," see Rick Moody, *The Black Veil: A Memoir with Digressions* (New York: Little, Brown, 2002). Moody offers a diagnosis of his own melancholia that seems to fit David's Christmas 1986 plummet as well:

> Melancholy isn't about anything. Melancholy has a style or manner but no subject. Melancholy is a way of thinking, a way of thinking about thinking, and it needs to consume the sufferer and thus needs layers and strata and veneers in perpetuity in which to cloak and conceal itself. Melancholy attempts to avoid detection. Melancholy is not a preoccupation with death, nor a recoiling from shop interiors or human fellowship, nor is it a lack of interest in things of the world, though these may be characteristics of melancholy. It's more a particular complexion to thinking, a tightening, a spiraling, a funneling, a drilling, an incising, a helixing, the direction of this cogitation being always down and in. . . . A preoccupation with death, a recoiling from society, an anhedonia, an obsession with conscience, these follow with melancholy, and they may advertise themselves fleetingly as its true subject, but any transient themes will soon give way to something worse, something darker and meaner, something less lucid, because the goal of melancholy is its direction and force and shape. (p. 137)

IV. FICTIONS

"Reiss Ranter: Investigative Polemicist," the story that David and Billy wrote together in the spring of 1986, was made into a movie, a short, independently produced feature. It was directed by a friend of David's and starred David's friend Rob in the role of David/Billy/Reiss Ranter. I remember a packed premiere at the Anthology Film Archives almost a year after David died. David would have loved the scene, I imagine; Billy later told me he had serious problems with the production.

On my trip to Israel I rented a car, drove north to Tel Dan, and followed the signs to the "Garden of Eden" just as David and Rina had done during David's last few days in Israel. At the time, I didn't know that this place had no claim at all to be the Garden of Eden from the Old Testament. According to the relevant sections of Genesis, the Garden existed at the confluence of four rivers, two of which—the Tigris and Euphrates—are nowhere near Tel Dan, which sits on one of the sources of the Jordan. Biblical archaeologists actually place the Garden in what is now southern Iraq, some forty miles north of Basra, in a town called Q'urna. The area was long known as lush and green and filled with life and water, but it was also filled with Shi'a Arabs who Saddam Hussein deeply mistrusted. In the 1980s, Saddam drained the marshes and let the place dry up; in a lame attempt to nevertheless capitalize on Q'urna's biblical claim, he built a Garden of Eden Hotel there, but few foreigners ever dared visit while he remained in power.

Interestingly, the most significant find at Tel Dan during two decades of excavation has been a small slab of writing in Aramaic that offers the only reference to the "House of David" found anywhere outside the Old Testament. See Avraham Biran's *Biblical Dan* (Jerusalem: Israel Exploration Society, 1994).

V. THE END

For an account of the Libyan side of the Lockerbie standoff and why the Libyans ultimately handed over the suspects for trial, see Khalil I. Matar and Robert W. Thabit's *Lockerbie and Libya: A Study in International Relations* (North Carolina: Macfarland and Co., 2004).

Most of my understanding of the evidence in the prosecution of Megrahi and Fhimah comes from the transcript of the trial at Kamp van Zeist. I picked through its ten thousand pages with the help of a CD-ROM provided to relatives of the victims by the Lockerbie Trial Families Project. It was produced by the College of Law of Syracuse University with a grant from the Office for Victims of Crime of the United States Department of Justice. All references to evidence or specific quotes from the trial come from this version of the transcript and from the Project's very useful daily and weekly summaries.